Exploring
Aotearoa

Many thanks to all those people who have provided information for this book. The patience and support of the good folk at New Holland is very much appreciated, along with the thorough and helpful editorial review by Gillian Tewsley. In particular, I would like to thank my friend Wojciech Kniaz for his company and advice while researching the North Island section of this book and despite the frequent bad weather, muddy tracks and endless detours to distant and forgotten pa sites, his enthusiasm and cheerfulness was unfailing and very welcome.

First published in 2012 by New Holland Publishers (NZ) Ltd
Auckland • Sydney • London • Cape Town

www.newhollandpublishers.co.nz

218 Lake Road, Northcote, Auckland 0627, New Zealand
Unit 1, 66 Gibbes Street, Chatswood, NSW 2067, Australia
86–88 Edgware Road, London W2 2EA, United Kingdom
Wembley Square, First Floor, Solan Road, Gardens,
Cape Town 8001, South Africa

Publishing manager: Christine Thomson
Editor: Gillian Tewsley
Design: Trevor Newman
Maps: Adapted from originals by Bruce McLennon/Island Bridge

Front cover photo: Pou and pallisading mark the entrance to Otatara and Hikurangi pa near Napier.
Back cover photos from top to bottom: Cape Reinga, Pania of the Reef statue at Napier, Rakaia Gorge, Canterbury.

National Library of New Zealand Cataloguing-in-Publication Data

Janssen, Peter (Peter Leon)
Exploring Aotearoa : short walks to reveal the Maori landscape / Peter Janssen.
Includes bibliographical references and index.
ISBN 978-1-86966-343-8
1. Trails—New Zealand—Guidebooks. 2. Maori (New Zealand people)
—History 3. New Zealand—Guidebooks. [1. Whenua. reo 2.
Taunahanahatanga. reo 3. Korero nehe. reo 4. Papatuanuku. reo
5. Purakau. reo] I. Title.
993.00499442—dc 23

10 9 8 7 6 5 4 3 2 1

Colour reproduction by Pica Digital Pte, Singapore
Printed by Times Offset (M) Sdn, Bhd, Malaysia, on paper sourced from sustainable forests.

Exploring Aotearoa
Short walks to reveal the Maori landscape

Peter Janssen

NEW HOLLAND

CONTENTS

Introduction	6
How to Use This Book	13
Glossary	15
English/Maori Place Names	17
NORTH ISLAND/TE IKA A MAUI	19
Northland	20
Auckland	33
Hauraki Gulf	52
Coromandel	59
Waikato	65
King Country	82
Bay of Plenty	87
Rotorua	102
Central North Island	109

East Cape, Gisborne and Waikaremoana 116

Hawke's Bay   123

Taranaki   130

Whanganui, Rangitikei, Manawatu,
Horowhenua, Kapiti   139

Wairarapa   146

Wellington   148

SOUTH ISLAND/TE WAI POUNAMU   157

Marlborough, Kaikoura and Nelson   158

Canterbury and West Coast   170

Otago and Central Otago   187

Far South   197

Bibliography   205

INTRODUCTION

As children growing up on the banks of the Waikato River, we frequently explored the farm across the road. A favourite place on the farm was an old hilltop pa: not that large, it was protected on three sides by steep banks and on the fourth by a deep ditch. There were just a few small terraces ringing the peak, but by lying in the old kumara pits we became invisible. It was a marvellous place, full of mystery. We could see for miles, along the river, over the lakes, and keep an eye on what everyone in the neighbourhood was up to. Below the pa in a small valley an old eel trap blocked a small stream. No one knew much about the pa – even the name had been lost over time.

That pa held a fascination that never left me; and over the years, in the course of researching a number of books, I have become increasingly aware of the huge number of pa sites around the country. A bit of homework on these pa has opened up a whole different view of this country that I and many others, both Pakeha and Maori, are only dimly aware of. Here was a world of gods and taniwha, love and hate, war and peace. Often only fragments of history remain and in many places not only is the history lost, but not even the name of the pa is remembered.

Pa sites are just part of the story. Our landscape, from the mountains to underwater reefs, is intertwined with marvellous legends that make this land come alive. These traditional stories are in turn further overlaid by a complex human history of great explorers, heroic warriors, brave women, bloody battles and love stories of sacrifice and passion.

Having personally discovered this history by exploring the landscape, I didn't want to write another book that was to be read quietly sitting in a chair, but a book that would act as a catalyst for those wanting to learn more. To really understand the past we need to get out and experience it firsthand – and this is a book that I trust will help people do exactly that.

All the entries in this book are linked to walks: most are very easy, while others are a bit more demanding. Using this book, the reader can stand on the very shore inhabited by taniwha, walk through the bush that is home to the patupaiarehe, or stand on the grounds of a pa that once was the scene of a great battle or a heart-wrenching love story.

The book is written primarily for Pakeha so they can take a fresh look at the landscapes they live in and begin to discover and understand what went before. This, of course, has limitations as well – it is impossible to tell the entire history of this country in a book of this nature. The entries are concise and short, more aimed at whetting the appetite than providing the whole meal.

The discovery of Aotearoa New Zealand

Opinions on when people first arrived in Aotearoa are a matter of much discussion, and as time and research continue, so will this discussion. You will find within the book varying and conflicting dates of early exploration, as I have gathered information from a wide range of sources, all credible, but with substantially different conclusions.

Kupe was an extraordinary sailor and can be credited with the discovery of Aotearoa. While the stories of Kupe vary considerably, they all agree that the land was empty when he arrived. Just when Kupe arrived is a matter of great debate, with dates as early as 500 AD through to 1100 AD, just prior to the main migration. The later date is plausible, as Kupe's discovery, and his return to his homeland in Eastern Polynesia, would have been the likely catalyst for the subsequent immigration. Archaeologists generally date the arrival of humans to around 1100 AD. However, many traditional Maori stories and whakapapa trace their ancestry to a much earlier date than this, and refer not only to Kupe but to several early navigators and waka. Ancestors who at first glance appear mythical are quite likely to be real people. As in traditional stories in all cultures, important ancestors were attributed with extraordinary abilities as a mark of respect and to enhance their importance. Even in the Bible, Methuselah lives for over 900 years, Daniel survives the lion's den, and Joshua brings down the walls of Jericho by playing loud trumpets and stamping feet.

It is entirely possible that Polynesian voyagers reached this country well before 1100 AD and, as waka only accommodated very small numbers of travellers, they would leave very little in the way of hard archaeological evidence 1500 years later. Of course they may also have returned to their homeland and left no trace at all. There are even some who believe that this country has been inhabited for as long as 3000 years by an ancient stone-based culture, though there is no real evidence to support this theory.

Where exactly the immigrants came from is more certain, as there are strong linguistic and cultural links between Maori and Eastern Polynesia

(Cook Islands, Tahiti, Marquesas Islands). Moreover, the discovery of Aotearoa also fits closely with the discovery of the Hawai'i islands, which were first settled by voyagers from the Marquesas Islands between 500 and 800 AD.

In every part of the country from Fiordland to Northland are place names associated with Kupe and his waka *Matahourua*. Given the wild nature of the seas around New Zealand, it would have taken great seamanship for Kupe to visit all these places. Some versions have Kupe landing first in the Wellington region, while others attribute the first sighting of New Zealand to Kupe's wife (or daughter) when she saw low cloud over what is now Great Barrier Island and called out 'He ao, he ao' (a cloud, a cloud). Place names attributed to Kupe are especially common around Wellington, as are many references to his wife and daughters who travelled with him.

While the theory of a single immigration by seven waka has now been discounted, it seems clear, from both Maori oral traditions and archaeological evidence, that from around 1150 to 1350 AD was a period of great immigration to Aotearoa. In addition to the numerous stories of settlement and discovery dating from this period, there are many accounts of waka making several journeys to and from Hawaiki, the homeland somewhere in the Pacific. Several accounts of the arrival of these great waka, including the *Tainui*, make reference to the people already living here.

Again Hawai'i provides a clue, as around 1300 AD a wave of immigrants arrived to settle there from the Tahitian islands.

It is unrealistic to think that significant numbers of people would have journeyed across the vast and dangerous Pacific Ocean without some knowledge of a certain destination. According to one traditional story, Turi, the captain of the *Aotea*, specifically settled at Patea on the advice of Kupe that this was good land. Taking into account their sailing skills, it is also very possible that, as well as discovering Aotearoa, some explorers made the journey to Australia – which after all is a good deal bigger than New Zealand – and were absorbed into the Aboriginal population.

In 1964 a fish lure was found in the sand dunes at Tairua. What was so unusual about this lure is that it was made of black-lipped pearl oyster, a species found only in the tropics. Moreover, the style of the lure indicated that it was made in Eastern Polynesia, most likely in the Marquesas Islands, and dated to end of the thirteenth century, as the location of the lure provided evidence that it wasn't dropped there at a later date.

The precise age of artefacts is often difficult to determine. The mysterious korotangi, a small bird carved in stone, is said to have come on the *Tainui* waka from Hawaiki, but it is impossible to tell the age of the carving, let alone its origin. Some Maori consider the korotangi neither old nor of Maori origin. On Mokoia Island is an ancient carved statue named Matuatonga, which protected the kumara crops and is said to have come on the waka *Takitimu*. Likewise the unusual carving of Uenuku is said to have come from Hawaiki on the *Tainui*, though it is carved from New Zealand totara. There is no doubt that the carving is reminiscent of Eastern Polynesian style and is at least 500 years old. Equally the Kaitaia carving is so similar to carvings from Eastern Polynesia that it must date back many hundreds of years to the early days of settlement.

One thing is certain: by 1400 AD, long-distance voyaging both for exploration and settlement appears to have completely ceased, with no real explanation.

Maori population

Although no firm figures exist, the pre-European population of New Zealand was estimated to be in the vicinity of 100,000–120,000, concentrated in the northern half of the North Island. Severely limited by the inability to grow kumara in the colder climate, the population of the South Island may have been as low as 5000, concentrated around Banks and Otago Peninsulas and the warmer northern coast. The West Coast may have had only 500 people, largely dependent on trading pounamu for food.

During the 1820s inter-iwi warfare, known as the Musket Wars, took a huge toll on life with the loss of an estimated one-fifth of the population, and the entire country was convulsed by displaced people. Eight iwi are said to have been completely wiped out and large areas of the country were virtually depopulated; some areas, such as the Coromandel Peninsula and the Tamaki isthmus, never recovered.

However, the introduction of European livestock and crops – especially the potato, which was easier to grow than kumara – meant that for the first time food was plentiful. At the time of the signing of the Treaty of Waitangi the Maori population was around 70,000 to 90,000 (Europeans numbered just 2000). Less than 20 years later the Maori and European populations were equal, at around 60,000 each.

From that point, through war and disease, numbers dropped

dramatically so that by 1896, the Maori population was 42,000. Other figures show the population had dropped even further, with estimates in 1871 numbering just 37,500. Sir Walter Buller thought in 1884 that the Maori population was only 30,000. The first census in 1906 showed a population of 47,700.

Slowly the population began to recover, though the influenza epidemic in 1918 resulted in the deaths of around 1000 Maori. After 1950 the numbers grew dramatically and the Maori population is now estimated to be well over 600,000, with the 2006 census figure at 565,000 and a further estimated 70,000 living in Australia.

The pa

For many, the pa is the most pervasive reminder of the Maori past, found in almost every part of the country and frequently in the most dramatic locations. While many are highly visible, many more have disappeared under forest or have been obliterated by farming, quarrying or roadworks. As a substantial number of walks in this book are to pa sites, a bit of further information will be helpful.

While pa existed before 1700 AD, it was around this time that large numbers were built all around the country; today over 7000 pa sites have been identified. Pa are not known elsewhere in Polynesia, and the theory is that two interrelated factors caused a radical shift in Maori society and culture at that time, which gave rise to the pa.

The first and most obvious is that the population had by that time reached a point where resources came under pressure, and with that pressure came the need to protect what already existed and to acquire more resources from neighbours, usually by force.

Early Maori were not natural conservators and their arrival had an immediate impact on the fragile environment. When Aotearoa was first discovered by Polynesian explorers, 85 percent of the land was covered in dense native forest. Through clearing land for crops and accidental burning of forest, Maori reduced the forest cover to 55 percent by the time Europeans arrived. (Europeans were within a much shorter period of time to diminish the native forest by a further 30 percent.)

For so long isolated from the rest of the world's land masses, New Zealand became a land of birds, and that very isolation spelt disaster for bird life with the arrival of people. Between Polynesian settlement and the arrival of Europeans, 38 species of birds became extinct through hunting and the introduction of the kiore or Polynesian rat. This accounted for the disappearance of all the largest birds, including all 10 species of moa, two adzebills, the New Zealand swan, the flightless New Zealand goose and the giant Haast eagle, and many species were restricted to the dense bush and offshore islands. (The arrival of Europeans led to the extinction of a further 19 birds.)

Another easy source of food, the fur seal, was hunted to near extinction and only survived in any numbers on the inhospitable Fiordland coast and remote offshore islands.

Like the Europeans who came later, Maori learnt the hard way that the land's resources were not infinite. Their response was twofold: the pa to protect and tapu to preserve.

While tapu is known throughout Polynesia, it is in Aotearoa and Hawai'i ('kapu'), that it became most highly developed. The primary reason for the extensive use of tapu and the attendant harsh penalties for breaking it (usually death) was that radical action was necessary to preserve food resources for the future. Tapu was highly successful in preventing overexploitation of the environment, and its use was often governed by periods of abundance and times of scarcity.

Most pa were small, between 1 and 10 hectares, and mainly functioned to protect small hapu in times of trouble and for the storage of the precious kumara crops. Often they were built on the boundaries of territories, especially if that boundary coincided with a valuable resource such as a large sheltered harbour or fertile soils. Most people lived in kainga, small villages close to their gardens or fishing areas, and very few people if any lived in the pa permanently. Pa were not continuously occupied, many being abandoned either permanently or for a long period, to be rebuilt at a later time. Even the larger pa sites that we see today are most likely to represent several pa built over a long period rather than just one pa, so it is often difficult to determine their original size.

The three classic types of pa are the headland, hilltop and ridge pa. All were positioned to maximise natural defence features such as cliffs, steep hillsides and isolated headlands. In addition to the defensive position, almost every pa had the widest and best view possible in order to see any enemy approaching from the furthest possible distance. Today the most obvious tell-tale signs of an old pa are deep defensive ditches, wide terraces to accommodate whare, kumara pits and house sites.

The Musket Wars produced the first radical change in the design of the pa, which underwent a transformation to accommodate attack by gun-wielding enemies. Many traditional pa were abandoned during this period and never reoccupied. Later, during the New Zealand Wars, the defences became yet more sophisticated to protect the pa from rifle and cannon fire. However, by the 1860s the days of the great fortified pa had come to an end and one by one their inhabitants drifted away, never to return.

Anyone wishing to investigate further the structure and layout of pa and kainga should visit the replica Maori village and fortified pa site at Te Hana, just north of Wellsford, http://www.tehana.co.nz/MAORI+VILLAGE.html.

Myths and legends

Given the limitations of space, recounting myths and legends connected to the landscape presented a real challenge: this book only touches on the rich tradition of storytelling. By necessity many of the stories have been simplified, though I hope that in the process the heart of them has not been lost. Almost every story has at least one variation, and some have multiple versions; it has not been possible to include them all here. I have included the best known versions and have added in variations where space permitted.

Spelling of Maori names

Spelling presented a similar challenge with numerous variations of personal and place names depending on the source. Some iwi use the double vowel, others macrons, some names are hyphenated or capitalised, while other sources exclude these. Much of the source material is from old records and books where the spelling is often radically different from modern texts and frequently contradictory. As with traditional stories, I have used what I determined to be the most common spelling, and I apologise in advance for any inaccuracies that may have crept in.

HOW TO USE THIS BOOK

Visiting sites

Most, if not all of these walks are on land open to the public, but many of these places were highly tapu in the past and a bit of respect goes a long way. In some places tapu still exists and you are asked not to enter.

Pa sites in particular were often the location of bloody battles, and all will have an associated urupa close by. When visiting pa sites refrain from eating, though drinking water is fine. Hilltops and peaks are often the representation of an ancestor, so if you do take food and drink with you, avoid sitting down to eat right on the very top.

Grade

The walks are simply graded **Easy, Medium** and **Hard.**

Easy walks are suitable for all ages and for family groups. They are mostly flat, well maintained and very easy to follow.

Medium walks require a bit more effort with a bit of uphill, but well within the range of a person of average fitness. They may not suit very young children; and occasionally the track might be a bit rough and muddy.

Hard in nearly all cases means that the track is uphill, though the grades and conditions of these tracks vary considerably from very good to a bit rough. They are unsuitable for very young children. Good footwear is recommended.

Time

The times given in this book are for the walks to be undertaken at a very leisurely pace and anyone of good fitness can take 25 percent off the time.

How to get there

Simple maps and instructions are provided, but if you don't know the area, a good road map or a GPS system will be very helpful. Each walk is numbered on the map for each region and these numbers relate to individual entries.

Gear

No special gear is required for these walks, but New Zealand weather is notoriously fickle and the condition of the tracks varies considerably, so be prepared. The weather in the South Island can turn cold quickly, even in summer; while the northern areas of the country are often exposed to the tail-end of tropical cyclones that can bring high winds and heavy rain, though these storms are usually short-lived.

Shoes: Tramping boots are not necessary. You will be much more comfortable with a good pair of trainers that you don't mind getting dirty; but make sure they have a good tread as the tracks are often muddy or have slippery sections over rocks and wooden steps.

Jacket: Invest in a jacket that is rainproof. Many jackets are only showerproof or windproof and it rains a lot in New Zealand. In wetter seasons, keeping a few dry items of clothing in the car is a good idea so that if you do get wet, you have something warm to change into.

Security

An unfortunate fact of life in modern New Zealand is that car burglary is now common in walk carparks. Some very popular attractions now even have security guards. Short of leaving someone with the car at all times, there are a few things you can do to lessen the chances of having your car broken into. Lock your car even on the short walks, and double-check your windows are closed (it is easy to forget the back windows). Make sure that all valuables are out of sight, and if possible carry your most valuable items with you (wallet, camera, phone, video camera). Invest in an inexpensive steering lock: this won't stop your car being broken into, but it will indicate to thieves that you are security-conscious and it will almost certainly stop them actually stealing the car.

Mobile phones

Mobile phones can be very useful if you are lost (which is highly unlikely on these short walks), but be aware there is not always coverage in some of the more remote places.

GLOSSARY

haka	vigorous dance with actions and rhythmically shouted words
hangi	underground oven of heated stones, also called an umu
hapu	a group of related families
hongi	greeting by pressing noses and mingling breaths
hui	meeting or gathering, usually a formal occasion
inanga	whitebait
iwi	tribe(s)
kokopu	freshwater fish, cockabully
kokowai	red ochre
kainga	village
kai moana	seafood
kaitiaki	guardians of the natural world
kaitiakitanga	the responsibility of taking care of the environment
kapahaka	Maori performing group
karakia	prayer, invocation
kaupapa	fundamental principles or usual way of doing things
Kingitanga	kingship; the Maori King Movement
Kingite	a supporter of the Maori King Movement
kiore	Polynesian rat
ko	digging stick
kuia	elderly woman, grandmother
kumara	sweet potato
kuri	dog
maketu	curse
mana	power, authority, status, dignity, respect derived from the gods
marae	strictly speaking, the area in front of the wharenui but the meaning can now also encompass the wharenui, associated buildings and even the local community
mauri	essential life force, spiritual power
mere	short flat club
moana	sea
noa	free from tapu

pa	fortified village or fort and more recently a Maori settlement
paua	abalone
puha	edible soft thistle
patu	weapon, usually a club
patupaiarehe	small people with supernatural powers/fairy people
pouwhenua/pou	carved marker post
pounamu	greenstone, jade
rua	kumara pit
rahui	ban, embargo; 'no trespassing' sign
rangatira	chief
rohe	tribal region
runanga	tribal council
tangata whenua	'people of the land', those who hold mana in an area
taniwha	water monster, ogre
tangi	funeral, to mourn
taonga	prized possessions, both material and non-material
tapu	sacred, forbidden
taro	leafy plant with a large edible fibrous root
tekoteko	main carved figure on a meeting house
toetoe	large native grass
tohunga	priest/magician
umu	oven, earth oven
urupa	burial ground, cemetery
utu	revenge, retribution
waka	canoe
wahi tapu	sacred place
waiata	song
wairua	spirit
waka taua	war canoe
whakapapa	genealogy
whanau	family, both immediate and extended family
whare	small house
wharenui	meeting house

ENGLISH/MAORI PLACE NAMES

English	Maori
Napier	**Ahuriri**
Mt Cook	**Aoraki**
Great Barrier Island	**Aotea**
Banks Peninsula	**Hakaroa**
Hastings	**Heretaunga**
Levin	**Horowhenua**
Coopers Beach	**Koekoea**
Hamilton	**Kirikiriroa**
One Tree Hill	**Maungakiekie**
Mt Wellington	**Maungarei**
Mt Eden	**Maungawhau**
Greymouth	**Mawhera**
Invercargill	**Murihiku**
Southern Alps	**Ka Tiritiri o te Moana**
New Plymouth	**Ngamotu**
Christchurch	**Otautahi**
Dunedin	**Otepoti**
Mt Albert	**Owairaka**
Thames	**Parawai**
Mt Roskill	**Puketapapa**
Mt Edgecumbe	**Putauaki**
Huntly	**Rahui Pokeka**
Stewart Island	**Rakiura**
Mt Hobson	**Remuera**
Auckland	**Tamaki Makaurau**
Mt Egmont	**Taranaki**
Taupo	**Taupo nui a Tia**
Tauranga	**Tauranga Moana**
Foveaux Strait	**Te Ara a Kiwa**
Te Mahia Hawke's Bay	**Te Matau a Maui**
Cook Strait	**Te Moana a Raukawa**
Oamaru	**Te Oha a Maru**
Palmerston North	**Te Papa i Oea**
East Cape	**Te Tairawhiti**
Northland	**Te Taitokerau**
Timaru	**Te Tihi o Maru**
Wellington	**Te Whanganui a Tara**
Meola Reef	**Tokaroa**
Doubtless Bay	**Tokerau**
Gisborne	**Turanganui a Kiwa**
Blenheim	**Wairau**
Canterbury	**Waitaha**
Raglan	**Whaingaroa**
White Island	**Whakaari**
Masterton	**Whakaoriori**
Nelson	**Whakatu**

NORTH ISLAND/
TE IKA A MAUI

NORTHLAND

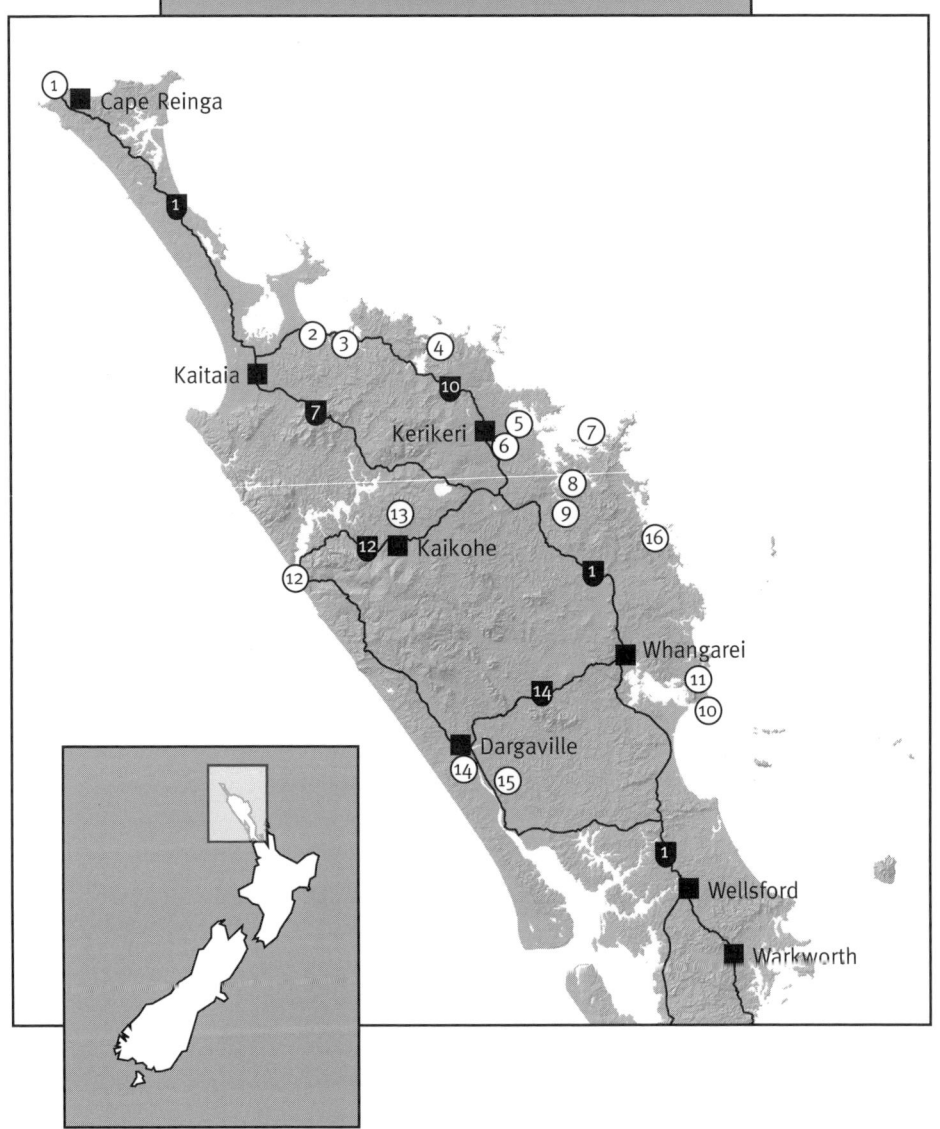

1 Cape Reinga

Kaitaia

Kerikeri

Kaikohe

Whangarei

Dargaville

Wellsford

Warkworth

1 Cape Reinga

The cape is renowned for the spectacular and wild seascapes where the Tasman Sea and the Pacific Ocean meet. The cape is also one of the most important wahi tapu (sacred sites) as it is the final departing point for the spirits of the dead on their journey to the underworld domain of Hinenuitepo, the goddess of death. Along the west coast the twisted and gnarled vegetation is evidence of the travelling spirits' desperate attempt to cling to this world. On the very point, right at sea level, is a small and battered pohutukawa said to be over 800 years old and to have flowered only once. Here the spirits finally step down the roots of this tree and into the underworld. A gentle way to say that someone has died is to say they have 'slid down the pohutukawa root'.

As the point is highly tapu, access has been restricted, though the importance of this site to Maori has also kept the area free from commercialisation despite the number of bus tours that crowd the cape around the middle of the day.

An easy walk on a sealed path leads down to the lighthouse with spectacular views in every direction.

Grade: Easy
Time: 20 minutes return
How to get there: This is the very end of SH1 – you can't go any further.

2 Taumarumaru Scenic Reserve

This reserve at the western end of Koekoea/Coopers Beach is the location of three pa. Taumarumaru is the oldest and largest of the three and occupies a high ridge in the centre of the reserve. While the rectangular outline of the pa still remains, the defensive ditches at either end have largely disappeared, though the ridge is lined with numerous rua or kumara pits.

On the headland looking east along the beach to Rangikapiti is Ohumuhumu, which was built by Korewha and Puneka, descendants of Tukiato. The outstanding feature of this pa is two ditches protecting the land side, which are exceptionally deep and steep and even today are difficult to clamber up. Topped with palisading, the trenches would have offered superb protection to the living terraces on the seaward side.

The third pa, Otanenui, faces west. The name of the pa reflects the coastal location and means 'the place of the huge old-man snapper'. This is the pa built by Tukiato after he was banished from Rangikapiti for killing the shark protected by his father Moehuri.

It will take around an hour to visit all three pa along wide grassy paths that make for easy walking, though it is a scramble to get up onto Ohumuhumu. There is also a track up onto the reserve from the western end of Coopers Beach.

 Grade: Easy

Time: 1 hour

How to get there: 3 km west of Mangonui on SH10 with good carparking and information. At the time of writing the sign marking the entrance had disappeared, but the reserve is directly opposite the Coopers Beach Bowling Club.

3 Rangikapiti Pa, Mangonui

Rangikapiti pa overlooks both Spirits Bay and inland along the Mangonui Harbour, and was the principal pa in this area. According to Ngati Kahu tradition, it was here that the voyaging waka *Ruakaramea*, commanded by Moehuri, first landed. It is now turned to stone and is still visible just below the pa at low tide. The name Rangikapiti means 'gathered together'.

The *Ruakaramea* was guided by a great shark across the open ocean to the safe harbour. To honour the shark, Moehuri not only named the harbour Mangonui (big shark), but gave orders that the shark was to be protected. Directly in opposition to his father's orders, Moehuri's son Tukiato and a group of friends killed the shark and, as punishment, Tukiato was expelled from the pa to the other end of Coopers Beach where he built the pa Otanenui.

Grade: Easy

Time: 15 minutes return

How to get there: Between Coopers Beach and Mangonui turn off SH10 into Mill Bay Road and then immediately left into Rangikapiti Road and the pa is at the end.

4 Ohakiri/St Pauls Rock, Whangaroa Harbour

Tararata was a handsome mountain, and being handsome he had two loving wives who took care of his every need. One day Maungataniwha, who lived to the west and was both a taniwha and a mountain, asked Tararata if he could have one of his wives, as he was still single. Not only did Tararata refuse the request, but he laughed in his face and mocked the bachelor to such a degree that Maungataniwha swung his huge tail and whipped off Tararata's head with such force that it sailed over the harbour and landed on the hill now known as Ohakiri or St Pauls Rock. The headless Tararata still stands today as the flat-topped mountain to the west of Whangaroa Harbour.

The harbour, correctly spelt Whaingaroa ('what a long wait'), takes its name from a woman whose husband had gone off to war and had been gone such a long time that she had lost her patience waiting for his return.

For those familiar with the tidal upper Whangaroa Harbour, the beauty of this bush-clad and almost enclosed bay will be a pleasant surprise. The views are spectacular of the fiord-like harbour far below, stretching out to the narrow entrance and beyond that Stephenson Island is clearly visible. The barren rock is an old pa site. Even today the track is a steep uphill climb with a final rocky scramble to the summit, though chain handrails assist in the steepest places. Despite the signs warning of limited parking and turnaround space, there is in fact good parking and an easy turnaround just 50 metres beyond the beginning of the track at the end of the road.

 Grade: Hard

Time: 45 minutes

How to get there: Take the road to Whangaroa off SH10 north of Kaeo. Take Old Hospital Road to the right 500 metres past the Marlin Hotel and before the main wharf. The track begins at the top of this road.

5 Ake Ake Point

This small headland pa with spectacular views over the Kerikeri and
Te Puna inlets and out to the Bay of Islands is today largely covered by
regenerating bush, though the terraces and a very deep defensive ditch
are still clearly visible. The pa was the home of the chief Tareha, who
was famous for his exceptional bravery and fighting skills. Allied with
Hongi Hika, and supportive of the establishment of the mission station,
he was also famous for both his physical size and his great appetite.
Samuel Marsden, who invited Tareha to visit the ship *Dromedary*,
commented that 'there was not an armchair in the cabin in which he
could sit'.

This easy loop track with a short flight of steps at the beginning
leads to a small beach in Te Puna Inlet and then on to the pa site on
Tareha Point. The lookout itself is cleverly shaped like a ship's prow.
On the return trip take the cliff-top option, which will reward you with
excellent views along the Kerikeri Inlet, and which emerges just 300
metres from the boat ramp. A short detour takes you down to a beach
of fine shingle.

Grade: Easy
Time: 40 minutes return
How to get there: The track begins at the end of Opito Bay Road.

6 Koropito Pa

The Kerikeri Mission was deliberately established adjacent to Koropito
pa, home to one of the most powerful chiefs in the north, Hongi Hika.
Without Hongi's patronage and protection, the mission had little chance
of survival. Hongi's main base was at Waimate, however, and when the
missionaries arrived in 1819 this pa was no longer fortified as it had
been in the past. No doubt those in the pa, with their uninterrupted
view back to Kemp House and the stone store, would have been able to
keep a good eye on the comings and goings of the Pakeha living there
and reported back to Hongi. By 1830 Maori had all left the area and
the pa was deserted.

All the major earthworks of the pa still remain, including the
defensive ditches and banks and wide terraces, and these are
complemented by excellent interpretive panels that give the visitor a
good idea of life in this pa 200 years ago.

Grade: Easy
Time: 20 minutes return
How to get there: At the end of Kerikeri Road, Kerikeri; well signposted from SH10.

7 Urupukapuka Island

The largest island in the Bay of Islands, Urupukapuka Island has a long history of Maori occupation, possibly dating back almost 1000 years. Eight pa have been identified on the island, and French explorer Marion du Fresne in April 1772 noted on a map of Urupukapuka a number of palisaded villages. At the time of du Fresne's visit Ngare Raumati lived on the island, though by the early nineteenth century Ngapuhi were in occupation.

A series of easy walking tracks links a number of small sandy beaches on this island in the outer reaches of the bay. The archaeological walk, which links sites of early Maori occupation, was undergoing a major upgrade at the time of writing. There is also a café and overnight accommodation on the island.

Grade: Easy
Time: Allow 2 hours
How to get there: There is no regular ferry service to the island, though there are tour companies and water taxis from both Paihia and Russell. Check with the i-SITE on the wharf for updated information.

8 Maiki/Flagstaff Hill, Russell

Russell began life as Kororareka, and the early settlement, known as the 'hellhole of the Pacific', was notorious for grog shops, brothels and general lawlessness. Despite its reputation it was even the capital of the fledgling colony for a brief nine-month period.

As tensions grew between the Maori and the British, mainly over trade and the imposition of duties and tariffs, Ngapuhi chief Hone Heke was well aware of the symbolic nature of the British flag flying over Russell, regardless of the fact that he had actually gifted the flagpole in the first place. Inspired by talk of revolution by American Captain William Mayhew, Hone hacked down the pole for the first time on 8 July 1844. When it was replaced, he cut it down again twice in January 1845 and actually flew the US flag from his waka.

The fourth time the flagpole was erected, the lower portion was clad in iron, but this did not deter Hone from cutting down the pole on 11 March 1845; and then, for good measure, he followed this up by sacking the town, burning down many buildings including the Duke of Marlborough Hotel.

Later, in an act of reconciliation, those involved in cutting down the pole erected a new flagstaff in 1857; and in January 1958 a British flag was raised, with the flagpole being named Whakakotahitanga, 'being at one with each other; unity'. This flagpole still stands today.

The first part of the walk is tide-dependent so it is best to start from this point and avoid having to return uphill if you find yourself cut off by the tide. Walk north along the beach and around the rocks to the beginning of the track that winds up through regenerating bush. At Titore Way turn right, and then take the track uphill to the summit. The views from the top are impressive. On the return trip, walk down to the carpark and then take the steps down to Wellington Street, which leads back to town. If the tide is not favourable, then walk up Wellington Street to the top.

Grade: Medium

Time: 45 minutes return

How to get there: From the north end of the beach at Russell, continue past the boat ramp and along the rocky shore to the beginning of the track.

9 Ruapekapeka Pa

Late December 1845 saw the final battle in the war of the north, when a British siege of Ruapekapeka (the bat's nest) began with a heavy artillery bombardment of the pa.

The British, outnumbering the Maori three to one, were confounded by Te Ruki Kawiti's innovative defences, which – unlike traditional pa – featured underground bunkers and foxholes to protect the defenders from both cannon and musket fire.

On Sunday 11 January 1846, the British became aware that the pa appeared very quiet, and when a small party of soldiers breached the palisades they found the pa virtually empty. As British reinforcements were called up, Maori warriors tried to recapture the pa, and after four hours of fierce fighting the Maori defenders finally abandoned the fight.

There are two possible reasons why the pa was almost empty. One story has it that the Maori defenders, believing the British would not attack on a

Sunday, had gone off to a Christian service and were caught off guard; the other theory is that the pa was deliberately left empty to lure the British into a trap, but that this plan went badly wrong.

The outline of the pa is very clear and complemented by good information boards with great views over the surrounding countryside. Note that the carpark is a little way from the site, and the British position is not to be confused with the actual pa, the entrance of which is marked by a fine carved gateway.

 Grade: Easy

Time: 45 minutes return

How to get there: 35 km north of Whangarei on SH1 turn right at Towai into Ruapekapeka Road. The pa site is 4 km down this road, which is unsealed and narrow in places.

10 Te Whara/Bream Head

The Bream Head Reserve stretches from Te Whara along an undulating ridge and down to Smugglers Bay and Busby Head.

At 476 metres, Te Whara is named in honour of Manaia's principal wife. It was renamed Bream Head by Captain Cook when he mistook tarakihi for bream. A pa was once located in the area where the radar station was located in World War II, though little now remains. The Te Whara track from Bream Head to Urquharts Bay is an old Maori trail linking the pa with the sheltered waters of the harbour.

At the southern end of the reserve is Busby Head, and this is the site of a much older pa. Not large, this pa was located on the narrow ridge along the headland, protected by a deep defensive ditch and with narrow terraces for small houses running the length of the headland. In the sandhills behind the beach at Smugglers Bay are old Maori middens, easily recognised by the large numbers of pipi shells in the dunes.

The coastal views from both Te Whara and Busby Head are exceptional.

The Te Whara track that runs the length of the reserve will take a good five hours one way and is hard work as it follows the ridge, which is very steep in places.

Two much shorter walks are up Te Whara as far as the old pa, and to Busby Head. The track to Te Whara starts at the Ocean Beach carpark and is a steady uphill walk on a good track through open vegetation with views all the way.

To get to Busby Head, the track is well marked from Urquharts Bay. From the carpark first take the track to the left around the gun emplacements and continue past the gun emplacements to a junction where the track to the pa leads along the ridge to the right. After visiting the pa, return to the junction, then turn down to the right and back along the beautiful Smugglers Bay where, if the weather is right, you can spend some time on the beach.

Te Whara Pa Site/Radar Station
Grade: Medium
Time: 1 hour 45 minutes return
How to get there: The track entrance is from the beach access carpark at Ocean Beach, 40 km from Whangarei and 3 km from Urquharts Bay.

Te Whara Track
Grade: Hard
Time: 5 hours one way
How to get there: One end is at the Ocean Beach carpark and the other at Urquharts Bay.

Busby Head and Smugglers Cove
Grade: Easy
How to get there: The track to the cove begins at the carpark at the very end of Urquharts Bay Road.

11 Mt Manaia

This distinctive mountain (460 metres) is easily recognised by the numerous volcanic outcrops that define the peak.

In the distant past Manaia was a proud rangatira who had his pa on the very summit of this mountain. Manaia was not happy and he was very envious of the chief Hautatu who lived on the other side of the harbour, for Hautatu was married to a very attractive woman, Pito. Manaia became so consumed with jealousy that he connived to send Hautatu on a raiding party, and while he was gone Manaia constructed a rock causeway across the harbour, then raided Hautatu's pa, kidnapping Pito.

On his return, Hautatu was furious. In his anger he attacked Manaia's mountain-top pa, forcing Manaia to escape along with his two children and Pito. In hot pursuit Hautatu quickly caught up with Pito and was about to strike her with a club when they were all turned to stone by a lightning bolt from the god of thunder – and there they remain today.

It is all uphill, but it is not as hard as it looks as the track is excellent and the grade steady for the most part. Take your time as the great views from the top are reward for the uphill climb.

Grade: Hard
Time: 2 hours return
How to get there: From the city take Riverside Drive out towards Whangarei Heads, and the beginning of the track is from the carpark of the Mt Manaia Club, 30 km from the city.

12 Hokianga/Arai Te Uru Coastal Walkway

First discovered by Kupe, the long finger of the Hokianga Harbour stretches far inland. The sheltered waters were a vital transport link for Maori and, later, for Pakeha. While geologists will tell us that the harbour is a river valley drowned by rising sea levels, the traditional story of how the Hokianga was formed is a good deal more interesting. There are two different versions, and both involve two taniwha.

The first story is relatively simple, and tells that two taniwha live on either side of the harbour entrance: Niwa makes his home on the high sandhills on the north head; Arai Te Uru lives in a cave on the south head. These two taniwha have just one important task: using their long and very powerful tails, together they stir the water at the entrance to the harbour, creating treacherous waves and strong currents and thereby protecting the people of the Hokianga from enemies invading by sea.

The second story involves just Arai Te Uru and his children, of which he had 11 and, like all big families, the children found their home in a cave above the beach just too crowded and started to fight among themselves.

One of the children, Waihou, decided to leave home and off he went burrowing his way far inland until finally he was so tired that he made himself a hole, lay down and slept. This hole filled with water and became Lake Omapere. When Waihou didn't return his brother Waima began searching for him, creating inlets as he went, until he became hopelessly lost and remains forever in the Punakitere swamp.

Next Utakura left to find his brothers . . . and on it went until all the taniwha's children had left home, never to return, and in the course of their travels created the 11 major waterways of the Hokianga.

This short walk on the South Head of the Hokianga Harbour winds through wind-stunted manuka, flax and toetoe and has incredible views north over the giant golden sandhills on the northern shore, and north-east along the inland waterway that is the Hokianga Harbour. The hard sandy soil has been shaped by persistent wind, and below the lookout is a lovely sandy cove that can be accessed by a good track starting at the carpark.

Grade: Easy

Time: 20 minutes return

How to get there: Signal Station Road off SH12, 4 km east of Omapere

13 Hone Heke Memorial Park, Kaikohe Hill

The name Kaikohe is a short version of kaikohekohe (to eat the berries of the kohekohe tree). This name stems from the aftermath of a battle when the pa Pakinga fell to attacking Ngapuhi led by Tuohu, and the survivors subsisted on the berries of kohekohe trees growing on the hill. It was also on this hill where the warrior Hone Heke Pokai retreated to mourn the fall of Ruapekapeka in 1846 and the death of his friends killed in the battle.

Now the hill is crowned with a monument and gardens in honour of Hone Heke Ngapua, the great-nephew of Hone Heke and great-great-nephew of Hongi Hika. Graduating as a lawyer, Hone began working for the Native Land Court in 1891 and as a staunch supporter of the Kotahitanga (Unity) Movement, he became leader of the Federated Tribes of New Zealand in 1892. From there he became MP for Northern Maori, a position that he held until his death in 1909. Hone is credited with introducing rugby to the North, and today local teams still compete for the Hone Heke Cup.

The walk starts through a fine carved gateway that incorporates both Maori and Pakeha motifs. It slopes gently uphill past magnificent old trees and through gardens to the monument.

Grade: Easy

Time: 15 minutes return

How to get there: From the centre of Kaihoke, drive west for 1 km along Broadway (SH10) and turn into Orrs Road. After 400 metres turn left into Monument Road and drive to the carpark at the end.

14 Poututerangi, Dargaville

Located on a high bluff overlooking the Wairoa River, this pa was known as Poututerangi, which is also the name for the tenth lunar month and means 'the post that lifted up the sky'. As you walk from the museum, the path first crosses the main defensive ditch that protected the large flat area in the central part of the pa, which is located on high steep bluffs that give superb views east and south over a wide bend in the river.

A legend tells of a magical log known as Rangiriri that floated along this part of the Wairoa River, and had been cursed by a powerful taniwha, Pokopoko. Whenever Rangiriri floated ashore near any village, someone would die within a few days, and it was certain death if anyone was brave or foolish enough to cut off even the minutest piece of the log.

 Grade: Easy
Time: 10 minutes return
How to get there: From the Dargaville Museum carpark

15 Tokatoka

During the bitter and bloody war that raged between Ngapuhi and Te Roroa, a hapu of Ngati Whatua, this pa above the Wairoa River was a Te Roroa stronghold under the rangatira Taoho. Ever alert to attack, Taoho knew when he saw smoke columns from Maunganui Bluff that the scouts he posted there were warning of Ngapuhi warriors coming up the long beach. Knowing a battle was imminent, Taoho sang a war song that urged his warriors 'to be as firm as the rock on Tokatoka'. It was Taoho who turned the tide of the battle of Moremonui when he killed the Ngapuhi chief Pokaia, though he himself was wounded during the fight.

The distinctive shape of Tokatoka is impossible to miss on the road from Ruawai to Dargaville, though the actual pa site is now occupied by an old cemetery with some earthworks still visible overlooking the river.

For the best view of the pa and the surrounding countryside go to the top of the peak, which at a distance looks quite difficult to climb, but in fact the track from the eastern side is not that hard, even though it is not well formed and is a bit of a scramble near the top. However, it is worth the effort, as the views from the top are superb and encompass a long stretch of the river, the Kaipara Harbour to the south and the rugged bush-clad ranges to the east.

Grade: Medium

Time: 40 minutes return

How to get there: At Tokatoka Tavern north of Ruawai, turn right into Tokatoka Road. The track begins about 1.5 km on the left by the 'Scenic Reserve' sign.

16 Mimiwhangata Regional Park

This beautiful but isolated park was the site of a great battle between Ngapuhi and Ngati Manaia.

Mimiwhangata was originally settled by people arriving on the waka *Mahuhukiterangi*, who eventually formed the iwi Ngati Manaia. Although they later intermarried with Ngapuhi, the relationship was not always an easy one.

Tensions boiled over when Te Waero of Ngapuhi deliberately destroyed a fishing net belonging to Ngati Manaia and, in an act of utu, was killed by them. Ngapuhi were incensed at the murder and in reply planned to attack the three Ngati Manaia pa on the Mimiwhangata Peninsula: Te Rearea, Taraputa and Kaituna.

To create the greatest confusion Ngapuhi, under their rangatira Te Rangitamaru, decided to attack all three pa simultaneously in the middle of the night. Te Rearea was attacked from the land, while the other two pa were invaded by sea and totally caught by surprise. Ngati Manaia suffered a devastating defeat with a huge loss of life, though their rangatira and some people managed to escape. Kaituna is still considered tapu today.

Today a sprawling farm park covers the rolling hills of the Mimiwhangata Peninsula. There are tracks though, the signage is erratic, but you can't get lost as it is all open farmland. Long sandy beaches make this an ideal destination for walking, but it is a long drive to get there. The only facilities at the park are toilets.

 Grade: Easy

Time: Allow 2 hours

How to get there: From Helena Bay take Webb Road for 5.5 km and turn left into Mimiwhangata Road. Continue for another 5 km along this narrow, winding gravel road to the carpark.

AUCKLAND

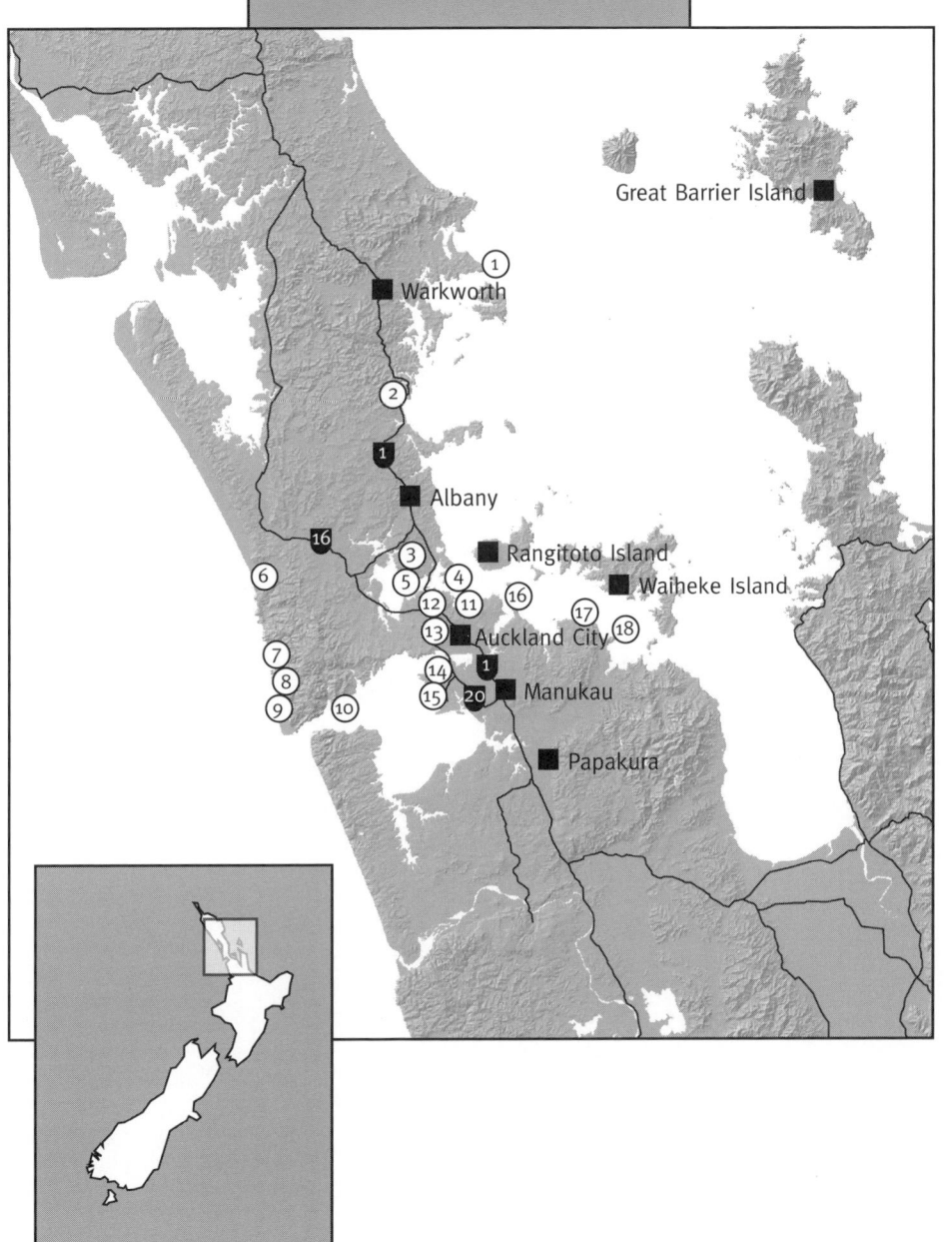

Great Barrier Island ■

①
■ Warkworth

②

1
■ Albany

16

③ ■ Rangitoto Island
⑤ ④
⑥ ⑪ 16 ■ Waiheke Island
⑫ ⑰
⑬ ■ Auckland City ⑱
⑭ 1
⑮ 20 ■ Manukau
⑦ ⑩
⑧
⑨ ■ Papakura

1 Tokatu, Tawharanui Regional Park

When travelling along the coastline, Maori, like all navigators, used distinctive landmarks to guide them. Tawharanui was known to these travellers as Takatu ('gannet'; now incorrectly spelt Tokatu), which is the name of the rock formation at the very tip of the peninsula.

The name Tawharanui refers to the edible flower bract of the kiekie vine, which grew abundantly here. Anchor Bay was originally known as Waikokowai, as the cliffs at the eastern end of the bay were a source of red ochre widely used for decoration and in rituals. Near the entrance to the park is the site of Oponui pa, though little remains.

In December 1874 a large group of Maori warriors escaped from Kawau Island, where they had been held prisoner after the defeat of the Maori King Tawhiao at Rangiriri. Coming ashore on the south coast of the peninsula, the men stayed only briefly before seeking refuge with Kingite sympathisers in the Kaipara. Thereafter their landing place became known as Maori Bay. The park, a mixture of farmland and bush remnants, has a maze of excellent tracks. The walk to Tokatu Point lookout starts from Anchor Bay and follows the northern coast to the very end of the peninsula with spectacular views of the Hauraki Gulf along the way.

To reach Maori Bay, park at the lagoon carpark and take the Maori Bay Coast Walk along the southern coastline. Parts of the walk are affected by the tide and may involve some rock hopping. An easier alternative is to follow the South Coast Track and then drop down into Maori Bay.

The two walks together form a loop that encompasses the entire park and will take around 3.5 hours.

Grade: Easy

Time: Tokatu Point Walk, 2 hours return; Maori Bay Coastal Walk, 2 hours return; North and South Coast Loop Walk, 2 hours

How to get there: Tawharanui is 26 km from Warkworth – the directions to the park are clearly signposted from SH1. The last 5 km of road just before the park is unsealed, narrow and winding.

2 Wenderholm Regional Park

The people who originally settled this land are descendants of the great explorer Toi who explored this area. Through intermarriage and occupation, various peoples settled along the coast and offshore islands and by the eighteenth century it was under the control of the iwi Te Kawerau. The situation began to change as Hauraki tribes began to push north – not for land, as was usually the case, but for possession of the sea and with it the rich shark-hunting grounds.

Around 1780, to avoid a direct confrontation between Te Kawerau and the Hauraki iwi Ngati Paoa, a meeting was held at Kakaha pa, located high above the beach. As part of the peace arrangement, it was agreed that a high-born Te Kawerau woman would marry a Ngati Paoa rangatira and, in return, Te Kawerau would be gifted a pounamu mere. However, that very night Te Kawerau returned the mere and took back the bride-to-be, as they believed that Ngati Paoa had placed a makutu on them that resulted in a storm that had sunk a number of their waka. Strategically this turned out to be a grave mistake by Te Kawerau, as the return of the mere greatly insulted Ngati Paoa and fighting broke out once more. Te Kawerau were finally defeated in a battle north of Matakana.

Peace was not to last when, in 1825, Ngapuhi swept out of the north and, after scoring a decisive victory at Kaiwaka, moved south. One after another, pa and their rangatira fell to the Ngapuhi onslaught, with many fleeing south to take refuge with their relatives in the Waikato. It was another decade before some of the people returned and, when Europeans arrived, only very few Maori lived in the area.

All the walks begin behind Couldrey House and are marked by a handsome carved pouwhenua. The tracks are well formed and marked, with the exception of the section of the Perimeter Track that drops down to Kokoru Bay on the Waiwera River, which is steep, very rough and very muddy even in summer. At the top of the Couldrey House Track, just before the junction with Maungatauhoro Te Hikoi Track, is the site of a former pa, though it is difficult now to make out any of the earthworks. There are also a number of lookout points over the coast and along the Waiwera and Puhoi rivers.

Grade: Medium
Time: To the lookout, 45 minutes return; Perimeter Loop Track, 2 hours
How to get there: Wenderholm Regional Park is just north of Waiwera on SH1.

3 Te Kauri Pa, Kauri Point Centennial Park

While the great hilltop pa gracing Auckland's prominent volcanic cones are well known, this pa is virtually unvisited.

Te Kauri is the only remaining fortified headland pa on the Waitemata Harbour, and little is known of its history apart from from the fact the area was once settled by the people of Te Kawerau (there are remains of a badly damaged pa at Northcote Point under the Auckland Harbour Bridge).

A defensive ditch protects the pa from the mainland, and steep cliffs on the other three sides gave the pa natural protection from attack by sea. Beyond the ditch is a large flat area now covered in trees with few other signs of habitation. An old pohutukawa tree clings to the cliff at the very end of the point. The views over the Waitemata Harbour are superb, with the pa looking directly south over Meola Reef. Below, Kendalls Bay would have provided a sheltered bay for landing waka and a warm microclimate for growing kumara.

This track doesn't have a lot of signage and it is easy to take the wrong path. Five minutes after starting the walk, ignore the track that branches off to the right and continue straight ahead. At the next junction take the track to the left marked 'Lower Entrance' and a bit further on take the track to the right signed 'Kendalls Bay'. After a short distance an unmarked track leads off to the left and this will take you to the pa. The track can be slippery when wet.

 Grade: Easy

Time: 30 minutes return

How to get there: Kauri Point Centennial Park, Onetaunga Road, Chatswood. The simplest access is the information board at the entry point opposite Chelsea View Drive.

4 Takarunga/Mt Victoria

Takarunga/Mt Victoria was the main pa in the area around Devonport; it is curious that Maunga Uika (North Head) was not fortified by Maori in pre-European times, though there is evidence of occupation and cultivation of the rich volcanic soil.

Tradition tells that when the great ocean-going waka *Tainui* explored the area, they found people already living there; and over the centuries the area, valued for its warm fertile soil and excellent fishing grounds, was occupied by numerous iwi. Around 1793 Te Haukapua (Torpedo Bay) saw several bloody clashes between Ngati Paoa and Ngapuhi, culminating in the defeat of Ngati Paoa. Although victorious, Ngapuhi did not settle permanently and returned north. Conflict between the two iwi continued in a long series of battles until 1828, when the great Ngapuhi fighting chief Patuone married Takarangi, the sister of Te Kupenga, a Ngati Paoa chief. Patuone moved to the area when he was gifted land at Takapuna, and when he died in 1872, aged 109, he was the first person to be buried in the cemetery on the flanks of Mt Victoria.

Start this walk at the cemetery. After visiting the grave of Patuone, make your way up to the track that winds its way to the top. Typical of hilltop pa, the summit of Takarunga is crowned by a series of wide terraces that once would have supported houses and been encircled by protective palisading. Fortifications built in the nineteenth century, and extended during World War II, have erased or damaged the Maori earthworks at the very top. As expected, the views over Auckland, the North Shore and the sea are impressive. Return down the road that will take you down to Devonport, from where you can walk back to the start.

Grade: Easy
Time: 30 minutes
How to get there: The cemetery is right by the roundabout on the corner of Albert and Lake roads. The road from the summit emerges onto Victoria Road, right above the main shopping area of Devonport.

5 Te Tokaroa/Meola Reef

Maori tradition tells two different stories to account for the long rocky reef that snakes almost all the way across the Waitemata and was known to Maori as Te Tokaroa (long rock).

The first story concerns the patupaiarehe, who are frequently described as fairy people, a description that implies a certain degree of cuteness, when in fact patupaiarehe were usually belligerent and unfriendly, not only to humans, but frequently to each other. Long ago two patupaiarehe iwi who lived in the deep, wet Waitakere bush clashed one night on the shores of the harbour just west of Te Rae (Point Chevalier). The losing side was gradually pushed back to the shore and with their route back to Waitakere cut off, decided that they would make their escape by building a bridge of loose rocks to the other side of the harbour. Covered by water at high tide, this causeway would confuse their enemies as to where they had escaped. Hauling heavy rocks, their stone bridge creeping ever deeper into the harbour, the patupaiarehe forgot about the dawn until suddenly the sun rose over the eastern horizon. With the bridge incomplete, the patupaiarehe were trapped forever and turned to stone by the sun's rays; some even say that the tree branches sticking out from the lava reef are the gaunt bones of those caught by the sun.

A similar story, but this time involving humans and with a happier ending, involves a siege of a pa on the summit of Owairaka (Mt Albert), then known as Te Puke-o-Ruarangi (the hill of Ruarangi). The people trapped in the pa escaped by a lava cave that ran from the northern slopes of the pa to Te Wai Orea (Western Springs lake; 'orea' is the native longfinned eel). From there they fled to the coast where they picked up rocks, built a causeway and crossed over to safety on the northern side of the harbour.

This is an easy, flat loop walk through open grass fields and regenerating coastal vegetation. Towards the exposed reef the track ends and mangroves give way to oyster-covered rocks. You will need very good, strong footwear if you intend to walk out any distance onto the reef itself. This is best done at very low tide and is much more difficult than it looks from a distance.

Grade: Easy
Time: 20 minutes
How to get there: The track is clearly marked on Meola Road between Westmere and Point Chevalier.

6 Otakamiro, Muriwai

Today the gannet colony on Otakamiro Point attracts thousands of visitors to Muriwai Beach. Interestingly, the area has long been associated with prolific bird life.

Motutara (island of seabirds), the small island directly offshore, today is inhabited by thousands of gulls and terns. The Te Kawerau people who once occupied this area made several references to moa, which they called Te Manu Pouturu, 'the bird on stilts'. Ngati Whatua, who came later, also make reference to hunting moa south of the Kaipara Harbour. Around 1700 AD a moa was sighted, and the fact was so unusual that a child was named after the event – Te Kura Reia, 'the startled moa'. Te Hokioi is the name given to an area just to the north of Muriwai Stream and is also the name of the extinct giant eagle, while a nearby ridge bears the name Karearea, referring to the native falcon.

However, the gannets for which Muriwai is now famous are a recent arrival as it wasn't until early in the twentieth century that these birds began establishing nesting sites on Oaia Island, followed by Motutara Island; finally, in 1979, they also settled themselves on Otakamiro Point on the mainland.

Long occupied by Maori, there were once two pa on the northern slopes of Otakamiro Point, though little evidence remains. While birds would have been an important food source, fur seals would also have attracted early Maori to the area. There is a seal colony on Oaia Island and seals can occasionally be spotted on the beach at Maori Bay.

This short loop walk begins from the main carpark for the gannet colony, overlooking Maori Bay, and leads out to Otakamiro Point. After viewing the birds, take the track back to Muriwai, and just before the road down to the beach, another track leads off to the right. This track climbs the hill, passing through the old pa sites on its way back to the Maori Bay carpark.

Grade: Easy

Time: 30 minutes return

How to get there: End of Motutara Road, Muriwai

7 Kitekite Falls

The traditional name of the falls is Ketekete and the valley Whatiwhati. Both place names are closely connected to a battle in the seventeenth century. In a revenge attack for the death of his father Tawhiakiterangi, Taimaro ambushed a group from the South Kaipara who were visiting the falls. The attack was signalled by Taimaro clicking his tongue, 'ketekete'. Most of those from the Kaipara died in the attack, but a few survivors escaped down the Whatiwhati valley.

This broad track follows the picturesque Glen Esk Stream through luxuriant bush and goes steadily uphill to the falls. The Kitekite Falls drop in three cascades, and the entire waterfall is best seen from the viewpoint on the track just before the falls. The track also offers views back down the valley over the tops of regenerating kauri. The lower falls tumble down a rock face into a small pool suitable for swimming, and the broad rocky area right by the falls is a good, if lumpy, spot for a picnic. The return track is down the other side of the stream.

Grade: Easy

Time: 1 hour return

How to get there: Take the road to Piha and at the bottom of the hill before the beach turn immediately right into Glen Esk Road. The track begins from the carpark at the top end of this road.

8 Te Ahua Point, Ahuahu Track

Once there was a beautiful chieftainess, Hinerangi, who fell in love with a chieftain from Karekare and moved there to be with him. But then as now, the west coast was notorious for dangerous surf, and one day Hinerangi's husband and two companions were swept off the rocks and drowned while fishing at the southern end of Te Unuhanga-o-Rangitoto (Mercer Bay).

Searching desperately for her husband, Hinerangi climbed to the top of this headland to scan the sea. She refused to leave the spot, and eventually died of a broken heart. Her sad face is now forever outlined in the rocks below the headland on which she sat, which became known as Te Ahua-o-Hinerangi (the likeness of Hinerangi).

Situated between Karekare and Piha beaches, Te Ahua Point is a superb lookout atop towering volcanic cliffs that drop hundreds of metres into a wild sea. To the south the view is along the coast to the dangerous bar that marks the entrance to the Manukau Harbour. The Ahuahu Track is well formed and well marked. A grassy knoll at the turnaround point is a good place for a break, though this area is exposed to strong westerly winds. For a longer walk, follow the track downhill to Karekare Beach.

Grade: Easy

Time: 40 minutes return

How to get there: The track begins at the end of Te Ahuahu Road/ Log Race Road, which turns left off Piha Road just before the road descends into Piha.

9 Te Rua o Kaiwhare/The Gap, Piha Beach

Kaiwhare the taniwha had a mixed reputation. On the one hand he was considered a guardian of the coast around the Manukau Harbour entrance, while on the other hand he could also be spiteful, churning up the sea with his mighty tail and overturning waka. At other times Kaiwhare created unexpected fluctuations in the tide, and floods that caused damage and even death.

To appease Kaiwhare before setting off on a journey, local fishermen would make a tiny house with food on top which would be floated off into the tide; this gave the taniwha his name, Kaiwhare, which means 'house eater'. However, this was often not enough, and Kaiwhare started eating men who had been thrown overboard. A brave warrior, Hakawau, decided to kill Kaiwhare in his lair in the area now known as The Gap. Hakawau stretched a net across the exit to the sea, and when the taniwha left his home to cause mayhem he became entangled in a net. Trapped, Kaiwhare thrashed about wildly before he died, in the process creating the large flat area between The Gap and the cliffs.

The first part of the track leads to a lookout high above Piha with excellent views along the beach to Lion Rock and further north along the coast. From this lookout the track branches to the left, leading to the second lookout above Te Rua o Kaiwhare. Here, in rough weather, the sea pounds through the rocky gap, though the beach below is surprisingly sheltered. Taitomo Island itself is privately owned Maori land and the land beyond the beach is also privately owned. To reach the beach below it is a bit of a scramble down the bank, especially at the very bottom. From the beach you can return to Piha along the rocky shore, but only at low tide. This coastline is notorious for rogue waves that wash people off the rocks, often to their death, so don't walk back along the shore if the weather is rough.

Grade: Easy (with some steps)

Time: 20 minutes return to first lookout; 30 minutes return to second lookout; 50 minutes return along the shore (low tide only)

How to get there: Take the road to Piha and at the bottom of the hill at Piha turn hard left into The Strand. The track begins at the carpark at the end of the road.

10 Puponga Point, Monument Track

Long ago there lived a taniwha on the coast of the Hauraki Gulf who, unlike most taniwha, was so good-natured that he was a favourite pet of the local people. However, the neighbouring Waikato people were very jealous of the pet taniwha and one day requested that he attend a big feast in his honour at Puponga on the Manukau Harbour, where the Waikato were fishing for shark.

It was a long journey and he was reluctant to leave his home but finally, at the urging of the hosts, the taniwha set off, first to the far north, around the top of the island, and finally down the coast to the Manukau. At the harbour entrance he was met by a welcoming party, but the kindly taniwha was unaware that the hosts had set a trap. On each side of the harbour were one thousand warriors holding the ropes of a huge net strung across the water at its narrowest point off Puponga – a net into which the taniwha now swam. For two days the taniwha struggled to free himself, churning up the sea with his thrashing tail and scouring out the harbour bed with powerful body movements, and for two days the exhausted warriors hung grimly on to their ropes.

Utterly spent, the taniwha finally died, but today the deep waters off Puponga Point are still wild and dangerous, a reminder that the kindly taniwha is gone but not forgotten.

Puponga Point juts far out into the Manukau Harbour and is so close to the southern heads that it is not hard to make out people on the far shore. This short walk goes up through regenerating bush and old pine trees to a monument to early settlers. There are good views over the harbour, though the pine trees obscure much of the vista.

Grade: Easy

Time: 20 minutes return

How to get there: At the very end of Cornwallis Road, off the road to Huia.

11 Takaparawhau/Bastion Point

When Europeans began settling the Tamaki isthmus around 1840, the previously large Maori population had been substantially reduced by the impact of the devastating Musket Wars a generation earlier. Ngati Whatua, hoping that a European presence would protect them from further Ngapuhi invasions, were exceptionally generous in both gifting and selling land cheaply to the government and the Anglican Church. However, as Auckland grew so did the demands for land and Ngati Whatua were now under pressure to sell yet more land to both settlers and the government.

By 1854 all that remained in Ngati Whatua hands was less than 300 hectares. Anxious to preserve this small amount, they obtained an agreement through the Native Land Court that this land would not be sold – an agreement that lasted until 1898, when even that land was taken by the government.

In the 1950s, Ngati Whatua still occupied the land behind Okahu Bay and this was the site of a Maori settlement including a marae and wharenui, but the land was low-lying and prone to flooding and most of the housing was in a poor state of repair. Subsequently all the buildings were pulled down and the people were relocated to state housing on land just above the bay. The land was then taken by the government and turned into a public park, and all that now remains in Ngati Whatua hands is a small church and urupa.

A new marae was established on Bastion Point on the last remaining Ngati Whatua land of less than one hectare, and this adjoined a substantial area on Takaparawhau Point that had originally been given to the government by Ngati Whatua for defence purposes in the nineteenth century. In 1941 the government no longer required the land and rather than return the 24 hectares to Ngati Whatua, the original owners, the land was gifted to the Auckland City Council.

When in 1976 the government decided to sell the remaining land to the highest bidder, action was taken to prevent the subdivision and the campaign began to have the land returned to Ngati Whatua. Activists, led by Joe Hawke, occupied the land for 507 days. The occupation finally ended in May 1978 when the police and army removed the protestors and in the process arrested 222 people. However, the occupation was not without its tragedy: five-year-old Joanne Hawke died in a fire on 28 September 1977 when a makeshift building caught fire and burned down. Ten years later the land was returned to Ngati Whatua.

Start this walk at the small carpark at the bottom of Hapimana Street (the road to the Savage Memorial). From there follow the wide grass track up to the right and continue to walk west roughly in the direction of Kelly Tarlton's. The track wanders through regenerating native trees and long kikuyu grass and as it veers around to the left it becomes more overgrown. This is a surprisingly large area and it feels a million miles away from downtown Auckland which is just a few kilometres away. The track emerges into a large grassy area. From here, continue straight ahead until you find a gap in the trees and beyond this is a track down the hill to the Orakei Domain. In the centre of the domain is a small cemetery and chapel and it is here that young Joanne Hawke is buried among her whanau. Return along Tamaki Drive to Hapimana Street.

Grade: Easy
Time: 1 hour
How to get there: Hapimana Street, Orakei

12 Maungawhau/Mt Eden

Maungawhau takes its name from the whau, a small tree that used to grow on the hill. Whau is an exceptionally lightweight wood that was frequently used to make fishing floats.

Covering an area of around 30 hectares, Maungawhau was famous for its rich gardens; it supported a large population of possibly more than a thousand people. The main crater is known as Te Ipu-a-Mataaho, 'Mataaho's cup', and was named after a man so large that he needed a cup of this size. Apihai Te Kawau included Mangawhau in the 3000 acres he sold to the Crown in 1840 to establish the settlement of Auckland, which he saw as protection from further Ngapuhi raids.

Maungawhau was also the home of Puhihuia, and the story of her love for Ponga is one of the great Maori love stories.

Long ago the people of Maungawhau were in conflict with the people living at Awhitu on the Manukau Harbour, and even though they were related, they could not agree on who had the rights to the rich shark-fishing grounds at Puponga on the southern side of the Manukau.

To resolve the conflict the people of Maungawhau invited the Awhitu people to the pa to resolve their differences. Among the visitors was Ponga, a brave warrior, but one of the lesser chiefs. While at Maungawhau, he set eyes on the beautiful Puhihuia and the two secretly met and fell in love. However, Puhihuia was admired by many others of considerably more mana than Ponga, so the two eloped and Ponga returned to Awhitu with Puhihuia. When Puhihuia set foot on land, the chief of Awhitu was horrified and, realising that serious trouble lay ahead, insisted that Puhihuia return immediately to Maungawhau. However, when they saw that Puhihuia had not been kidnapped and was deeply in love with Ponga, they allowed her to stay despite deep misgivings.

Meanwhile back at Maungawhau, the pa was in turmoil and a similar argument raged between those who wanted to fight and bring back Puhihuia and those who deeply wished to prevent war. While the men discussed and prevaricated, Puhihuia's mother decided that immediate action was required and together with a large group of other women, they dressed as warriors, boarded their waka at Onehunga and set out across the Manukau for Awhitu to bring back Puhihuia.

Standing on a high cliff, Puhihuia and Ponga nervously watched as the waka of Maungawhau drew near. As the waka came close Puhihuia recognised her mother and quickly realised that the warriors were in fact all women. Against Ponga's wishes she went down to the shore to confront the women of Maungawhau. One by one in hand-to-hand combat the valiant Puhihuia, driven by her love for Ponga, defeated each of her opponents. Impressed by the strength of her love for Ponga, the people of Maungawhau relented and a great feast blessed the marriage of Puhihuia and Ponga and brought peace between Maungawhau and Awhitu.

As with so many of Auckland's volcanoes, the evidence of terraces, house sites and kumara pits is very clear. One of the most popular lookout points in Auckland, Maungawhau becomes very crowded with cars and tour buses at times, so walking up is a more pleasant option as the pathway avoids the road for the most part. While it is uphill most of the way the walk is not difficult. It crosses numerous terraces and earthworks, giving a much better impression of how large this pa is than those who drive up get.

Grade: Medium

Time: 1 hour

How to get there: There are several tracks to the top, but the easiest one to find is the walkway that begins on Clive Road, Mt Eden.

13 Maungakiekie/Cornwall Park and One Tree Hill Domain

Maungakiekie (mountain of the kiekie, a native vine) was the most populous pa on the Auckland isthmus, supported by the fertile volcanic soil and ready access to the rich fishing grounds on both the Waitemata and Manukau harbours. All over the slopes of the hill are terraces, kumara pits and house sites, though not all of the hill would have been fortified at any one time. A defensive ditch very near the summit may indicate that only the very summit was heavily fortified. This aside, the earthworks cover an enormous area of 45 hectares; most pa were tiny in comparison.

Maungakiekie was for a long period occupied by the iwi Te Wai o Hua until the early seventeenth century, when Ngati Whatua invaders from the Kaipara became the dominant iwi on the isthmus. However, Tamaki Makaurau was devastated by the subsequent invasion by Ngapuhi, who were heavily armed with muskets. When European settlers began to arrive, the pa on Maungakiekie was abandoned and the entire isthmus was only lightly populated.

The tree after which One Tree Hill is named has itself had a turbulent past. Originally a totara tree, 'Te Totara-i-Ahua', stood on the summit. It was cut down in the nineteenth century – though at this point the story becomes murky. One version goes that the tree was felled by a settler for firewood; however, according to two other sources, the totara had already disappeared and it was a pohutukawa that was cut down. Another variation of the same story says that the tree was cut down by a drunken European in an act of sheer vandalism, while yet another version says that the tree was cut down by workmen protesting the lack of food rations.

John Logan Campbell tried to replace the native tree on the summit, using pines as a shelterbelt; but while the native trees failed to take hold, two of the pine trees flourished. One of the pair was cut down in 1960 with no fuss, leaving just the single tree to match the name. It was this lone tree that was attacked by a Maori activist in 1994. The tree was later removed by the Auckland City Council because it was unstable, and since then local authorities and iwi representatives have been unable to agree on a replacement.

Sir John Logan Campbell, who named the area One Tree Hill after the totara tree and donated the park to Auckland City, is buried on the summit next to the obelisk, which is dedicated to the Maori people.

Tucked away behind a cascading waterfall is a very rare relic of a Maori shrine. Kumara was vital to Maori for their survival and, to ensure the success of the crop, a carving – occasionally in stone – of Rongo, the god of cultivation, was erected near to the gardens to enlist the help of the god with the growth of the crop. This narrow column of stone originally formed part of a shrine on Te Tatua-o-Riukiuta (Three Kings) and was called Te Toka-i-tawhio, 'the stone that has travelled around', as it was originally located in the upper Waitemata Harbour and was later moved. The stone had been dumped on the side of a road where it was found by John Logan Campbell, who then had it placed on a plinth in the park.

Cornwall Park and One Tree Hill Domain lie side by side, and to visitors it is immaterial where one park starts and the other finishes. Begin the walk at Te Toka-i-Tawhio, which is located to the left of the large barbecue area not far from the entrance off Greenlane Road West. From here walk along Twin Oak Drive and continue clockwise around the mountain to the narrow road to the summit, where the extensive earthworks of the pa are the most obvious. After taking in the view at the top, take the steps down to the road and go through a small gate on the northern side of the obelisk. A substantial defensive ditch is just below this gate and as you make your way downhill to the road, take note of the numerous wide terraces that ring the hill.

Grade: Easy
Time: 1 hour
How to get there: The main entrance to the park is off Greenlane Road West, Greenlane.

14 Mangere Mountain

One of the largest and least modified of Auckland's 50 volcanic cones, Mangere is a quiet haven compared with the better-known volcanoes. The rich volcanic soils sustained a large Maori population in pre-European times; the first tribe to occupy Mangere were Nga Iwi, a subtribe of Te Wai o Hua. Kumara and taro flourished in the gardens around the mountain, and with easy access to kai moana in Manukau Harbour, the people of Mangere were well fed. Maori land boundaries indicated by low stone walls fan out from the base of the mountain, and kumara pits and house sites are clearly visible inside the crater.

Maori were well aware of the volcanic nature of the isthmus, and the legend about the cause of this activity involves a great love story.

Hinemairangi lived with her Hunua people on the coast near Maraetai and fell in love with Tama Ireiea, who lived in the Hikurangi pa in the Waitakere Ranges. Against her parents' wishes, Hine eloped with Tama and went to live with his people on the west coast. Displeased by his disobedient daughter, Hine's father was determined to bring her back and set off with a large group of warriors in the dead of night for the rugged hills of the Waitakere Ranges.

To protect Hikurangi, the rangatira Tiriwa turned to a powerful tohunga, who helped in a most spectacular way. With great magic the Hikurangi tohunga conjured up volcanic eruptions that engulfed all of Tamaki Makaurau – only to find that the Hunua tohunga, with magic of his own, fought back by directing streams of boiling lava towards Waitakere. Now the tohunga from Hikurangi called on the gods, who doused the fiery rivers of lava with torrential rain so heavy that clouds of steam rose up from the earth and obscured the sun. When the clouds cleared, the war party from Hunua were burned to death by the scorching heat of the sun. Eventually the two peoples were reconciled and Hinemairangi returned to Maraetai, where a large rock is named in her honour.

There are excellent views out of the Manukau from the top of Mangere Mountain. The track follows the rim of the crater, but as the whole park is open grass, you can just stroll anywhere.

 Grade: Easy

Time: Allow up to 1 hour

How to get there: Main entrance at end of Domain Road off Coronation Road, Mangere Bridge. The Visitor Centre off Coronation Road is an alternative starting point, though the displays there are mainly geared to schoolchildren.

15 Otuataua Stonefields

While undoubtedly an area of significant historical and archaeological importance, to the untrained eye the Otuataua Stonefields are difficult to make sense of. Settled originally by Te Wai o Hua, and covering 100 hectares, the stonefields highlight the importance of kumara and taro to early Maori.

Despite this country's equable climate and rich soil, there are few edible native plants; even those such as fernroot and karaka berries take a huge amount of preparation before they are edible. On arrival from their tropical homeland, the first Polynesian migrants found that only kumara and taro could grow in this cooler climate, and these crops were dramatically restricted by climate. This in turn had a significant impact on where Maori could live. Pre-European Maori populations were largely restricted to the northern part of the country and to coastal areas further south.

Both taro and kumara need a long period of warm sunny weather to mature. One method of maximising the heat required by these delicate tropical plants was to plant the crops very close to rock walls or in a small circle of rocks, thereby taking full advantage of the sun's heat reflected off and held by the rocks. Here at Otuataua, what appear to be merely random stone piles are in fact the remains of carefully constructed walls and mounds designed to enhance the growth of kumara and taro.

The site also contains the Otuataua pa, although to the casual visitor this pa is much more difficult to spot than those on the volcanic cones.

This easy walk through rocky outcrops and farmland is enhanced by the excellent information panels, which certainly help to interpret what at first glance appears to be a landscape without much form.

Grade: Easy

Time: 30–40 minutes

How to get there: From George Bolt Drive (the road to the airport) turn right into Ihumatao Road, right again into Oruarangi Road and finally left into Ihumatao Quarry to the carpark at the end.

16 Te Naupata/Musick Point

Long occupied by Ngai Tai, Te Waiarohia pa covered the very tip of the long peninsula known as Te Naupata. The pa was encircled by a series of defensive trenches that protected it from attack from the land, and even today these ditches are particularly clear near the end of the point. However, the defences were no match for Ngapuhi invading the Waitemata in 1821 and in the face of an enemy heavily armed with muskets, the pa was abandoned and never reoccupied.

The area is now known as Musick Point: the English name is not a spelling mistake but the surname of a pioneer flying-boat aviator, Captain Edwin Musick.

The short track, which is quite rough in places, begins behind Musick Point Air Radio Station and winds around the point, with a flight of steps leading down the cliff for those keen on further exploring the rocky shoreline. There are excellent views of the inner gulf islands and especially the volcanic cone of Browns Island, which lies just offshore.

Grade: Easy

Time: 20 minutes return

How to get there: The entrance to the point is through the Howick Golf Club, Musick Point Road, Bucklands Beach.

17 Omana

Omana is a short version of O-Manawatere, 'the dwelling place of Manawatere', and was a pa occupied by the iwi Ngai Tai. Manawatere was the founding ancestor who travelled from his homeland, not by waka, but by 'gliding over the waves on taniwha'. Manawatere is also remembered in the name of an ancient pohutukawa at Cockle Bay, called Te Tuhi-a-Manawatere.

This small pa is protected on the seaward side by steep cliffs with the two sides facing the land protected by very deep ditches that are still there today. Originally the ditches were much deeper and topped by a bank on which stood thick palisading, making it very difficult for enemies to breach the defences.

Around 1837 William Fairburn established the Maraetai Mission Station here, which included a farm and a small school for Maori.

The pa site is a short easy walk from the carpark.

Grade: Easy

Time: 20 minutes return

How to get there: The track begins at the main carpark of Omana Regional Park, which is on Omana Beach Road off the Whitford–Maraetai Road about 1.5 km from Maraetai.

18 Whakakaiwhara/Duder Regional Park

Around 1300 AD, the waka *Tainui* travelling north from Waihihi anchored at the very end of this peninsula while sheltering from a severe easterly storm. It is remembered in the place name Te Tauranga-o-Tainui, the anchorage of *Tainui*. Spending a few days here, the crew gathered food in the bush, in particular the edible parts of the kiekie (whara), and thereafter the whole peninsula became known as Whakakaiwhara or 'to eat whara'. The *Tainui* continued on to the Waitemata, where a number of those onboard decided to settle and gradually over time also came to occupy the Whakakaiwhara Peninsula. Eventually the people were known as Ngai (or Ngati) Tai, with 'tai' said to refer to either the *Tainui* or the ancestors Taihaua and Taimanawaiti.

The pa, also called Whakakaiwhara, was strategically located at the very tip of the peninsula, and the terraces, kumara pits and a defensive ditch are still visible today. The Duder family purchased the land in 1866 and continued to farm it up to 1994, when it was sold to the Auckland Regional Council for a park. Today the peninsula is almost entirely farmland with small patches of regenerating bush that are slowly being expanded.

The Farm Loop Walk is best undertaken anticlockwise following the south coast of the peninsula, as this is a comfortable steady climb to the trig, which has grand views over the Firth of Thames, the gulf islands of Waiheke, Ponui, Browns and Rangitoto, and to the east the blue-tinged Coromandel. A further track leads out to the point, which will add another 50 minutes.

Grade: Medium

Time: 1.5 hours to the pa at the end of the peninsula

How to get there: From SH1 travel towards Whitford and on to Maraetai, then follow the coast south to Umupuia Beach. From the southern end of Umupuia Beach turn right into North Road, and the entrance to the park is on the right a short distance down this road.

HAURAKI GULF

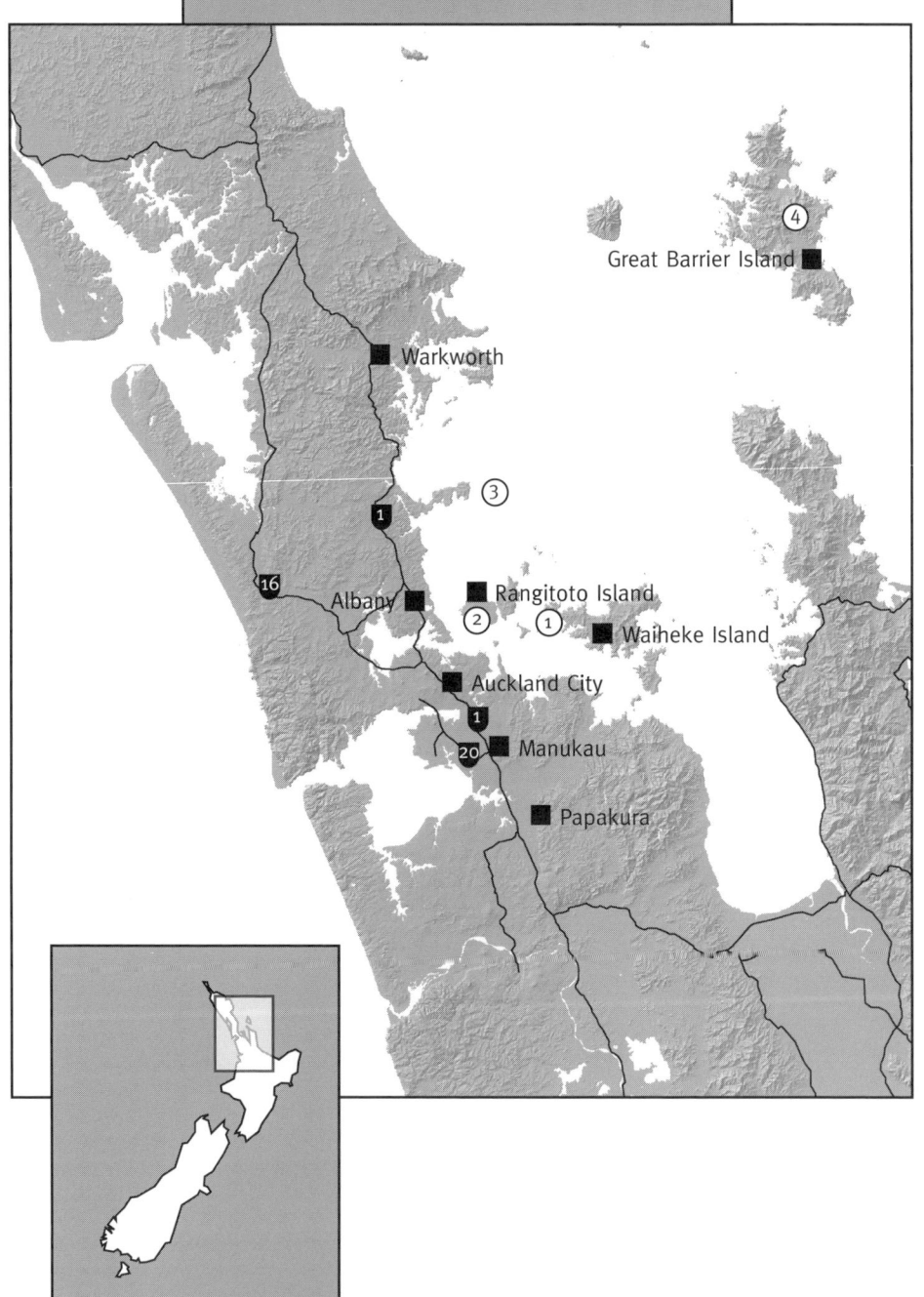

Great Barrier Island ④

Warkworth

③

① 1

Albany
Rangitoto Island
② ① Waiheke Island

Auckland City
① 1
⑳ Manukau

Papakura

1 Waiheke Island

There is no consensus as to the origin of the name Waiheke, or 'cascading water'. Local historian Paul Monin contends that by the time Pakeha began recording local names, those Maori who would have known the original meaning were dead. Some say that the name is either a mistake or a joke, as the island does not have rivers or waterfalls that would remotely qualify. The mistake theory is supported by some who claim that when a surveyor asked a local Maori the name of the island, the man thought he was just asking the name of the stream by which they were both standing. Taimoana Turoa, in his thorough tome *Te Takoto o te Whenua o Hauraki,* is on the side of humour, and states that when Kahumatamomoe, the son of the captain Tamatekapua, came ashore from the waka *Te Arawa,* he needed desperately to urinate – and that's how the island became known as 'cascading water'.

An older name for the island, Te Motu-arai-roa, 'the long sheltering island', makes a good deal more sense.

The earliest people appear to be Te Uri Karaka, who were later overwhelmed by settlers arriving with the great voyager Toi. Subsequently the island came under control of Ngati Huarere, who were in turn superseded in the eighteenth century by Ngati Paoa, who were in occupation when Cook anchored off the island in 1769. In the early nineteenth century the population was estimated at around 1000 people, but that population halved following the invasion by Ngapuhi in 1821.

Fifty pa sites have been identified on the island and the Matietie Historic Reserve Walk passes, in a very short distance, four headland pa, all small but perfectly positioned.

Ideal for those who are going to Waiheke for the day on the ferry and do not want to venture too far afield on the island, this walk follows the coast around to Cable Bay and then returns inland to Matiatia, where the wharf is located. The walk begins to the north of the carpark by the wharf. If the tide is high, then the first part of the walk is a scramble over rocks and tree roots for about 100 metres. This is by far the most difficult part of the track. From the small bay just beyond the wharf, the walk first goes past the large red shed and then follows the markers around the coast.

The first two pa are reached within 10 minutes' walking: the first is recognisable by the flat area on top of the headland; while the next pa, not more than 100 metres further on, is a little harder to recognise. However, take some time and the several flat terraces dropping down the hillside will become more noticeable. Further along is another headland pa, though this pa is cut off by the high tide. Surrounded by water and encircled by steep rocky cliffs topped by stout palisading, this pa would have been difficult to attack. The last pa is easy to miss and is located on high cliffs just before the track drops down to Cable Bay. The area is relatively flat, and what identifies the headland as a pa is the narrow defensive ditch that runs parallel to the track.

All four pa are readily accessible by short tracks and along the entire walk the views are superb, to downtown Auckland and the islands of the inner gulf, Rangitoto, Motutapu, Motuihe, The Noises and Tiritiri Matangi, and Little Barrier in the far distance.

At Cable Bay, easily identified by the triangular cable sign, turn right uphill until you hit the road, and then turn left and continue down the road to the track which leads off to the right just past the locked road gate; this takes you back to Matiatia. For those wanting a longer walk from Cable Bay, continue up the steep track uphill and on to Owhanake Bay and then turn inland, where the track takes you back to Oceanview Road leading to the wharf. This longer walk will take about 2 hours.

Another walk on the island is at Whakanewha Regional Park on the southern side of the island. The Loop Track leads up from the beach to a lookout point with views over Whakanewha, or Rocky Bay, and back towards Auckland city. From the lookout the track passes through regenerating and mature bush fragments to an old pa site, with kumara pits clearly visible. From here the track leads down to Poukaraka flats with its old pohutukawa trees and broad grassy area ideal for picnics.

Matietie Historic Reserve Walk

Grade: Medium

Time: 1 hour 10 minutes

How to get there: The walk begins and ends at Matiatia, the main Waiheke ferry wharf. The start of the walk is not marked as such, but the access is via the shoreline beyond the Matietie Reserve sign, to the left of the carpark.

School Loop Track
Grade: Easy
Time: 30 minutes
How to get there: Whakanewha Regional Park

2 Rangitoto Island

The largest and youngest of Auckland's volcanoes, Rangitoto erupted from the sea about 600–700 years ago and was last active just 350 years ago. Despite the close proximity of Motutapu, the eruption of Rangitoto was more disruptive than catastrophic to those living there, and while the island was coated in a thick layer of ash, this ash was very fertile and ideal for cultivation. Footprints of people and dogs returning after the eruption have been found on Motutapu, and over 300 Maori sites have been identified on the island.

The full name of Rangitoto is Te Rangi-i-totongia-a-Tamatekapua, 'the day that the blood of Tamatekapua was shed'. This refers to a battle around 1350 AD in which the crews of the waka *Te Arawa* and *Tainui* clashed on the island and Tamatekapua, the captain of *Te Arawa*, lost the fight and presumably was injured.

Legends tell a different creation story from that of a volcanic eruption. In one version a race of giants lived along the west coast beyond the high hills of the Waitakere Ranges and these giants were fond of boasting about their strength and abilities. One giant, in a demonstration of his immense powers, picked up an entire hill at Karekare and carried the hill all the way to Takapuna, where he then placed it in the sea next to Motutapu. The area at Karekare by the creek where the hill came from is called Uruhanga-o-Rangitoto (the wind of Rangitoto).

Another story speaks of a quarrel between a husband and wife, who were the children of the fire gods. During the argument both rashly cursed Mahuika, goddess of fire, who in turn complained about the behaviour of the couple to Mataoho, the god of earthquakes. As a punishment, Mataoho created an earthquake to destroy the couple's home, and that struck with such a force that it created the hole that became Lake Pupuke, while at the same time forcing Rangitoto up out of the sea. When mist enshrouds the summit of Rangitoto, it is said to be the tears of the quarrelsome couple mourning the loss of their home.

The walk to the summit (259 metres) is a steady climb on a well-formed path and leads to a magnificent view over Auckland and the Hauraki Gulf.

The crater and summit are actually covered in reasonably large trees, as the original volcanic eruptions that created the cone occurred during the very early stages of the island's creation and the last eruptions were much further down the western slope. A side track just below the summit (20 minutes return) leads to extensive lava caves, some collapsed and some intact. It is possible to scramble through the caves – a torch is useful.

 Rangitoto Summit
Grade: Medium
Time: 2 hours return
How to get there: Fullers run a regular ferry to the island (www.fullers. co.nz), phone 09 367 9111), but take care not to miss your ferry back, as there is no overnight accommodation on the island and alternative transport to the mainland is expensive.

3 Tiritiri Matangi

Maori legend has it that Tiritiri Matangi, like all the other islands of the Hauraki Gulf, is one of the floats of a huge fishing net and the name of the island very appropriately means 'tossed by the wind'. The main pa on the island was known by the same name.

Occupation of the island by the Kawerau people goes back to the fourteenth century, though the entire population may never have been more than 100 people. They relied heavily on kai moana, especially the rich shark-fishing grounds surrounding the island. In the sixteenth century this coastline, including Tiritiri Matangi, became a battleground between local iwi and Ngati Awa moving north, and the Kawerau were forced off the island, though they returned around 1700 AD.

In 1821 the local tribes, armed only with traditional weapons, were no match for the Ngapuhi raiders carrying muskets, and the people of Tiritiri Matangi, like those on all the islands of the gulf and along the coast, abandoned their lands and fled south in the face of overwhelming firepower. While small numbers returned in the 1830s, arriving Europeans found the land largely empty.

Stripped of its native bush, the island was farmed from 1850 to 1970, with only a few coastal remnants remaining on this small, relatively flat island of only 230 hectares. In a bold move, the Department of Conservation embarked on a programme not only to reforest the island, but also to develop it as an open sanctuary with easy access for the public.

Today Tiritiri Matangi is best known as the country's most accessible island bird sanctuary and home to some of New Zealand's rarest birds.

There are two visible headland pa on the mainland: Tiritiri Matangi, which was the main pa, is located on the western side of the island; and the much smaller Papakura pa is in the north. The latter pa is inaccessible, but the Tiritiri Matangi pa, which still retains much of its defensive earthworks, can be visited. The pa is accessible either off the Ridge Road that runs down the spine of the island, or at the end of the Hobbs Beach Track which runs north from the wharf.

The island has a maze of tracks of varying length. The walk from the wharf to the lighthouse will take about 50 minutes return, while a walk around the island can take up to 3 hours. The island terrain is rolling, and none of the tracks is difficult.

 Grade: Medium
Time: Allow 2 hours
How to get there: 360 Discovery provides a ferry service from Auckland or Gulf Harbour: (www.360discovery.co.nz, phone 0800 360 3472).

4 Aotea/Great Barrier Island

Lying 100 kilometres to the northeast of Auckland, Aotea is the largest island in the Hauraki Gulf. It is a common belief that the discovery of this island gave the country the name Aotearoa, 'land of the long white cloud'. The story goes that Kupe's wife (or daughter) on board the *Aotea* waka, after the very long journey from their Pacific homeland Hawaiki, saw a long cloud on the horizon and cried out, 'He ao, he ao' ('a cloud, a cloud'), and from her call, Kupe named the island Aotea. Later, when the mainland was discovered, the name was extended to Aotearoa.

More likely, though, both the island and the mainland were named after the waka *Aotea*.

However, Maori never applied the name Aotearoa to the whole country and in fact never had a single name that encompassed all the islands we now call New Zealand. For Maori and early settlers alike, if the name Aotearoa was used at all, it applied only to the North Island. A nineteenth-century Maori newspaper specifically made reference to 'Aotearoa and the South Island'. In 1898 William Pember Reeves published a history of New Zealand entitled *The Long White Cloud Ao-tea-roa*, and this may be the first reference to Aotearoa being applied to the entire country. Now

Aotearoa is universally recognised as the Maori name for New Zealand.

The island Aotea has a long history of Maori occupation and was fought over by various iwi through the centuries. Ngati Rehua, who live on the island today, trace their history back to the mid-seventeenth century when they defeated Ngai Tai for control of the island. In 1838 the island was attacked by Ngati Kahungunu armed with muskets. Over 100 warriors died in the battle, which took place near Tryphena and was known as Te Mauparaoa. Most Ngati Rehua then fled the island, fearful of revenge.

Hirakimata (Mt Hobson) in the centre of the island is the highest peak at 621 metres, and on a clear day a trip to the summit is well worth the effort. The first part of the track to Windy Canyon is easy going. It becomes a little more difficult through the canyon, though the track is well formed. The last section to the summit is more challenging and is steep, narrow and rough in places, though at the very summit there are boardwalks to protect the fragile landscape. The views from the summit are exceptional, with the Coromandel Peninsula to the south and Auckland and the mainland stretching along the western horizon.

Grade: Medium/hard

Time: 4 hours return

How to get there: The beginning of the track is clearly signposted at the summit of the Whangapoua Hill on the Aotea road between Awana and Okiwi.

COROMANDEL

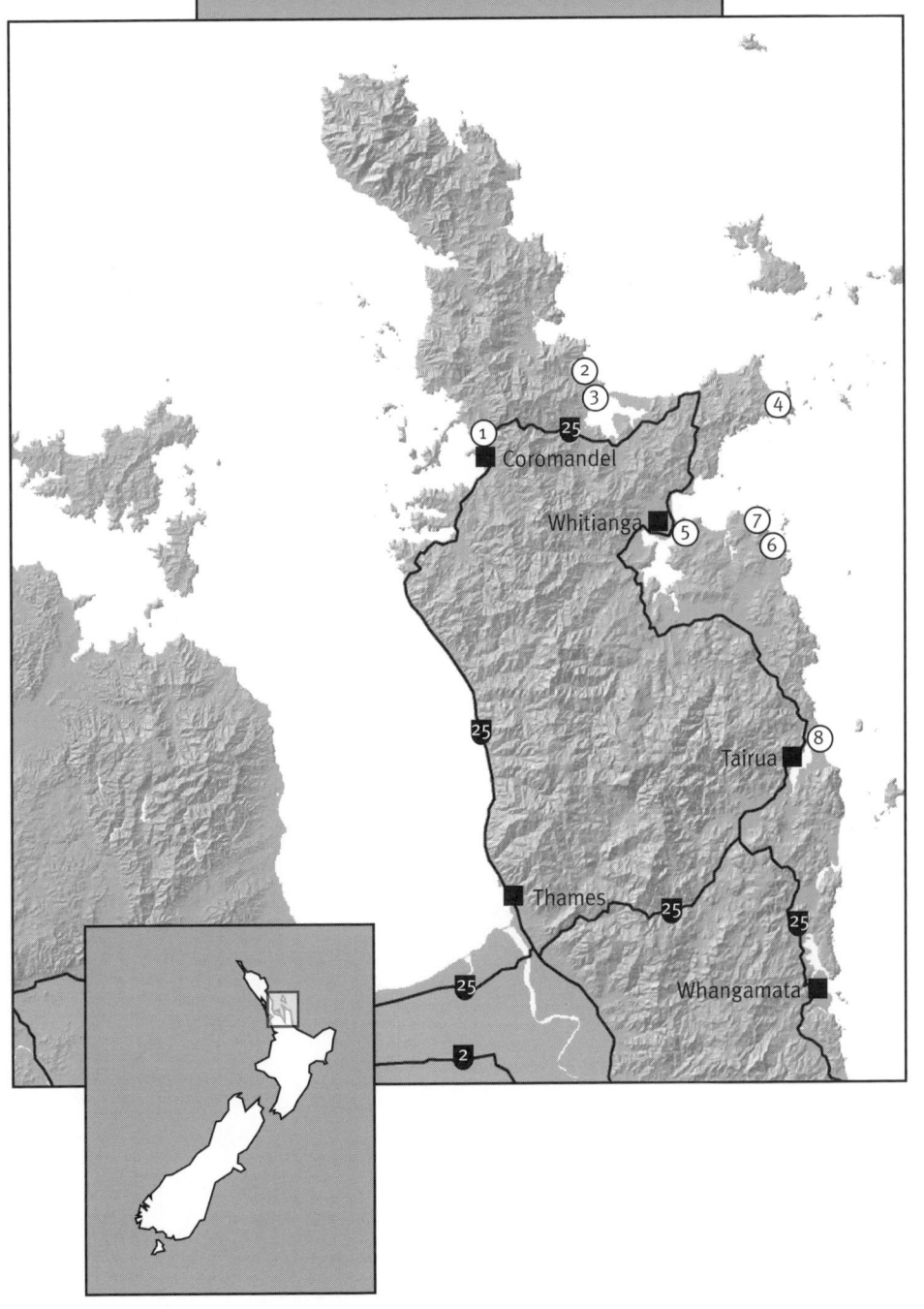

1 Coromandel Pa

The history of this pa is obscure and even the name is forgotten, but the site is so impressive and the views so spectacular that it is well worth the short walk from the town. The track is in excellent condition and while it's all uphill, the gradient is reasonably gentle. At the top few signs of the old pa remain, but the strategic position is obvious with the 360-degree view encompassing the Hauraki Gulf and its islands and back across the town to the ranges.

Grade: Easy
Time: 25 minutes return
How to get there: The track to the pa is off Wharf Road about 300 metres from the main intersection in town. There is no parking down the driveway that leads to the track but there is plenty across the road.

2 Motuto Pa

New Chums Beach is a beautiful untouched stretch of white sand just north of Whangapoua and a popular destination for many visitors, but few, if any, visitors are aware of the pa site that occupies the peninsula between New Chums and Whangapoua.

Built by Ngati Huarere, Motuto is a typical headland pa with steep cliffs providing defence from an attack by sea and a narrow isthmus connecting the pa to the mainland, which was easy to fortify and to defend.

The track leads off to the right from the main track to New Chums and it is a tricky scramble to get to the top. The main part of the pa faced the sea and today the well preserved terraces are clearly visible. As with most coastal pa, there are spectacular views along the coast.

Grade: Medium
Time: 50 minutes return
How to get there: Follow the beach from the northern end of
Whangapoua Beach, cross over the stream and then pick up the track
just above the high-tide mark.

3 Raukawa Pa, Te Rehutae/Opera Point

Built around 1700 AD and occupied by Ngati Huarere, the main features
of Raukawa pa are still very clear. Substantial earthworks remain with
wide terraces and kumara pits. There is a deep ditch to protect the
landward end, while the cliffs protect the seaward side. On one side
of the pa is the open sea; on the other the estuary and main channel of
the Whangapoua Harbour with views over the estuary, the Matarangi
peninsula and far out to sea. Not much is known about the history of the
pa, though, like many others on the Coromandel Peninsula, it either fell to
the musket-wielding Ngapuhi in 1818, or was abandoned in the face of
the invasion.

There is an easy track along the estuary to a small beach and then a bit
of a scramble up a grassy slope to the pa. If you are feeling adventurous,
there is a rough, unformed, but reasonably clear track that returns from
the headland back along the ridge to the carpark.

 Grade: Easy
Time: 25 minutes return for the estuary track; 40 minutes return via
the ridge track
How to get there: On the road from Whitianga to Coromandel turn-off
at Te Rerenga to Whangapoua. The carpark is 5km on the right just
before Whangapoua settlement.

4 Opito Pa

This magnificent pa occupies the whole of the headland that shelters the
southern end of Opito Beach. Steep slopes made attack difficult from the
north, and sheer cliffs made it impossible from the south, while a steep
bluff protected the landward side of the pa, which was further enhanced
by several defensive ditches. The headland itself has numerous broad
terraces and is pitted with rua (for storing kumara) and house sites. The
views across the beach and along the coast are spectacular.

Grade: Medium

Time: 1 hour

How to get there: At Kuaotunu take the Black Jack Road first to Otama Beach and then to Opito, and follow the road to the very end (parts of this road are winding and gravel). The staircase to the pa is a short walk along the beach.

5 Whitianga Pa

Whitianga is a contraction of Te Whitianga-a-Kupe, 'Kupe's crossing place'; as the name suggests, Kupe explored the area around 1000 AD. While tradition has it that his people settled here and built the pa, the area has been more closely associated with Ngati Hei. Hei was the captain of *Te Arawa* waka. He settled here, and what is now called Mercury Bay is known in Maori as Te Whanganui-a-Hei, 'the great harbour of Hei'.

However, when Captain James Cook visited the area in November 1769, the pa had fallen into disuse, the blacked stumps of the palisades a sign that the pa had been burnt. Local Maori told Cook that about 30 years earlier the pa had fallen to an attack by Ngati Rangi, an iwi from the Tauranga area. Following the capture of the pa, the Tauranga chief married the wife of the Ngati Hei chief who had died defending Whitianga. Even though the pa was in ruins, Cook was impressed by the defences, especially the very deep defensive ditches which would originally have been topped by a bank and crowned by stout palisading. Cook commented:

A little with[in] the entrance of the river on the East side is a high point or peninsula jutting out into the River on which are the remains of one of their Fortified towns, the Situation is such that the best Engineer in Europe could not have choose'd a better for a small number of men to defend themselves against a greater, it is strong by nature and made more so by Art.

Even today the pa is very impressive and surprisingly large. The main defensive ditch remains, though substantially diminished in size, and is now part of the track to Back Bay. Like all headland pa, Whitianga relied heavily on the steep cliffs and the water for defence.

An unusual feature of the pa is the shallow holes in a flat slab of rock in the middle of the pa: the best guess is that the holes supported poles for some type of platform, possibly a watchtower.

Grade: Easy
Time: 25 minutes return
How to get there: Take the ferry from Whitianga township over to Ferry Landing. The pa is immediately to the right of the landing. If you are coming from Cooks Beach, the pa is at the end of Purangi Road.

6 Stingray Bay

In the legend of Maui's great fish, the whole of the North Island, Te Ika a Maui, was a giant stingray and the peninsula which is now called Coromandel is known as Te Tara o Te Ika a Maui, 'the jagged barb of Maui's fish'.

In Maori mythology the stingray is descended from Punga, a son of Tangaroa, god of the sea. Unfortunately, Punga is considered the father of all ugly creatures, including not just stingrays but insects, reptiles and sharks. However, Maori highly valued stingrays for food, as they were not only plentiful but also easily caught.

A good place to see these graceful fish is at the appropriately named Stingray Bay, which is a short track that branches off the popular walkway to Cathedral Cove. From the track above the bay, stingrays are frequently seen gliding through the shallows along the beach.

 Grade: Easy
Time: 25 minutes return
How to get there: From Hahei Beach Road turn left into Grange Road South and continue to the carpark at the very end. In summer the walk to Cathedral Cove is so popular that the small carpark is quickly overwhelmed and in peak times a shuttle bus runs from the town to the beginning of the track.

7 Te Pare Historic Reserve, Hahei

A stronghold of Ngati Hei, who arrived in the area on the waka *Te Arawa* in 1350 AD, this reserve includes two pa sites: Hereheretaura pa on the headland and Hahei pa on the high ridge to the right. Hereheretaura pa must be one of the most beautifully situated pa in the country, with broad terraces occupying a rocky headland, the sea on three sides and with a magnificent outlook over Mercury Bay and Hahei Beach.

Hahei pa is quite different and is less accessible but easily recognised by the north-facing terraces that fan out down the hillside, though there are no visible signs of defence earthworks. Hereheretaura, on the other hand, has both a ditch and steep banks to protect the pa from attack.

Grade: Easy
Time: 30 minutes return
How to get there: The track to the pa site begins at the end of Pa Road, or leads up from the southern end of the beach at low tide.

8 Paku Peak, Tairua

Discovered by Kupe around 1000 AD, the Coromandel coast has a long history of Maori settlement. They were originally attracted to the area by the now extinct moa and the abundant kai moana. The only known artefact linking Aotearoa to Eastern Polynesia, a fish lure, was found in the sand dune behind Tairua Beach in 1964. The lure is made from black-lipped pearl oyster shell. These oysters are not found in New Zealand and so, given the location of the find, this must have been brought to the area by an immigrant from Eastern Polynesia.

Originally a Ngati Hei stronghold, Tairua succumbed to Ngati Maru invaders in the seventeenth century. Their tenure was not to last as musket-wielding Ngapuhi swept down the coast in the 1820s. Ngati Maru escaped inland to take refuge with their Tainui relatives, where most settled permanently.

A short rocky scramble leads to the top of the volcanic peak Paku, with dramatic coastal and inland views. It is easy to see why, once an island, this peak was the ideal position for a major fortified pa. Below the old pa site is an ancient pohutukawa tree. Tradition tells of a chief who left his wife to go off to battle and when her husband did not return, his wife, consumed with grief, climbed into the tree and there she died. Thereafter the tree was named Pikiariki or 'the climb of the chieftainess'.

Grade: Easy
Time: 30 minutes return
How to get there: From the Tairua shopping centre off SH2, turn into Manaia Road, then left into Paku Drive and follow the road to the carpark just below the summit.

Above left: Cape Reinga is the departing point for spirits to the underworld and is one of the most tapu sites in the country.

Above right: Protecting Ohumuhumu pa are two very deep and distinctive defensive ditches.

Left: Flat-topped Tararata (in the distance) lost his head in a fight with Maungataniwha over wives.

Below: A carved arch incorporating Maori and European motifs marks the entrance to the Kaikohe Hill walk.

Above left: Two taniwha guard the entrance to Hokianga Harbour by creating wild waves and dangerous currents.

Left: The pa on the lower slopes of Tokatoka Peak has spectacular views over the Wairoa River.

Below: An ancient pa crowns Busby Head overlooking Smugglers Bay.

Above: A carved pouwhenua marks the beginning of the track up to an old pa site at Wenderholm.

Above right: Maungakiekie/One Tree Hill, in the heart of Auckland city, is one of the largest pa in the country.

Right: A rare carved stone representing Rongo, the god of cultivation, now in Cornwall Park, Auckland.

Above: The Gap at Piha beach was created by the taniwha Kaiwhare as he struggled to escape from a net.

Right: In legend Rangitoto Island was created as the result of a domestic dispute.

Below: At the end of Musick Point are the remains of a headland pa, Te Naupata.

Left: The Wairere Falls near Te Aroha, where 12-year-old Tarore was killed and her Gospel of Luke stolen.

Below left: Two limestone carvings feature on the walk around Lake Hakanoa in Huntly.

Below right: Sacred to the Tainui iwi, Taupiri Mountain is also an important pa site and burial ground.

Left: Superbly sited overlooking the Waikato River, Pohaturoa pa is just south of Tokoroa.

Middle left: The gunboat *Pioneer* was a key part of the attack on Waikato Maori by the British and is today a war memorial in Mercer.

Below: Hourere pa, crowned by a lone pohutukawa, has excellent views over Aotea Harbour north of Kawhia.

Above: Rocky cliffs dropping into the sea are an integral part of the defences of Hahei pa.

Above right: The sand dunes below the volcanic peak of Paku, Tairua, yielded the only artefact found in this country that can be directly traced back to Eastern Polynesia.

Right: Gate Pa in the heart of modern Tauranga was the scene of a major victory by 250 Maori over 2000 government troops.

Below: Karangaumu is just one of eight pa in the Papamoa Regional Park in the Bay of Plenty.

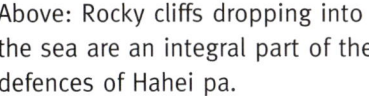

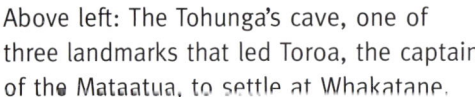

Above left: The Tohunga's cave, one of three landmarks that led Toroa, the captain of the Mataatua, to settle at Whakatane.

Above right: This small graveyard at Opepe near Taupo marks the site of the battle between government soldiers and Te Kooti's men.

Lower left: Maori rock drawings at Lake Tarawera depicting waka motifs were created with red ochre.

Right: South-east of Turangi, two redoubts mark the site of Te Kooti's last stand.

WAIKATO

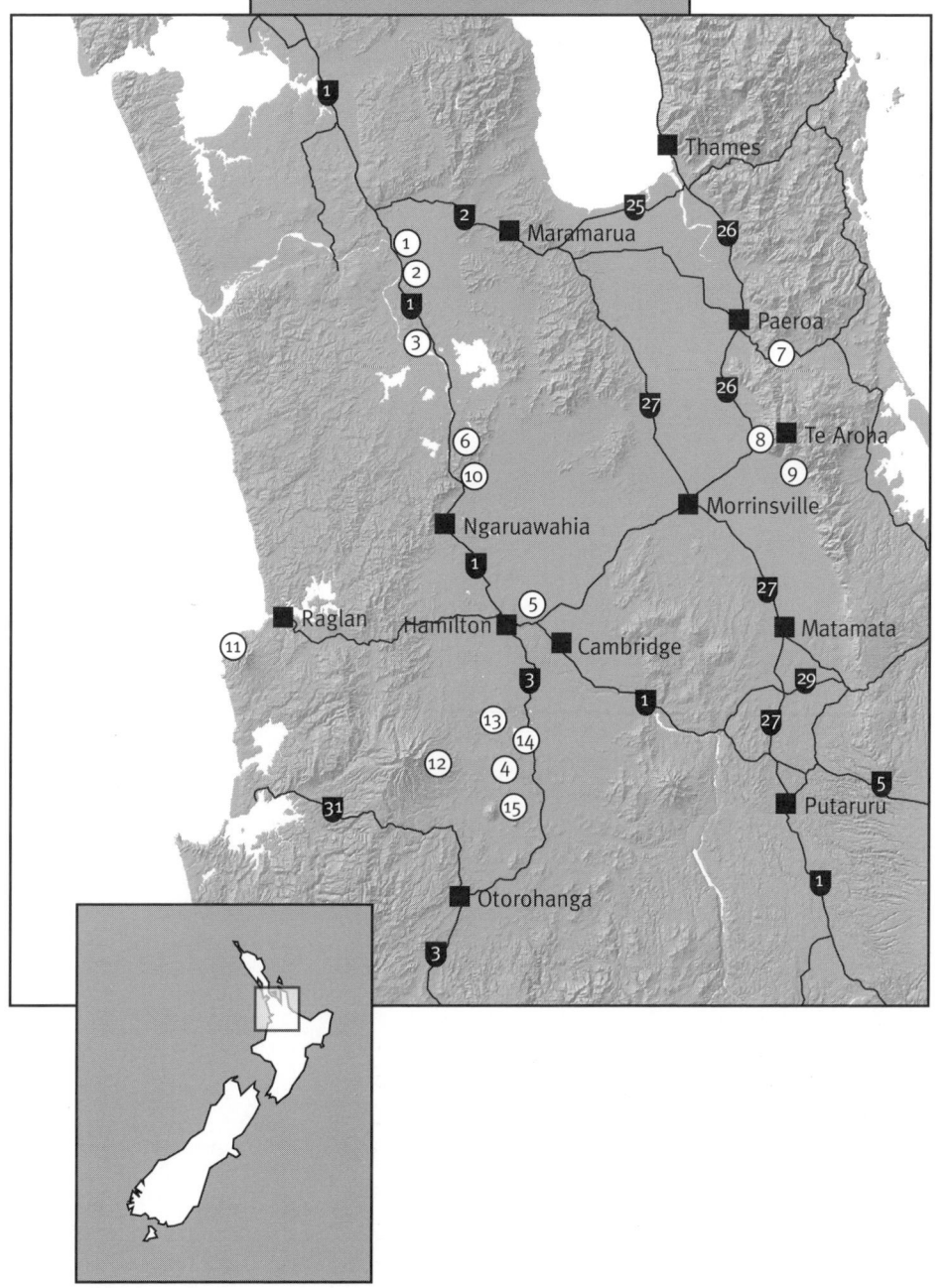

The war in the Waikato

The years before the Treaty of Waitangi were generally a period of cordial relations between Maori and European settlers, and Maori were enthusiastic adopters of European technology. Iron tools were in great demand and new crops and livestock revolutionised Maori agriculture; the potato in particular made a huge impact on the quality of life in the cooler regions. Maori encouraged European settlers, often gifting and selling land so that they could trade more easily and, during the bitter Musket Wars, European settlers were seen as offering some sort of protection to local Maori.

After the Treaty the situation changed rapidly. What Maori had not anticipated and what quickly alarmed them was the sheer numbers of settlers who began arriving and showed no signs of stopping. In 1840 the European population was estimated at around 2000; by 1859 Maori and European populations were equal at around 60,000. When four ships bringing settlers arrived in Wellington, a local chief asked if all the tribe of England had come to New Zealand.

Far-sighted Maori leaders understood the need to hold on to their land, and others saw that political solutions were also necessary in this rapidly changing environment. Just three years after the signing of the Treaty, Maori clashed with settlers over the issue of land.

The Kingitanga movement was one such solution: what could be better than to emulate the greatest power in the world at the time by setting up their own royalty? At the heart of the Kingitanga movement was Maori unity, driven by a desire to halt the loss of land. This, however, was seen by the British as almost treasonable and that, combined with the pressure to provide land to the increasing number of settlers, made conflict in the Waikato inevitable.

Throughout 1862 and 1863, the British prepared for war, building a string of redoubts across South Auckland and pushing the Great South Road from Drury to Pokeno where, in early 1863, yet another redoubt was constructed, provocatively called the Queen's Redoubt. Try as he might, Governor Grey could not provoke the Maori King to fight. When war broke out in Taranaki early in 1863, Grey saw his chance to sort out the King movement once and for all, and on 12 July 1863 British troops finally crossed the Mangatawhiri Stream, which Maori had declared to be their northern boundary.

1 Te Teoteo's Pa and the Whangamarino Redoubt

The first serious clash between the British and Maori troops occurred at Te Teoteo's pa, where Maori, led by Te Huirama, had hurriedly constructed a defensive position. They were attacked by 500 British troops, leaving 30 Maori dead. The pa defenders abandoned their positions and retreated a short distance south to the Meremere pa. The British then quickly built the Whangamarino Redoubt, from where they bombarded the Maori position at Meremere.

The pa site is now somewhat overgrown but the views are extensive along the Waikato River. The redoubt, however, is well preserved and from here Meremere, the next objective in the war in the Waikato, is clearly seen just to the south.

An easy track leads up from Oram Road across farmland. The redoubt is on the right and Te Teoteo's pa is on the left overlooking the river.

 Grade: Easy
Time: 30 minutes return
How to get there: Oram Road, 2 km south of Mercer.

2 Meremere Redoubt

Originally there was a pa here. Waikato Maori were well aware that the attack at Meremere would come from the river. The defenders had constructed several lines of rifle pits and had also acquired three ship's guns – but all the preparations and strong fortifications were made redundant when the pa was outflanked by 600 British troops landing upstream during the night of 31 October. The defenders realised that their rifle fire would be ineffective, the pa was abandoned and the warriors slipped south to reinforce their position at Rangiriri.

On 1 November, the British built another redoubt on the site of the pa. Today the redoubt appears rather plain, rectangular and relatively unsophisticated compared to other redoubts such as Alexandra.

Grade: Easy
Time: 15 minutes return
How to get there: Meremere Lane, Meremere

3 Rangiriri

Rangiriri was the first major clash of the Waikato campaign. Maori forces were estimated to be fewer than 2000, and opposing them were over 12,000 British and Colonial troops, armed with artillery, under General Cameron. In addition two heavily armed gunboats, the *Avon* and the *Pioneer*, were moving up the river in support of the ground troops.

Maori had prepared well for the attack, with a huge trench running from the Waikato River to a deep lagoon adjoining Lake Waikare. The central redoubt, cleverly designed by the Waikato chief Te Wharepu, stood 8 metres high above deep trenches and was constructed to withstand rifle and cannon fire.

The British attacked with almost 1500 troops against 500 warriors, but were unaware of the strength of the central redoubt. The Maori repulsed no fewer than eight concerted attacks. In one of those strange twists of war, a white flag flown on one of the gunboats was mistaken by the chief Wiremu Te Kumete as a sign that the British were signalling for a truce, and the defenders allowed the fully armed British to enter the pa uncontested, before realising their mistake.

The British troops paid a high price, however, with 130 dead or wounded in comparison to 50 Maori casualties. While many Maori managed to escape south, the capture of over 180 warriors dealt a serious blow to the Maori King's ability to resist the British invaders.

Only a small part of the Maori defences now survive at Rangiriri, and while time has considerably reduced the earthworks, even this small area gives a hint of the complexity of the trenches and redoubt.

A site that is seldom visited is Te Whero's Redoubt off Talbot Street in Rangiriri. This was also part of the defence complex and lies 1.5 kilometres from the main redoubt, which gives some idea of how extensive the Maori line really was. There is also a small cemetery, opposite the Rangiriri Hotel, where many of the British and some Maori were buried.

Grade: Easy
Time: 10 minutes
How to get there: Clearly marked on SH1 at Rangiriri

4 Alexandra Redoubt, Pirongia

After the fall of Rangiriri, King Tawhiao's position at Ngaruawahia
was impossible to defend and slowly the Maori were forced ever further
south. Moving deeper into Waikato territory, the British troops found the
settlements along the river empty, while Maori gathered at the heavily
defended Paterangi pa. However, as at Meremere and anxious to avoid
the losses of Rangiriri, the British troops outflanked Paterangi and moved
south to Rangiaowhia, which fell with little fighting.

The final battle came at Orakau, though by this time the Maori
defenders numbered just 300 against 1200 well-armed British troops.
After bitter fighting, the pa fell with 160 Maori dead and just 17 British
killed. While this engagement effectively ended the fighting in the Waikato,
tensions continued, with the Maori simmering with resentment in what is
now known as the King Country.

Pirongia, then called Alexandra, was a frontier town and in 1868, a
redoubt was built in anticipation of further hostilities. Four years later a
larger and more sophisticated redoubt was built on a low rise; the Anglican
church of St Saviour was moved from the site to accommodate the
fortifications. This is the best preserved redoubt in the Waikato. It forms a
square with arrowhead-like parapets in each corner all encircled by a deep
trench. The redoubt was less than 2 kilometres from Whatiwhatihoe, the
headquarters of Tawhiao, just over the aukati or confiscation line.

Grade: Easy
Time: 10 minutes return
How to get there: From the southern end of the main street in Pirongia
(Franklin Street), turn into Bellot Street and the redoubt is on the left.

5 Kirikiriroa, Waikato River Walk

After the battle at Orakau, the British lost their enthusiasm to pursue
Tawhiao into the rugged, dense bush country south of Te Awamutu.
Besides, the British finally had what they were after and, to punish the
rebels, confiscated almost 500,000 hectares (of which 20,000 hectares
were returned at a later date). Even more convenient for the invaders was
that most Maori fled south with the King, and much of the confiscated
land was also empty.

The main Maori settlement in what is the modern city of Hamilton
was Kirikiriroa, located on the hilltop where the Anglican cathedral now

stands; there were further settlements at Pukete and Miropiko. The name Kirikiriroa means 'long stretch of gravel', and even today the stretch of the river below the old pa site has a gravelly, sandy bank at this point. The Kirikiriroa pa had less than 100 inhabitants and, as with other pa along the river, was abandoned in the face of the invading British after the fall of Rangiriri.

Directly across the river is the site where the militia first landed in 1864, marked by a plaque. Just a short distance downstream are the remains of the gunboat *Rangiriri* anchored in the riverbed. Though it was named after the battle, the gunboat did not see action at Rangiriri; the gunboats in action were the *Avon* and the *Pioneer*. The gun turrets of the *Pioneer* still survive – one is a war memorial in Mercer, and the other is in the park at the confluence of the Waipa and Waikato rivers at Ngaruawahia.

The *Rangiriri* was built at Port Waikato and was deployed on the river until 1892, when it was scuttled on the riverbank. Clad in thick armour and heavily armed, the gunboat was driven by a paddlewheel astern and was designed to be highly manoeuvrable on the narrow stretches of the river.

Waikato Museum, at the beginning of the walk, houses a magnificent waka taua as well as significant Maori taonga. From the museum, walk south along Victoria Street, with the Anglican Cathedral occupying the site of Kirikiriroa on the right. Turn left over the bridge and on the other side take the steps to the left. Turn right into Memorial Park, which is the site of the first landing of the militia in 1864, and continue along the river to the wreck of the *Rangiriri*.

 Time: 1 hour
Grade: Easy
How to get there: Start at the Waikato Museum at the southern end of Victoria Street.

6 Lake Hakanoa

The area around present-day Huntly belonged to Ngati Mahuta and Ngati Whawhakia. The large shallow lakes of Kimihia, Hakanoa, Waahi, Whangape and Waikare were rich in eels, a critical food source for inland iwi. However, as time wore on the eel catches began to diminish through overfishing, and as the supply of eels dropped, tension between the two tribes began to rise.

To prevent trouble the rangatira Potatau Te Wherowhero imposed a rahui to limit the season for catching eels from the river and lakes. The period of prohibition was determined by a stick laced with notches, which was gradually driven into the ground. Once the stick was driven below ground level, fishing could recommence. In addition, a pokeka or special flax cloak was used to signal whether fishing was allowed or forbidden.

Several place names in the Huntly area relate to this fishing arrangement; the Maori name for the Huntly area is Rahui Pokeka. During the fishing period the chief divided the catch between the tribes and this was known as wahi; the lake on the western side of the river is known as Lake Waahi. Lake Hakanoa to the east of the river takes its name from the lifting of the tapu on fishing – noa – and the haka performed to celebrate the lifting of the tapu.

The Hakanoa Walkway encircles the lake. The entrance is marked by a carved gateway and an excellent information board. Flat all the way, the walk takes in wetlands, grassy picnic areas and several formal gardens as well as informal plantings. While the lake itself is shallow and muddy, the excursion around the lake is very pleasant.

Grade: Easy
Time: 50 minutes
How to get there: The walk begins at the south end of the Huntly Park Domain on Taihua Street.

7 Ohinemuri River, Karangahake Gorge

There are two very different stories regarding the origin of the name Ohinemuri – though, as the name suggests, they both involve young women and the word means the same thing in both stories.

Hinemuri was the youngest of three daughters of the chief Te Onekiteakua, but when she fell in love and wanted to marry, her father refused to allow the marriage to go ahead until her two older sisters had married. Hinemuri was heartbroken and her tears formed the river, which took her name, 'the woman left behind'.

In the second story, the chief's daughter was out gathering food in the bush when the pa was suddenly attacked by an enemy tribe. Unprepared, the people of the pa fled into hiding, and when the woman returned to the pa she found it in possession of the enemy and tried to find somewhere to hide. A taniwha living nearby saw her distress and rescued the young woman by taking her to his cave, disguising their hiding place by rolling a huge rock in front of the entrance. After the pa had been retaken by her father and it was safe to return, the taniwha rolled back the rock so she could return home. The river was then named after the incident, O-hinemuri, 'the place of the woman left behind'.

The Ohinemuri runs through the picturesque Karangahake Gorge, and a track, following the line of the old Paeroa to Waihi railway, passes through the most rugged part of the gorge. Flat and easy walking, the track runs from Karangahake through to the Waikino Visitor Centre, though the most popular section of the walk is a loop in the middle of the gorge.

The loop starts over the bridge from a popular picnic area, the Karangahake Reserve, and follows the south bank of the river and the old railway bridge and tunnel on the north side.

Even though the tunnel is lit, a torch is handy as the lights are at irregular intervals and the track is a bit rough under foot.

Grade: Easy

Time: 45 minutes

How to get there: Karangahake Reserve is on SH2 between Paeroa and Waihi about 7 km from Paeroa.

8 Whakapipi/Bald Spur, Mt Te Aroha

The literal translation of Te Aroha is 'love'; however, for those expecting a tale of romance and passion, the 'love' in this case is quite different.

Te Mamoe (or Kahumata Mamoe) was the son of an Arawa chief living at Maketu. On an expedition west of the Kaimai Range, Te Mamoe became hopelessly lost in the vast swamp that once covered the Hauraki Plains. Climbing to the highest peak in the range, he became homesick when he saw Maketu shining in the distance. As an expression of the love he felt for his home, he named the mountain 'the love of Te Mamoe'.

Te Mamoe left behind his mauri, or spirit, and this caused a spring to well up from the heart of the mountain and emerge in the foothills as hot springs – which later became famous for their therapeutic properties. A pool of clear water in a cliff on the mountain was known as 'the mirror of Mamoe' and attracted newly married couples to make a wish.

Whakapipi (Bald Spur) was once a patupaiarehe pa; the dense bush and misty peaks make the perfect home for these mysterious people.

The same thick bush became a refuge for local people when they were attacked by Ngapuhi in 1815. Later, during the New Zealand Wars, wounded Maori warriors came here to recuperate in the healing waters of the springs. The Mokena geyser, the only hot soda water geyser in the world, takes its name from the Maori chief who once owned the land on which the town of Te Aroha now stands.

There are no two ways about it: the walk to the top is unrelentingly steep and you need a good level of fitness to climb the 952 metres to the summit. The only view along the way is from Whakapipi, and near the top the vegetation becomes distinctly subalpine.

The track, however, is clear to follow, in reasonable condition and, as Te Mamoe found, the views from the summit are spectacular: on a good day, Ruapehu and Taranaki can be glimpsed on the southern horizon.

If the summit is beyond your reach, the trip to Whakapipi is a very good second option. While it's a solid climb to 350 metres, the track is well formed, zigzagging through the bush to a lookout that has excellent views over the town below and the Hauraki Plains beyond.

Of course a reward for both is a good soak in the hot pools.

 Te Aroha Summit
Grade: Hard
Time: 4–5 hours return

 Whakapipi
Grade: Hard
Time: 1.5 hours return

How to get there: The track begins behind the Mokena Bath House in Te Aroha Domain.

9 Wairere Falls

Tarore lived with her father Ngakuku in a pa near Waharoa. Taught to read by local missionaries, she was given a book, Te Rongopai a Ruka, the Gospel of Luke. In 1836, at just 12 years old, Tarore set off with her father and a group of Maori Christians for Tauranga. They stopped for the night near the falls. Here the small band was attacked by Arawa warriors who, seeking utu for an Arawa man murdered at Waharoa, killed Tarore, took out her heart and stole her gospel.

Rather than continue a cycle of revenge killings, Ngakuku told his followers not to seek utu; instead he said, 'There lies my child. She has been murdered as payment for your bad conduct, but do not rise to seek a payment for her. God will do that. Let this be the finishing of the war with Rotorua. Now let peace be made.' Ngakuku's forgiveness and the words of the stolen gospel brought peace between the two belligerent iwi. Tarore is buried in a small cemetery near Waharoa.

Set in attractive native bush, these spectacular 153-metre falls drop in two stages. The falls are visible from a wide area of the Waikato, but are hidden for the entire walk, only to be finally revealed from the viewing platform. Following the stream, the track meanders through bush. Huge boulders litter this small valley – some the size of a small car. The walk is a steady uphill grade until you reach a long flight of steps just before the viewing platform. If you want to go to the top of the falls, it is a further 45 minutes from this point.

 Grade: Medium
Time: 1.5 hours return to the falls lookout
How to get there: The track to the falls starts at the end of Goodwin Road off Te Aroha–Okauia road, about 20 km south of Te Aroha township.

10 Taupiri Mountain

Ko Waikato te awa
Ko Taupiri te maunga
Ko Te Wherowhero te tangata.

Waikato is the river
Taupiri is the mountain
Te Wherowhero is the man.

The importance of Taupiri to the Tainui people cannot be overstated. The name means 'beloved' or 'the close-clinging lover'. In legend, Taupiri is the wife of the great Pirongia, and the smaller peaks Kakepuku and Te Kawa near Te Awamutu are their children. In some versions of Maui hauling up his great fish, it is Taupiri that is the first point of the fish to break the surface.

A pa crowned the lower hill below the summit, and once was the home of the great chief Te Putu. At war with Ngati Raukawa, who were gradually encroaching on their territory, and after scoring a decisive victory on the bank opposite Taupiri, Te Putu agreed to a request that he meet with the defeated rangatira Ngatokowaru. The two men met just below the pa and as they greeted each other with a hongi, Ngatokowaru fatally stabbed Te Putu in the neck with a dagger fashioned from the barb of a stingray.

Furious at the death of the chief, Te Putu's son Tawhiakiterangi sought revenge. But before setting out to attack his enemies, he met with a powerful tohunga near Waahi to acquire extra powers. The Waikato war party set off upriver, and when they came near Taupiri, a ghost canoe joined the flotilla. Although this waka was invisible, the chanting of the warriors and the splash of the paddles could be easily heard. The Waikato fleet followed the wake of the ghost waka upriver to meet the enemy. So powerful was the magic entrusted to Tawhiakiterangi that when they arrived they found the people of Ngati Raukawa lying on the ground and so helpless that Tawhiakiterangi's warriors were able to kill them with just the stems of toetoe.

Te Putu's mana was so great that his spilt blood made the area below Taupiri so tapu that the pa was abandoned and never reoccupied. European travellers later remarked that when approaching Taupiri they had to cross to the other side of the river to avoid touching tapu ground.

Te Wherowhero, who later became the first Maori King, had a pa at Taupiri, but this was abandoned during the Ngapuhi raids in 1826 and never fully reoccupied. After the land confiscations in 1864 when Waikato Maori were allowed to return to their homes, the people were dismayed to see that a road had been built around the foot of Taupiri. The construction of a railway line and later even a quarry further desecrated the tapu ground.

Today a small meeting house sits on the banks of the Mangawara River below the mountain. The lower slopes are the principal burying grounds of Tainui, and all the Maori kings and queens are buried here.

Though Taupiri Mountain is highly sacred to Tainui, they have allowed access to the summit. There are two tracks forming a loop, and both are marked by small wooden gateways. The first is just by the carpark and is the steeper and rougher of the two tracks. The second entrance is about 500 metres along the gravel road: this is not so rough and has a gentler grade, though it will take longer to get to the top. From the summit on a crisp sunny winter's day, snow-capped Ruapehu is clearly visible far to the south while, below, the Waikato River wends its way through fertile farmland.

The cemetery is not a tourist attraction and casual visitors are requested to respect this area and not walk among the graves.

Grade: Hard

Time: 1 hour 15 minutes

How to get there: The tracks begin by the small marae just south of Taupiri township where SH1 crosses the Mangawara River. Both tracks to the top lead off the access road.

11 Te Toto Gorge

It might come as a surprise that this steep exposed coastline was once extensively cultivated by early Maori. However, the wide slopes are well sheltered and face northwest for maximum sunshine. Moreover, the abundance of volcanic rocks allowed Maori to build walls and mounds that enhanced the warmth of the sun by reflecting the heat of the sun off the stones.

Traces of two small pa have been found – believed to have been occupied in the seventeenth century. In addition to the gardens, Maori also planted karaka trees to harvest their berries, and many of these trees are still growing today.

The name Te Toto in Maori means 'blood' and it is thought that the gorge was the scene of a dreadful atrocity in pre-European times.

The track begins at the end of the carpark and, although it's not marked as such, it is reasonably well defined. How far you want to go is determined by how far uphill you want to walk on the way back; the track eventually just peters out in the long grass. Stunted, almost prostrate manuka along this track are testament to the fierce westerly winds that sweep the lower slopes of Mt Karioi, an ancient extinct volcano. The views are superb both north and south along the exposed Waikato coastline. If you are up for something more demanding, the track to the Karioi lookout and summit starts on the other side of the road.

Grade: Medium

Time: Up to 30 minutes

How to get there: From Raglan follow the Wainui and Whaanga roads around the coast. After Manu Bay the road becomes narrow, winding and unsealed. The carpark is on the right, 1 km past the sign 'Te Toto Gorge Scenic Reserve'.

12 Mt Pirongia

Pirongia is a contraction of Pirongia-te-aroaro-o-Kahu or 'the fragrant pathway of Kahu' and relates to a journey that the tohunga Rakataura made across the mountain, following the scent of his wife Kahu. The full name of Mt Karioi, which lies just to the west – Maunga-o-karioi, meaning 'to linger' – also relates to the same story.

As with so many rugged mountains, Pirongia is closely connected to the patupaiarehe, the fairy people. Small, with pale skins and red hair, the patupaiarehe are known for cunning, trouble-making and love of music. They eat only raw food and are terrified of cooked food.

Ruarangi lived near the Hakarimata Range just to the north of Pirongia and one day his wife Tawhaitu was kidnapped by Whanawhana, a patupaiarehe chief, who took Tawhaitu off to his home on the summit of Pirongia and kept her there under his control by magical spells and enchanted music. Tawhaitu was allowed to return home during the day, but the spells forced her to return to Pirongia every evening and spend each night with Whanawhana.

Naturally Ruarangi was greatly distressed and was keen to put a stop to this arrangement. He consulted a powerful tohunga, who advised Ruarangi to build a hut of ponga ferns and coat himself and Tawhaitu and also the hut with a mixture of kokowai (red clay) and shark oil. He should also build an umu in front of the hut.

When Tawhaitu did not appear that night, Whanawhana came looking for her, but as patupaiarehe are afraid of both cooked food and the smell of kokowai and shark oil, his enchanting magic lost its power and after that night he was never seen again. However, the legacy of Whanawhana can still be seen today in that some Maori children are born with urukehu, fair or copper-coloured hair.

The track to the summit (959 metres) is a long slog and should be undertaken as a two-day trip with an overnight stay in the hut. However, a good alternative is the much easier walk to Ruapane (723 metres). From the carpark follow the sign that says 'Picnic Area and Lookout'; the Ruapane track peels off to the left about 30 metres into the bush. The track is a gradual climb, some of it through fine tawa forest, but not far from Ruapane it becomes steeper before arriving at a well-defined rocky outcrop giving fantastic views back over the lush Waikato. Beyond Ruapane the track leads to another rocky outcrop called Tirohanga, with even better views.

Grade: Medium
Time: 2 hours return to Ruapane
How to get there: The track begins at the carpark at the end of Corcoran Road, which is off Te Pahu Road.

13 Matakitaki Pa, Pirongia

On the northern outskirts of Pirongia stand the remains of Matakitaki pa, which in February 1822 witnessed one of the greatest battles of the Musket Wars.

After raiding the Tamaki isthmus, Hongi Hika turned towards the Waikato iwi, whom he accused of giving refuge to Ngati Whatua and Ngati Paoa survivors. Gathering a great war party of around 3000 men, Hongi crossed the Manukau, paddled up the Waiuku River and, after the army had dragged their waka overland, led his fleet up the Waikato River.

As Waikato fled south in front of the advancing Ngapuhi, their chiefs decided to make a stand at Matakitaki. This superbly defended pa was built on a headland where the Mangapiko Stream entered the Waipa River. It was protected by the water and the steep bluffs on the riverside, and also by several rows of ditches and palisading on the land side. Crammed full of refugees, Matakitaki sheltered as many as 10,000 people, a fact that had a major impact on the course of the battle.

Waikato warriors under Te Wherowhero seized the advantage and launched a surprise attack on the invaders, killing around 150 men and, more importantly, capturing 90 muskets. The victory was shortlived as Ngapuhi surrounded the pa and, with muskets, picked off any inside the pa who dared to shout insults from the parapets. Now under attack, the people inside the crowded pa grew alarmed. The unease turned to panic when Waikato warriors fired the captured guns inside the pa, causing the people to think that Ngapuhi had broken through the palisades. Total confusion reigned inside the packed pa, and hundreds were trampled to death in the ditches while trying to escape. Meanwhile Te Wherowhero tried to hold the position, but the situation in the pa was impossible and he was forced to withdraw to the south.

The battle left 1500 dead and many hundreds more taken prisoner. Following this overwhelming defeat, Waikato iwi abandoned traditional weapons and began to arm themselves with muskets.

It is a short easy walk across farmland to the pa – though originally it was much bigger and extended out to the main road. The main features still remaining are the deep defensive ditches on the landward side. Don't forget to close the farm gates behind you.

 Grade: Easy
Time: 15 minutes return
How to get there: The pa is located on SH35 at the northern end of Pirongia township.

14 Battle of Hingakaka, Lake Ngaroto

Lake Ngaroto is a small wetland lake not far south of Hamilton – and on its shores was fought the Battle of Hingakaka, said to be the largest battle ever fought in this country. The dates estimated for the battle vary between 1790, 1803 and 1807.

Tensions had been growing between coastal Tainui, closely allied with Taranaki, and their inland relatives Ngati Maniapoto and Waikato, allied with Hauraki. The issue finally came to a head over the uneven distribution of the fish harvest. Ngati Toa chief Pikauterangi, based at Marokopa on the coast, gathered together a huge war party of between 7000 and 10,000, crossed into Ngati Maniapoto territory and invaded the Waipa district.

Wahanui, a Maniapoto chief, sent out the call to his Waikato allies and gathered together a force of around 1600 to 3000. They decided to confront the invaders on a narrow ridge overlooking Lake Ngaroto. Pikauterangi and his warriors took up positions at the foot of the ridge and made the first attack, but clever tactics on the part of the defenders confused the invaders. The decisive point of the battle came when Pikauterangi was killed. Retreating towards the lake, the invaders were further ambushed, then in full panic were trapped in the swamp around the lake. Attempting to escape through the unfamiliar terrain or by swimming across the lake, thousands died. The name Hingakaka means 'fall of the kaka', as so many chiefs died that it was compared to a hunt for kaka (a native parrot).

In the past it was traditional to carry into battle powerful tribal talismans to assist in the fighting. In 1906 the sacred carving Te Uenuku was found hidden in the swamp at Lake Ngaroto; it is believed that it was carried into the Battle of Hingakaka and was quickly hidden by the fleeing warriors. This highly unusual carving embodies the spirit of the war god Te Uenuku, who appears in the form of a rainbow. Te Uenuku is made of totara and may date back as far as 1400 AD; the style is similar to Eastern Polynesian and Hawaiian carvings.

Lake Ngaroto was also known for its island pa, and the remains of these can be seen today.

The walk around the lake is flat and easy; for the most part, vegetation obscures the view of the lake. Two island pa sites can be seen on the eastern side of the lake, but the level of the lake is considerably lower than in the past and these pa are now little more than small hillocks on the shore. The track can be very wet in places.

The battle itself took place on a ridge south of the lake, and Bank Road, which leads to the lake, crosses the actual battlefield.

Grade: Easy

Time: 1.5 hours

How to get there: From the main street of Te Awamutu (Alexandra Street), head north 2 km and turn right into Paterangi Road. After 4 km turn into Bank Road; the lake is at the end of this road.

15 Kakepuku

Impossible to miss, Kakepuku dominates the landscape south of Te Awamutu and the name is a contraction of Kakepuku-te-aroaro-o-Kahu, 'the swollen stomach of Kahu'. The mountain was named by Rakataura, a tohunga on the voyaging waka *Tainui*, and honours the pregnant stomach of his wife Kahu.

There are five pa in the reserve area protecting the mountain, settled in around 1550 AD: Hikurangi, Tokatoka, Torewera, Omango, Arikiturere. In pre-European times most of the bush had been cleared from the mountain, but by the 1860s all the pa on the mountain were abandoned and the bush began to return.

Author James Cowan grew up in the district and was fluent in both Maori and English. He is best known for his books of Maori stories and legends published in the 1920s and 1930s.

The track is hard work, all uphill, rough and slippery (an upgrade is planned). The bush has completely returned and is now quite mature and the view from the top (449 metres), though partly obscured by trees, is well worth the trip. The most obvious pa site is on the summit, which is ringed by wide terraces. The track also passes through another pa site just as you reach the lip of the old crater, but the remains here are a little hard to detect.

 **Grade:** Hard

Time: 1.5 hours

How to get there: From Te Awamutu turn off SH3 into Fraser Street, which becomes Puniu Road and then Pokuru Road. Travel 6.5 km and turn left into Te Mawhai Road. After 1 km turn right into Kakepuku Mountain Road; the carpark is on the right.

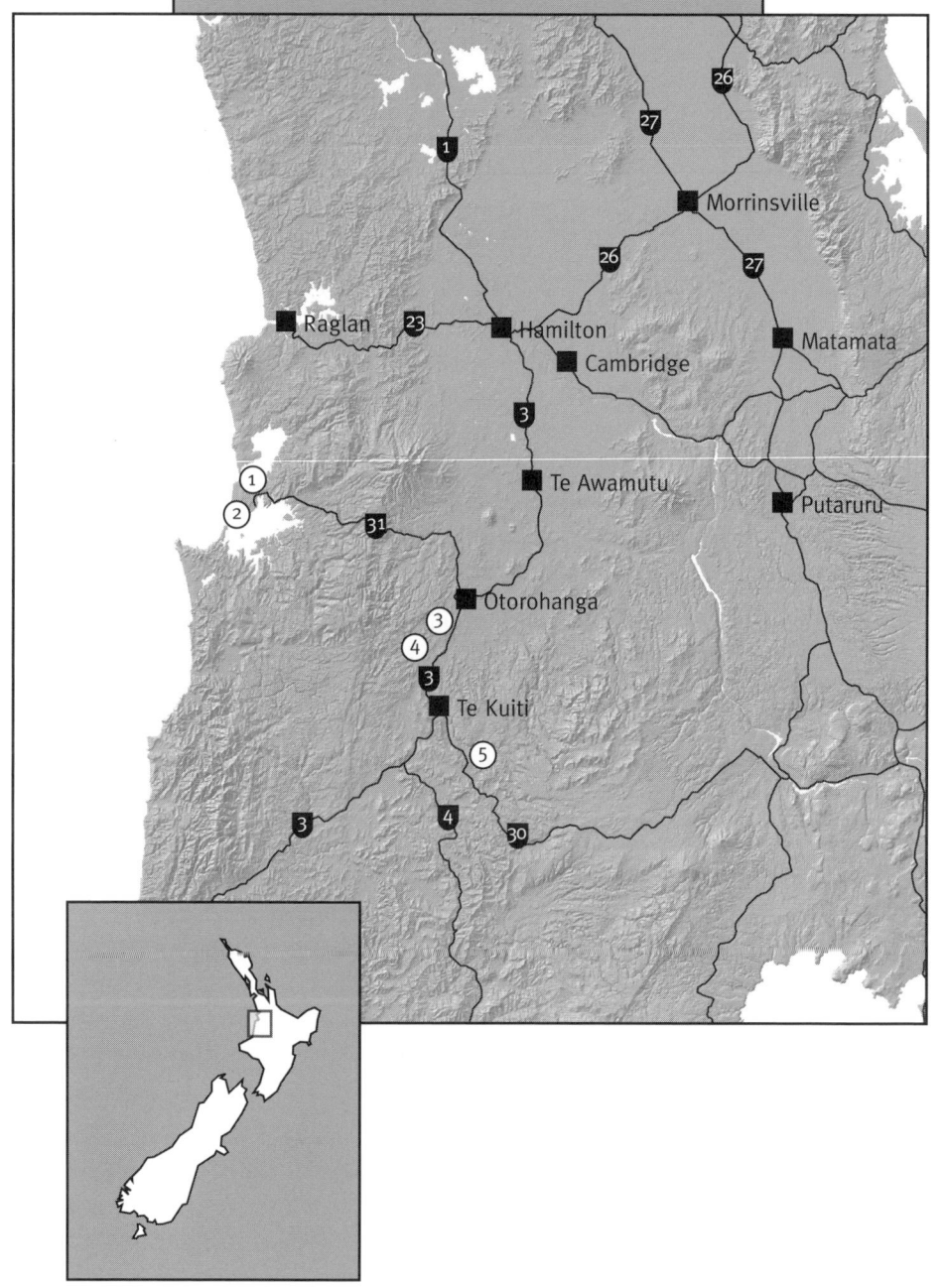

KING COUNTRY

1 Horoure Pa, Aotea Harbour

Aotea Harbour has a long Maori tradition dating from around 1300 AD and the arrival of the *Aotea* waka, after which the harbour is named. The *Tainui* waka arrived at Kawhia, just a few kilometres to the south, about 50 years later and for many generations the two people lived in harmony.

However, around 1600 AD the Kawhia people were expanding their territory, and when a Kawhia chief was killed on Aotea's south shore, the Kawhia chief Karewarewa attacked several pa on the northern side of Aotea. Eventually hostilities subsided, peace returned, and the two tribes were united when their rohe came under attack around 1800 from inland Tainui iwi.

The invaders first occupied Whaingaroa (Raglan) and then moved south, first taking the pa on the northern side of Aotea Harbour. Under Te Rauparaha the local tribes fought back, but the decisive battle for Aotea focused on Horoure pa, defended by the chief Rangipotiki. The defenders held their ground, but opposition collapsed when Rangipotiki was killed. The survivors fled south to take refuge in pa still controlled by Te Rauparaha, but when he was defeated at Lake Taharoa all the people trekked south to Taranaki and on to the Horowhenua.

For a long period after this defeat, the area remained empty until the defeat of Waikato by Ngapuhi at Matakitaki in 1826, when survivors from that conflict settled here.

The pa is above the small seaside town of Aotea. While there is not a track up to the pa, it is not too difficult to scramble up the grassy slope to the top – the views over the harbour are well worth it. The earthworks along the ridge include terraces, ditches and kumara pits, and the pa is crowned by a number of fine old pohutukawa.

Grade: Medium
Time: 30 minutes return
How to get there: Just before Kawhia township, turn off SH31 into Aotea Road and after 2.5 km turn left into Morrison Road. Follow Morrison Road to Aotea and turn right into Lawton Drive. The pa is at the end of this road.

2 Tangi Te Korowhiti, Kawhia

This large tidal harbour has a long and important Maori history. Kawhia is the final resting place of the *Tainui* waka, which is buried behind the historic Maketu marae and is marked by two stones, one at either end of the waka and over 20 metres apart. Hoturoa, the captain of the *Tainui*, is featured on the tekoteko (the figure at the top of the front gable) of the meeting house.

Kawhia is the home of the very popular Kai Festival. This annual festival of Maori food and culture is held in Omimiti Park on the weekend closest to Waitangi Day and attracts over 10,000 people. As well as traditional delicacies such as puha, paua, kanga wai (fermented corn), mussels, and hangi-cooked food there is also Maori craft, art, kapahaka and music.

Just along the beach from the marae a tree named Tangi Te Korowhiti marks the spot where the *Tainui* waka tied up. The tree was considered highly tapu and death was the penalty for anyone who touched it or even walked in its shadow. A storm in 1953 badly damaged the actual branch to which the *Tainui* was moored, and in the 1960s the branch finally broke and eventually the tapu was lifted. However, please treat the tree with respect and do not climb up into it or swing on the branches.

You can drive almost right up to the tree, but a much more pleasant option is to park by the wharf and take the coastal track around the harbour. There are numerous large pohutukawa along this walk, and Tangi Te Korowhiti is in the last group of trees just before Kaora Street.

Grade: Easy

Time: 20 minutes return

How to get there: From the wharf in Jervois Street walk south along the road until it merges into a track. The tree is at the end of this track not far from where it joins Kaora Street.

3 Opapaka Pa

Ngati Hia built this long ridge pa in the eighteenth century primarily to defend their lands in the valley below against incursions from Tane Tinorau, living to the south. After a battle near Waitomo, the chief of Tane Tinorau spread his dogskin cloak on the ground to signal a future of peace between the two iwi. After this, the area around the pa became known as Te Horahanga-o-te-kahu-o-Tane-Tinorau, 'the place where Tane Tinorau spread his cloak'.

The pa has very distinctive terraces and defensive ditches, but it is the kumara pits that attract most attention. Whereas in other pa sites the kumara pits are mere indentations in the ground, here at Opapaka the pits are enormous, measuring several metres wide and the depth of an adult. Moreover, the pits are located just outside the central part of the pa and were only lightly defended. Within the central part of the pa is an area known as the tihi, a special raised area where the chief lived.

Only part of the site is accessible; the western end is overgrown with vegetation. Good information panels make this site worth visiting.

From the carpark the walk is a steady uphill through mature bush, complete with tree identification information, so this is also a good opportunity to brush up on your tree knowledge. After about 20 minutes the track emerges out of the bush onto farmland and from there it is a short walk up to the pa site following the fenceline.

Grade: Easy/medium

Time: 1 hour return

How to get there: The entrance to the track is easily missed. It leads off the carpark of the Waitomo Adventure Centre, on the right 6.5 km from the Waitomo turnoff on SH3.

4 Ruakuri Walkway

The walkway was part of an old track that Maori used to travel from the coast to inland villages. It passed close to the Ruakuri caves, or 'the den of the dogs'. The name relates to the discovery of the caves by a man who was part of a local war party led by a chief called Tane Tinorau. While out hunting for birds, the warrior was savagely attacked by a pack of wild kuri (dogs) who had made their home in the caves entrance and he only narrowly escaped by throwing his catch to the dogs. Later he returned and, after killing and eating the dogs, he used their skins to make a cloak for Tane Tinorau. The first person buried in the caves was Tane Tinorau. In addition to burials the caves were used for the storage of important taonga, including pounamu, patu and pipitewai – cloaks of flax and kaka feathers. The cave was also used as a shelter by travelling Maori; there is evidence of fires and middens containing shellfish and kiore.

The short 30-minute walk along the Waitomo River is crammed with fantastic limestone outcrops, caves and a huge natural tunnel. The unspoiled bush features luxurious growth, in particular ferns, mosses and lichens. Easy to miss is the fantastic underground cavern, which is about 5 metres past the natural bridge viewing platform. Initially it appears to be just a hole in the ground, but let your eyes adjust and the short flight of steps quickly becomes apparent. This leads to a lookout point in a huge cavern high above the river as it disappears underground.

The area has glowworms at night, but don't forget your torch. The track is well formed, but walk it anticlockwise or else the signs won't quite make sense.

Grade: Easy

Time: 30 minutes

How to get there: 2 km from the Waitomo Glow Worm Caves, next to the entry to Aranui Cave.

5 Mapara Scenic Reserve and the Legend of the Kokako

Kokako hold a very special place in Maori myths, especially in relation to the demigod Maui. In the legend of Maui and the sun, when Maui traps the sun in his net in order to slow its crossing from east to west, it is the kokako who brings water in its long wattles to the struggling and thirsty Maui. To reward the bird for its great kindness, Maui gives the kokako long nimble legs so it can more easily hop through the trees to find food.

Mapara is one of the last strongholds of the endangered kokako, and this reserve is the most accessible place for those who want to hear or see this elusive, attractive bird. With persistent trapping of predators the kokako numbers in the reserve have rocketed to almost 100 breeding pairs, and Mapara has provided numerous birds to populate other reserves around the North Island.

The loop track in the reserve leads through the territories of several birds so the chance of hearing these birds is high, but you will need to be very patient to actually see one. The best chance is the period two hours after dawn, so you just have to get up early, especially in summer.

Grade: Medium

Time: 1 hour return

How to get there: Travel 26 km south of Te Kuiti on SH4 and turn left into Kopaki Road and then, after 2 km, turn right into Mapara South Road. The reserve is 5.5 km down this gravel road.

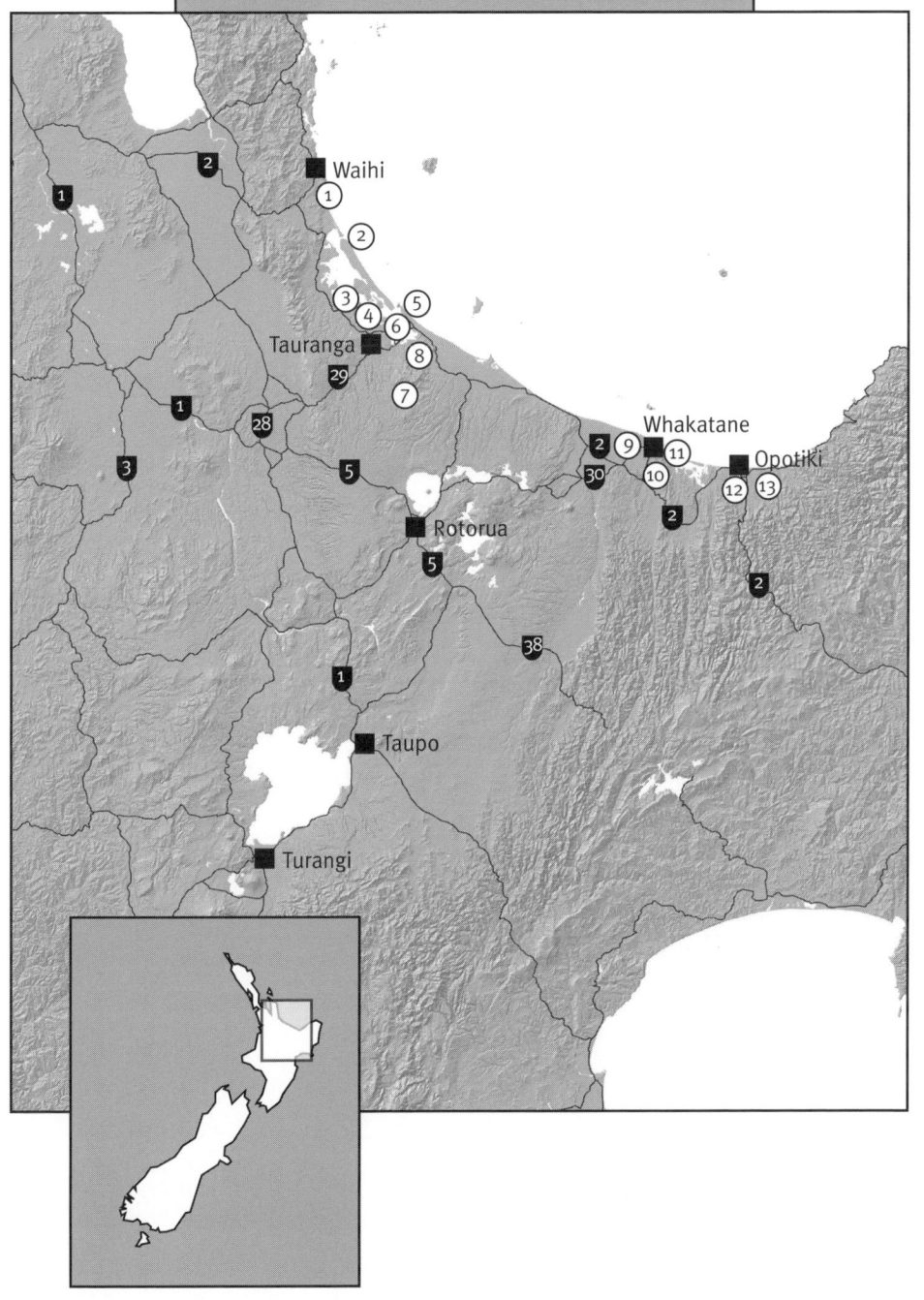

BAY OF PLENTY

1 Homunga and Orokawa Bays, Waihi

With over 7000 pa sites in New Zealand, many pa have little or no documented history and are unmarked and unprotected. Pa were mainly used in times of refuge for small local populations and were only occupied for short periods. They were often hastily constructed using timber that has long since rotted away, so the traces left by these pa are often minimal. By the middle of the nineteenth century, with the arrival of European agriculture and technology, the old-style fortified pa was almost redundant, and large numbers had been abandoned by this time.

This coastal track passes through two pa sites. Neither pa is named, neither has any signage, and it would be easy to walk straight past them. This coast was devastated by Ngapuhi raids during the Musket Wars when the population either fled ahead of the invaders or bravely defended their homes, only to be taken captive or killed during the raids. By the time of the Treaty of Waitangi in 1840, few Maori remained on the Coromandel Peninsula.

The best way to do this walk is to start from the northern end, but it will require a cooperative person to drop you off at the start. This means you walk down the very steep hill to Homunga Bay and then follow the coast back to Waihi Beach. This makes for a pleasant and relatively easy two-hour walk. Failing that, this is a four-hour return walk.

The first site is an unmarked headland pa just a short distance from Homunga Bay. The track passes right through the defensive trench, which looks distinctly man-made. There is a rough track to the left, which will take you on to the small pa protected on the sea side by rugged cliffs.

The second pa is more spectacular and is high on a steep hill behind Orokawa Bay. However, the pa is located on the northern slopes of the hill and is only visible from the northern end of the beach or from the track as it descends to the beach. Broad terraces drop down from the summit and are very obvious, though there is not a track to the top.

You can just do the return walk to Orokawa Bay, but the coastal stretch to Homunga is by far more attractive and the track is in better condition. The section from Waihi Beach to Orokawa is very muddy in parts.

Grade: Easy/medium
Time: 2 hours one way; 4 hours return
How to get there: At Waihi Beach the beginning of the track is right on the northern end of the beach and at high tide it will be a bit of a scramble to keep your feet dry.

At the other end the track starts at the very end of Ngatitangata Road. From Waihi take SH25 towards Whangamata and, after 1.2 km, turn right into Barry Street, which becomes Golden Bay Road and then Ngatitangata Road, a total distance of 9 km.

2 Otawhiwhi, Bowentown Heads

From a distance Bowentown Heads looks like one entity, but there are in fact two separate hills. The heads are known as Otawhiwhi, 'the entwining', which relates to a grisly incident where the intestines of a defeated chief were wrapped around a rock on the beach. The name Katikati was applied to a wide area that stretched from near the present town of Katikati through to Waihi, and this commemorates the visit to the harbour by Tamatekapua and the *Arawa* waka, when they stopped to eat. While his men ate their food very quickly, Tamatekapua ate so slowly that his men considered that their chief was merely nibbling (katikati) at his food and so named the place 'Katikati-o-Tamatekapua'.

One tradition has it that the great *Tainui* waka called into the bay below the heads and several on board the waka found the area so appealing that they settled there.

Te Hoa is the name of the pa on the highest point, though very little of this remains today. In contrast, the pa near the carpark, Te Kura a Maia, is very impressive. At first glance from the carpark all that is visible is the deep ditch-and-bank protecting the landward side of the pa, but beyond the outer defences, substantial terraces fan out down the slope towards the sea.

During the New Zealand Wars, British troops were stationed below the pa in what is now known as Anzac Bay, though no fighting occurred here.

From the upper carpark it is a 20-minute return steep climb to Te Hoa, while the walk to Te Kura a Maia is an easy stroll of 15 minutes.

 Grade: Easy
Time: Allow 40 minutes
How to get there: From Waihi Beach township, follow the road along the beach south to the heads.

3 Waihuri Pa, Omokoroa

Little is known about this small pa on a headland at the very end of the Omokoroa Peninsula, an area occupied by the Pirirakau hapu of Ngati Ranginui. Foreshadowing the present-day popularity of the Bay of Plenty with retirees, the great Ngati Haua fighting chief Te Waharoa and his wife moved to Omokoroa in their old age and died here in 1838.

The pa is easily recognised by the very deep defensive ditch that protected the pa on the landward side. Within the pa are a number of fine old karaka trees, highly valued as one of the few substantial native trees to provide edible berries.

While the road goes within a five minute stroll of the pa, a much more interesting walk is from the modern-day jetty on The Esplanade. Walk along the beach and past the boatyard, from where you will get an excellent view of the strategic position of the headland and the pa. From the beach a track goes up a small rise and through the Gerald Crapp Historic Reserve, with its fine old trees, to the pa.

Grade: Easy

Time: 30 minutes return

How to get there: From SH2 north of Tauranga, turn off at Omokoroa Road and drive the 5 km to the very end where the road drops down to the sea and, for a short distance, is called The Esplanade. Park at the end next to the store/café.

4 Ongarahu Pa, Huharua Park, Plummers Point

Like Waihuri pa just across the water, Ongarahu pa was the domain of the Pirirakau hapu of the iwi Ngati Ranginui. This was not the main pa on the peninsula, which may explain why Ongarahu is so small. Huharua pa, located half a kilometre to the southeast but now destroyed, was much larger. Tradition has it that Huharua and Ongarahu were linked by a long tunnel or covered ditch, though no evidence of such a tunnel has yet been found.

After the defeat of Ngati Ranginui at Gate Pa in 1864, this land was part of the Katikati Te Puna purchase, with only 50 hectares at Huharua remaining in Maori hands.

The pa may have been very small, but it was located on a superbly defended headland. Protected by steep cliffs, it is surrounded by a defensive bank and the landward trench is so deep that a bridge has been built to cross it. The small flat area beyond the ditch is an old urupa.

Ongarahu was featured on Maori TV's *Marae DIY*: the project included building modern palisading and a covered gateway.

Grade: Easy
Time: 15 minutes return
How to get there: From SH2 north of Tauranga, take Plummers Point Road and drive 4 km to Huharua Park.

5 Mauao/Mount Maunganui

The story of Mauao is a sad tale of unrequited love that will still touch the hearts of people today.

Mauao, originally a nameless slave mountain, once lived in foothills of the Kaimai Range and was desperately in love with beautiful Puwhenua. However, Puwhenua did not return his affections and instead was in love with the handsome mountain Otanewainuku. As time went on passion built up in the heart of the nameless one and finally, no longer able to endure the torment of seeing his beloved with another, he decided to kill himself by flinging himself into the ocean and drowning.

Mauao, however, needed help and called on the patupaiarehe to pity him and assist in ending his empty life. So as the sun went down, Mauao, the lovesick mountain, was secured by strong ropes and dragged to the sea by the patupaiarehe. It was a long haul and slowed even further by the mountain, who kept stopping to gaze one more time at Puwhenua – and suddenly the eastern sky began to glow with the light of dawn. Alarmed and fearful of being caught by the sun's rays, the patupaiarehe threw down the ropes and fled back to the forest, leaving the mountain just on the edge of the ocean. The hapless mountain at last had a name, Mauao, meaning 'caught by the morning sun', and is forever trapped, destined to gaze back at his lost love Puwhenua still in the arms of his rival.

According to tradition the *Takitimu* waka made landfall at the base of Mauao on its long journey from Hawaiki, and Tamatea the captain, together with all those aboard, climbed to the summit where they gave thanks for their safe journey by chanting ancient karakia and planting the mauri or life force of the people on the mountain.

Another legend involves the voyaging waka *Tainui*, which was sailing down the coast looking for a place to beach the waka, when Mauao loomed in front. Moving closer they saw savage waves crashing against rocks and, while steering clear, grounded the waka on a sandbank. The crew could not move the waka off the sand and into deeper water, and the captain Hoturoa decided that some greater evil was at work. He quickly concluded that an elderly woman, Wahinerua, was the cause, and he had her thrown under the waka. The crew then paddled with all their strength, rolling over Wahinerua's body. They finally floated free of the sandbank and found deeper water. Freed from the waka, the lifeless body of Wahinerua drifted with the tide and was finally washed up below Mauao; today it is the pinnacle of rock at the entrance to the harbour known as Te Kuia or Kuia Rock. To acknowledge Wahinerua and to show respect for the sea, it is tradition to toss a small offering of food when passing the rock.

Evidence of three pa has been found on Mauao. The mountain was once the stronghold of Ngati Ranginui, but after many attempts to wrest the mountain from their control, a final determined attack, called the Battle of the Kokowai, saw the pa fall to Ngaiterangi around 1700 AD. The last battle for the mountain came in 1820 when Ngapuhi, led by Te Morenga and armed with muskets, took Mauao. The pa was never reoccupied.

There are two choices for walking Mauao: up to the top or around the base. The base track follows the coastline on a broad undulating track that is an easy walk for old and young alike. The track skirts the rocky shoreline pounded by the open sea. Past Te Kuia standing just offshore and along towards the harbour are the telltale terraces of an old pa stepping uphill. Overhung with old pohutukawa, the track continues around to the sheltered waters of Pilot Bay, passing a statue of Tangaroa, god of the sea.

It is a steady climb to the 232-metre peak, but the tracks are mostly in excellent condition and not that difficult. The summit is a surprisingly large area of flattish land. The remains of an old pa are where the trig now stands and while not much remains on closer inspection, ditches and terraces can be discerned.

Summit Track
Grade: Medium
Time: 1 hour 15 minutes

Base Track
Grade: Easy
Time: 45 minutes

How to get there: The tracks begin in Mount Maunganui on the corner of Adams Terrace and Marine Parade.

6 Gate Pa

During the conflict in the Waikato, Maori sympathisers in the Tauranga area supported the Tainui war effort by providing supplies through the port and with food from their farms and gardens. When rumours of Maori reinforcements from the East Coast on their way to the Waikato reached Governor Grey, he decided to finally cut off supplies by sending troops to Tauranga.

Realising that war was imminent, Rawiri Puhirake, rangatira of the Tauranga-based iwi Ngaiterangi, instructed Henare Taratoa to draw up a list of rules that the combatants were to follow – a list that the Maori fighters religiously adhered to in the fighting. Issued on 28 March 1864, this extraordinary document read as follows:

To the Colonel,
Friend, – Salutations to you. The end of that. Friend, do you give heed to our laws for regulating the fight.
Rule 1. If wounded or captured whole, and butt of the musket or hilt of the sword be turned to me, he will be saved.
Rule 2. If any Pakeha, being a soldier by name, shall be travelling unarmed and meets me, he will be captured, and handed over to the direction of the law.
Rule 3. The soldier who flees, being carried away by his fears, and goes to the house of the priest with his gun (even though carrying arms) will be saved. I will not go there.
Rule 4. The unarmed Pakehas, women and children, will be spared. The end. These are binding laws for Tauranga.

By
Terea Puimanuka
Wi Kotiro
Pine Amopu
Kereti
Pateriki.
Or rather by all the Catholics at Tauranga

With the rules established, Rawiri then proceeded to construct a fortified pa at Pukehinahina, about 5 kilometres from the Te Papa mission where the British had set up camp. Designed by Pene Taka, this pa had traditional Maori elements of defence such as palisades and ditches, but significantly adapted them to take into account long-range rifles and, more importantly, cannon fire. Both the defeat and the high number of British casualties suffered in the attack were later attributed to this sophisticated design.

Consisting of two redoubts, the main pa occupied the top of the small hill, while a smaller redoubt was located 20 metres away. Between the two was a deep ditch which was to accommodate 600 warriors.

On 21 April General Sir Duncan Cameron finally arrived at Tauranga with over 600 troops and heavy artillery. He was joined a short time later by 430 naval personnel and, by 28 April, Cameron had almost 2000 men under his command. Opposing him were fewer than 250 Maori defenders.

The attack began on the morning of 29 April with a bombardment of the pa by mortars, howitzers, naval cannon and Armstrong guns, which continued through to the middle of the day and resumed a short time later, finally ending at 3 pm. With such substantial firepower against a fort of earth and timber, the British had every reason to feel confident when the advance assault party of 300 men attacked the pa at 4 pm.

What happened next is not entirely certain, but one thing is clear: the defenders had suffered few casualties during the bombardment as they had been safe deep underground in the superbly designed pa. In addition, a flagpole had been placed at the back of the pa and not in the centre, causing the British to aim for the pole, only to have the shells overshoot the main redoubt. Storming deep into the pa, the attacking force was met by withering crossfire, only made worse when General Cameron mistakenly believed that the pa had been taken and ordered a further 300 reinforcements into the small space.

With many of the officers killed or wounded, the British panicked and retreated from the pa and were then caught in the open by further crossfire from the smaller redoubt. By the end of the day the British had suffered about 100 casualties, compared to an estimated 25 Maori casualties. However, the Maori defenders realised that the pa was impossible to defend against such overwhelming odds and by dawn the next day it was deserted.

The battle was a disaster for the British and the blame rightly fell on General Cameron, though official accounts smoothed over the defeat. However, revenge was not long coming and on 21 June the British inflicted a heavy defeat on Ngaiterangi at Te Ranga, about 6 kilometres from Gate Pa. During the battle both Rawiri Puhirake and Henare

Taratoa were killed, resulting in a final surrender in July. Following the surrender came the inevitable confiscation of Ngaiterangi land by the government, which in turn sold the land to settlers.

Several stories of Maori chivalry are connected with the battle. Maori adhered to the guidelines drawn up by Henare Taratoa, and during the night after the battle Henare is said to have crossed through British lines to bring water to the British wounded. In 1900 Heni Pore made the claim that she had given water to the fatally wounded Colonel Booth during the same night.

Rawiri Puhirake, who died and was buried at Te Ranga, was later reburied in the Tauranga cemetery next to his foe Colonel Booth.

Today Gate Pa Domain, an attractive small park, occupies the site of the battle and a carved gateway leads to a short walk with excellent storyboards outlining the details of the battle. The main pa was on the high point where St George's Anglican church now stands, along with a small memorial to the dead from both sides of the conflict.

The name Gate Pa is derived from a gate placed in the boundary fence to let in supplies, and the main road through Tauranga, Cameron Road, is named after the leader of the British troops.

 Grade: Easy
Time: Allow 20 minutes
How to get there: Gate Pa Domain, Corner Cameron and Church Streets.

7 Otanewainuku

Rising to 640 metres, the bush-covered Otanewainuku is closely connected with two very famous Maori stories. Tutanekai, lover of Hinemoa, while being pursued by his enemies through this area, leapt spectacularly from the summit of Otanewainuku and avoided capture.

This is also the mountain that caused Mauao so much grief when the beautiful Puwhenua rejected him and chose Otanewainuku instead. Mauao then persuaded the patupaiarehe to drag him to the ocean to drown. Caught by the morning sun, he remains stranded on the edge of the sea forever, looking back at Puwhenua and Otanewainuku.

A loop track through magnificent virgin forest leads to the summit, which has a lookout tower giving spectacular views over the Bay of Plenty. The tracks are in very good condition with surprisingly little mud, considering the dense wet bush. The righthand side of the loop following the ridge is a steady but not steep climb, while the lefthand side of the loop to the summit is flatter, but much steeper at the end.

 Grade: Easy/medium
Time: 1.5 hours
How to get there: From SH29 at Tauranga take Oropi Road for 14 km, turn left into Mountain Road and continue along this road (part gravel) for a further 7 km to the carpark and shelter.

8 Te Rae o Papamoa/Papamoa Hills Regional Park Summit Walk, Te Puke

These hills are known to Maori as Te Rae o Papamoa. There are no fewer than eight pa in the park and a further three just outside of it. Occupation of these pa dates from around 1650 AD, which coincides with the rise of the pa in the seventeenth century. Over time three iwi have occupied these hills: Ngaiterangi, Ngati Pukenga and Waitaha a Hei.

Four pa are easily accessible on this walk. The largest, Wharo pa, covers 7 hectares; but the most spectacular is Karangaumu, which occupies the highest point in the park at 224 metres. Not only is it a large pa covering the top of the hill, but the ramparts, defensive ditches and terraces are all clearly visible. The heart of the main summit pa consists of a large flat area between two raised areas, surrounded by wide terraces and reached via a deep defensive ditch. Even to the untrained eye, the strategic advantage of this hilltop pa is immediately obvious. The whole bay is clearly visible and watchful lookouts would have missed nothing from this ancient fortress. A number of very old karaka trees grow just below the pa.

A steady uphill walk, this track begins through a mature pine forest which has an unusual understorey made up almost entirely of kawakawa. Take some time to chew a small piece of a new leaf and enjoy the peppery taste, followed by a mild numbness as you experience an anaesthetising effect. Early herbalists used this plant to alleviate toothache by packing the infected tooth with kawakawa leaf, thereby numbing the pain.

The trail eventually emerges from the trees to open farmland with increasingly broad views of the eastern Bay of Plenty. The loop track is not that obvious if you walk to the summit first, but it begins about 300 metres back down the track from the summit and links four pa, including Karangaumu.

Grade: Medium
Time: 1 hour 10 minutes return to the summit; 1 hour 45 minutes for
the loop walk
How to get there: 5 km east of Te Puke on SH2, turn left into Poplar
Lane and drive 1800 m to the carpark.

9 Kaputerangi/Toi's Pa

Toi was one of Polynesia's greatest voyagers, not only exploring the
coastline of New Zealand, but repeatedly crossing back and forward
across the South Pacific.

Kaputerangi is one of New Zealand's oldest pa sites; the strategic
value of this hilltop location is obvious. It was this pa that the male crew
members of the *Mataatua* were visiting when it slipped its moorings
and was saved by the actions of Wairaka (see Whakatane River Walk,
overleaf).

However, according to legend, the original inhabitants of this area
were known as Kakahoroa, descendants of Tiwakawaka, the grandson
of Maui the great voyager and fisherman. When Toi arrived, his people
intermarried with these earlier people and all the numerous descendants of
Toi were then known as Te Tini o Toi, the multitude of Toi.

Kaputerangi is also the place where kumara came to Aotearoa. Tradition
tells that one morning Te Kurawhakaata, the daughter of the chief
Tamakihikurangi, was walking along the river when she came across two
strangers lying on the shore and clearly exhausted. These two brothers,
Taukata and Hoaki, had journeyed from Hawaiki in a waka called *Nga
Tai a Kupe*, and Kurawhakaata took the tired and hungry men back to
Kaputerangi for food. However, when the meal of fern root, mamaku and
cabbage tree was placed before them, they were, despite their hunger, very
unimpressed.

Taukata asked for water and from his kit took some dried root, which
he crushed and stirred with the water into a paste. He then offered the
mash to his guests, who were so impressed with the flavour that they
clamoured to know what the food was and how they could get more.
When he explained that this was kumara and it could be obtained from
their homeland, the people of the pa, who at that time had lost the art of
building ocean-going waka, set about building a large waka with the help
of the two brothers. From a great totara tree emerged the waka
Te Aratawhao, and it was this waka that journeyed to Hawaiki and

brought back the kumara to Aotearoa.

The views from the summit are endless in all directions and, with the steep drop on the river side of the pa, the site was eminently defendable. The track is in excellent condition, with some stepped sections, and at the very beginning the walk crosses the top of Wairere Falls.

 Grade: Easy/medium
Time: 45 minutes return from Seaview Road
How to get there: The walk begins from the carpark on Seaview Road in Whakatane; if walking up from the town centre, take the long flight of stairs in Canning Place behind Pohaturoa Rock.

10 Whakatane River and Historical Walk

Toroa, the captain of the famous waka *Mataatua*, was given specific instructions by his father Irakewa before leaving Hawaiki to look for three distinctive landmarks: a cave, a waterfall and a tall rock; when he found all three, then that would mark the place to settle. Today, more than 800 years later, these three landmarks are within the central business area of Whakatane and are linked by an easy walk.

The first landmark is Muriwai's Cave (partially collapsed), where Irakewa's daughter lived. This cave was considered highly tapu until the tapu was lifted in 1963. The second is Wairere Falls, and while this is not so spectacular, it is nonetheless a very attractive waterfall, considering it is right in the middle of town. The final landmark is Pohaturoa Rock, which has at the base a highly tapu cave where tohunga performed sacred ceremonies.

When the waka *Mataatua*, captained by Toroa, arrived and moored in the estuary of the river, the men climbed up to Kaputerangi, leaving the women and children behind on the *Mataatua*. A swift outgoing tide put the waka in danger of being carried out to sea but, in a breach of tradition, Toroa's daughter Wairaka saved the day by picking up a paddle and exclaiming 'E! Kia whakatane au i ahau!' ('let me act like a man'), and with the other women she brought the waka back to safety. This action is the origin of the name of both the river and the town.

Start the walk by the Visitor Centre and follow the river towards the sea, past the busy Whakatane wharf and on to the landing place of the *Mataatua*, marked by a replica of this famous waka. From here continue to the heads and the bronze statue of Wairaka overlooking the narrow entrance to the river. Follow the road back to town, taking in Toroa's three landmarks – Muriwai's Cave, Wairere Falls and Pohaturoa Rock in the very centre of the business area.

Grade: Easy
Time: 1 hour
How to get there: Start the walk at the Visitor Centre in Kakahoroa Quay, Whakatane.

11 Tuwhare Pa

Tuwhare pa, built around 1700AD, is in fact three distinct pa sites all in very close proximity, and with views over the harbour and the sea.

Ohiwa harbour was the traditional boundary between Ngati Awa to the west and Whakatohea to the east, and while Whakatohea claimed the entire harbour, this important Ngati Awa pa reinforced their claim to important and rich food resources.

Located on a tribal boundary, Tuwhare pa saw more than its share of conflict. One of those conflicts was resolved in very dramatic fashion by a young woman, Mere Aira. The daughter of a Ngati Awa chief, Mere had married a Whakatohea chief, Kape Tautini, and they lived at Tuwhare. Not long after the birth of their son, Kape Tautini went out on a fishing expedition and failed to return. Even though she was grief-stricken at the loss of her husband, Mere couldn't help feeling that something was not quite right. That vague feeling of unease turned into fear when one day, totally unexpectedly, a fleet of Whakatohea waka taua was spied rapidly approaching the pa, and standing tall in one waka was none other than Kape Tautini.

Caught completely unprepared to fight, Ngati Awa had no choice but to try and plead with the belligerent Whakatohea. All the people gathered on the beach behind their chief. Expecting a fight, the invaders were at first taken aback, but they became increasingly aggressive, performing haka and recounting past insults and injuries. With a one-sided battle very likely, Mere Aira stepped forward and, holding her son high above her head, called out, 'The child I am holding in my arms is the symbol of our two tribes and could make peace or war. Unless the killing is stopped for now and all time, I shall throw my child on these rocks.' Whakatohea were so impressed by the courage of Mere Aira that a peace deal was immediately arranged on the beach.

From the carpark is a short easy walk to the pa where the extensive earthworks are still visible and from where there are excellent views over the Ohiwa harbour.

Grade: Easy

Time: 15 minutes return

How to get there: The track is on the right, 200 m from the Ohope Beach/Opotiki Road intersection.

12 Hukutaia Domain/Burial Tree

This small reserve of low rainforest was established in 1918 at the request of local Maori to protect Taketakerau, an ancient puriri tree believed to be over 2000 years old. In 1913, after the tree had been damaged in a storm, a large cache of old bones was discovered hidden deep inside the hollow of the old puriri. The tree was used by the local Upokorehe hapu to conceal the bones of the notable dead to save them from desecration by enemies, a common practice among early Maori (caves were also used for this purpose). After the tree was damaged the remains were buried elsewhere. Although the tapu has been lifted, please respect the tree.

The tracks are not well marked, but the reserve is very small and you can't get lost, though the puriri tree might take a little searching for.

Grade: Easy

Time: 30 minutes

How to get there: From Opotiki take the road to Whakatane. Just over the Waioeka River bridge turn left into Woodlands Road, and the reserve is on the left 7 km down this road.

13 Tauturangi Walkway

Opape lies east of Opotiki. Tradition tells that it was along this coast that the waka *Nukutere* landed on its long migration voyage from Hawaiki, bringing with it taro, kumara and ti (cabbage tree). It was also at Opape that a young woman received a love message carried by a shellfish that had travelled all the way from Kaiti (Gisborne), bearing words of love and devotion from a man living there (for the full story see Kaiti Hill, p119).

On 28 February 1870 war parties loyal to the defiant Te Kooti attacked Opepe and not only captured guns and ammunition, but also took 170

prisoners. However, when Major Kepa arrived shortly after in pursuit
of the men, the people of Opape refused to cooperate and were made to
suffer yet again. The captives from Opape were in the meantime dragged
through the rugged Urewera country and were constantly under the threat
of death if any disobeyed or tried to escape. Finally Kepa caught up with
the band on 25 March, and while Te Kooti and a small group of followers
escaped, the hapless people of Opape were either captured or killed in the
fighting. Many were later imprisoned as supporters of Te Kooti.

This well-formed track leads up from the tiny settlement of Opape and
around a coastal headland with excellent views out to Whale and White
Islands and far along the rugged bush-clad East Cape coast. The walkway
also passes the old pa sites of Kohinehine, Ruruarama and Tarakeha,
though these are not marked and are not accessible.

The start of the track is not easy to find. At low tide go down the boat
ramp and walk to the right along the beach. The beginning of the walk is
clearly marked just over the stream. At high tide, take the road to the right,
cross the bridge and follow the road to the left back along the stream. A
rough track skirts a small cemetery and, after a short distance, joins the
main track. The track stops just beyond the lookout so there is not much
point going any further.

 Grade: Easy
Time: 50 minutes return
How to get there: 14 km east of Opotiki on SH35, turn left into Opape
Road and park down by the beach. Park on the road to the left of the
boat ramp so the ramp is left clear for people launching boats.

ROTORUA

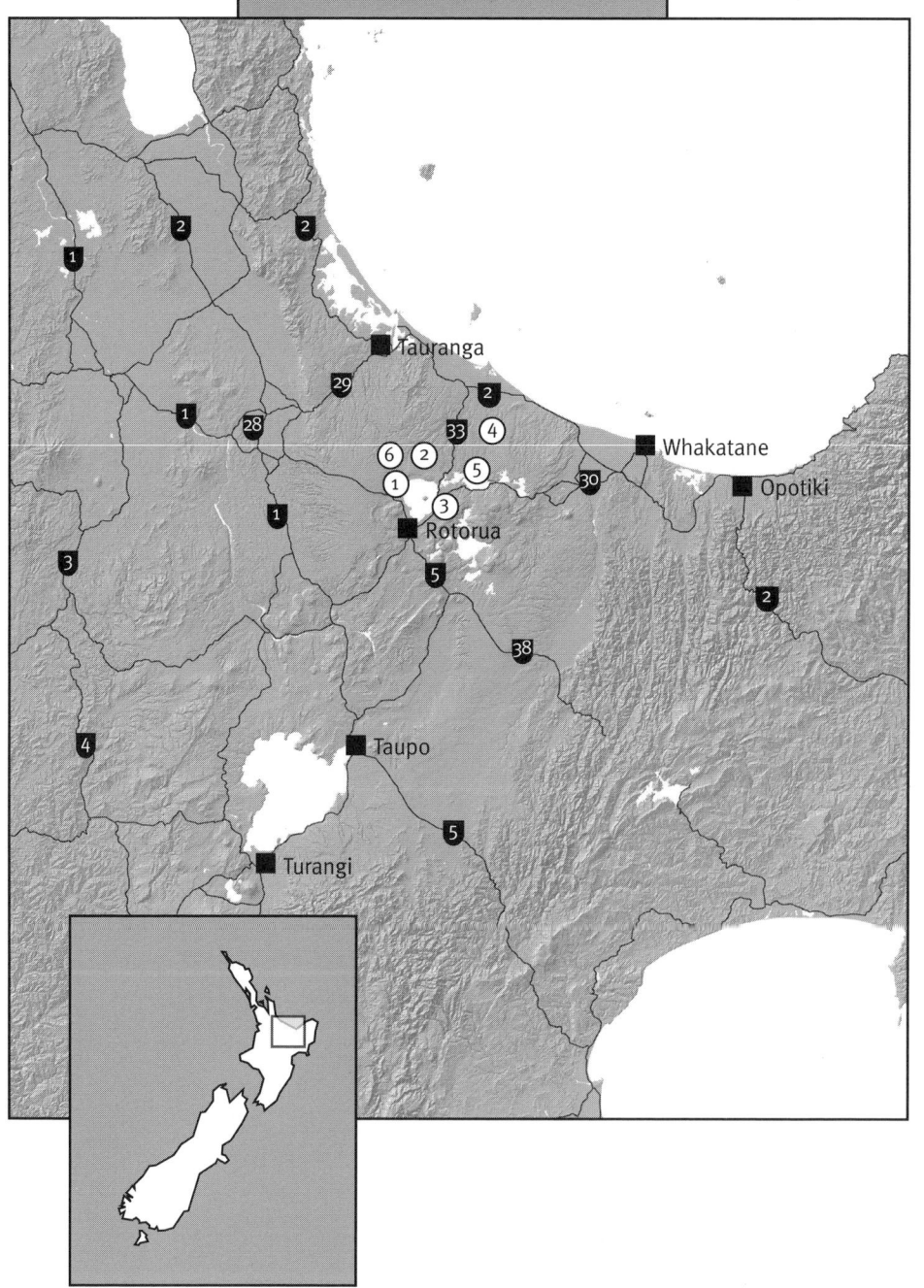

1 Rotorua City Walk

This short walk around the centre of Rotorua connects the modern city with its long Maori past. Start the walk at the Rotorua City Focus on the intersection of Hinemoa and Tutanekai Streets. These are two streets that bear the names of two of Rotorua's most famous ancestors, and here they are celebrated with huge carved statues by local artist Albert Te Pou. In addition to these two carvings are tall contemporary pou and two large carved panels by artists Manahi Skerret and Erin Tioke that celebrate the migration voyage of the *Arawa* waka and the great ancestor Ihenga.

From the City Focus head east on Hinemoa Street to the Government Gardens, which were established on land gifted by Ngati Whakaue 'for the benefit of the people of the world'. However, long before this, the hot springs by the lake were well known to Maori for their therapeutic value.

The lakefront is a short walk from the gardens and is the starting point for trips out to Mokoia Island, as well as the location for the popular *Opera in the Pa* concerts held here in the summer.

Continue west along the lakefront to Ohinemutu village. One of the most important Ngati Whakaue settlements, Ohinemutu has been the heart of Maori Rotorua for hundreds of years. Overlooking the lake is St Faith's Church, built in 1910 with Tudor-style overtones. The interior is decorated with fine weaving and paintings. Of special note is the window showing Christ as a Maori chief and placed in such a way that he appears to be walking on the waters of Lake Rotorua. Services on Sunday are held in English and Maori. Behind the church are the graves of returned soldiers in concrete tombs above ground, as there is too much geothermal activity for burials underground.

The heart of Ohinemutu is the beautifully carved meeting house Tamatekapua on Te Papaiouru marae, named after the captain of the *Arawa* waka, which brought the ancestors of the Arawa iwi to Aotearoa around 1350. Ohinemutu is a contemporary Maori community, not a tourist attraction, and while the local people welcome visitors, every respect should be shown to both the people and the place.

From St Faith's Church continue west past finely carved meeting houses and veer left into Ariariterangi Street, where steam floats up from stormwater drains and hot water bubbles in backyards. Then turn left into Rangipahere Street, which leads to Kuirau Park.

Kuiarau lived here with her husband Tamahika. As Kuiarau was bathing in a hot pool she was seized by a taniwha lurking below the surface, who then dragged her down to his lair. However, Kuiarau fought back and the gods, who witnessed her struggle with the taniwha, made the water boil and thereby destroyed the taniwha together with the helpless Kuiarau, who is now remembered in the name of the park (though slightly altered to Kuirau).

Thermal activity is concentrated in the northeastern section of the park, but this varies considerably from year to year and season to season. From Kuirau Park return to the City Focus.

Grade: Easy
Time: 1 hour
How to get there: Start at the City Focus, corner of Hinemoa and Tutanekai Streets.

2 Mokoia Island

Occupied by Te Arawa for over 700 years, Mokoia Island was prized as a strategic defensive site and a rich fertile area to grow the valuable kumara. In recent years the island was considered too isolated and the last residents left in 1953.

Of particular fame is the great love story of Hinemoa and Tutanekai. Hinemoa, forbidden by her family to marry the handsome warrior Tutanekai, swam one cold night from the shores of the lake to the island, guided only by the sound of Tutanekai's flute (now in the Rotorua Museum). On reaching the island, Hinemoa warmed herself in a hot pool, where she was eventually discovered by Tutanekai and taken to his whare. In the morning Tutanekai's people expected trouble but Hinemoa's family, impressed by her epic swim, gave the union their blessing.

Now a native bird sanctuary, the island has a number of easy walking tracks, and historic areas that include the site of Tutanekai's whare, Hinemoa's pool, and a rare and ancient stone carving of Rongo, the god of cultivation, placed there to safeguard the kumara crops.

The island is managed by a trust and can only be visited by guided tour, which lasts around 2.5 hours. For information and bookings, go to www. mokoiaisland.co.nz, or phone 07 476 0920.

3 Maori Rock Art, Lake Tarawera

This large lake of beautiful clear water lies at the foot of Mt Tarawera, and was substantially altered by the 1886 eruption. Nine days prior to the eruption a mysterious waka was seen on the lake by a party of tourists returning from the famous Pink and White Terraces, but as the boat came closer, the waka suddenly disappeared. Believed by many to be a waka wairua (spirit canoe) come to warn of the approaching doom, it is said that its reappearance will signal the next eruption.

The eruption itself was said to be caused by the powerful spirit Tamaohoi. The great Arawa tohunga Ngatoroirangi was travelling over the mountain when he clashed with Tamaohoi, who resented Ngatoroirangi crossing his land without permission. In the fight that ensued, Ngatoroirangi's magic was much greater and he managed to trap Tamaohoi deep underground inside Mt Tarawera. Finally in 1886, Tamaohoi burst out of his underground prison in the form of a violent volcanic eruption that brought disaster to the area around the mountain.

To the right of the carpark is a short track to the Wairoa Stream, the outlet for the Green Lake, and to the left another short walk leads to Maori rock drawings. These drawings were originally covered by the 1886 eruption, but were rediscovered in 1904. Executed in kokowai or red ochre, the drawings are at first indistinct, but on closer inspection, the image of a waka full of people, including standing figures, becomes increasingly clear.

 Grade: Easy
Time: 15 minutes return
How to get there: From SH30 towards Whakatane, turn right onto Tarawera Road at Te Ngae, and follow the road all the way to Tarawera Landing, 2 km past the Buried Village.

4 Hinehopu's Track, Lake Rotoiti

This well-formed track through attractive bush links Rotoiti and Rotoehu and takes around two hours return. There are three entrances, none of which is particularly well marked, though the best starting point is at the

Lake Rotoiti end. The highlight is the famous matai tree under which Hinehopu, when a baby, was hidden from enemies by her mother. It was also under this tree that she met her husband Pikiao, and many of the iwi Ngati Pikiao trace their lineage directly back to this couple. The tree is right by the main road, which does tend to detract from the atmosphere somewhat.

It was also along this track that Ngapuhi warriors, led by Hongi Hika, launched their attack on Rotorua; the track is also called Hongi's Track. Seeking revenge for earlier deaths, in 1823 Hongi Hika arrived in the Bay of Plenty and led a large war party towards Rotorua, only to discover that the Arawa people had all decamped to Mokoia Island and, for extra protection, had ensured that all waka were secured on the island. Not discouraged, Hongi travelled up the Pongakawa River to Lake Rotoehu and then dragged his waka along this track to Lake Rotoiti. Hongi's warriors were well armed with guns and the Arawa people, now trapped on Mokoia Island, were overwhelmed, and many were slaughtered.

Grade: Easy

Time: 2 hours return

How to get there: At the eastern end of Lake Rotoiti, turn off SH33 into Tamatea Street and continue for 500 m to the carpark where the track begins. There isn't any signage but the track is fairly obvious. There is limited carparking at the Lake Rotoehu end.

5 Te Koutu Pa, Lake Okataina

The full name of Okataina is Te-moana-i-kataina-a-Te Rangitakaroro, or 'the ocean where Te Rangitakaroro laughed'; it refers to an incident that occurred around 300 years ago. The chief Te Rangitakaroro was sitting on a rock on the shore of the lake with a number of warriors when one remarked that the lake was like an ocean, a comment that the chief found so funny that his laughter echoed around the lake.

Te Koutu pa was the most important of the numerous settlements around the lake, and was occupied by a number of iwi before Ngati Tarawhai made Te Koutu their home. The pa was on an important trading route with portages linking the lakes Tarawera, Okataina, Rotoiti and Rotorua.

Te Koutu was renowned for the skill of its waka builders, and was famous for carving. Carvers there were early and enthusiastic adopters of European carving tools, and one of the pa's most famous carvings is the magnificent gateway now in the Rotorua Museum. Once this huge gateway stood on the narrow isthmus that links the pa to the mainland, but anxiety over the deterioration of the carving saw it removed first to the Auckland Museum and, in more recent times, back to Rotorua.

During Hongi Hika's invasion of Rotorua in 1823, he sent a party of his men to bring back the head of Te Koutu's great tohunga, Tamakoha, so he could eat his brains and thereby acquire Tamakoha's mana. However, Tamakoha was more than a match for Hongi and conjured up a great storm on the lake that so terrified Hongi's men that they abandoned the attack and fled.

The level of Lake Okataina varies considerably, and in the past was 12 metres lower than it is today. During the Hawke's Bay earthquake in 1931, the lake abruptly dropped nearly 4 metres.

During the Tarawera eruption in 1886 Te Koutu was thickly cloaked in a heavy layer of ash, though by that time the pa was virtually abandoned. Today the pa is covered by regenerating bush, but all the earthworks are clearly visible and the pa is noted, in particular, for its stone kumara storage pits and burial caves carved into the hillside.

The walk begins through the archway by the carpark and follows the shoreline of the lake through the bush to the small peninsula where the pa is located.

Grade: Easy

Time: 1 hour return

How to get there: From the carpark by the lake at the end of Okataina Road.

6 Ngongotaha Summit

Ngongotaha was one of the greatest strongholds of the mysterious patupaiarehe, who were also known as iwi atua, 'the godlike tribe'. Patupaiarehe shunned human contact and were known for their trouble-making, and very seldom showed any kindness to humans. The tribe of patupaiarehe who occupied the mountain were known as Ngati Rua and numbered over a thousand living close to the summit, which was then known as Te Tuahuoteatua (the altar of the god).

Ihenga, the grandson of Tamatekapua, was exploring the country around Rotorua when he saw what looked like smoke rising from near the summit and decided to explore further. However, the climb through the dense bush was much more difficult than he first thought and soon Ihenga became very thirsty; but then as now, there were no springs or streams on the upper reaches of the mountain. Still he climbed, when suddenly to his great surprise he came across the Ngati Rua pa, catching the usually wily patupaiarehe unawares. Ihenga's thirst was by then so fierce that he immediately asked for water and, contrary to the usually unfriendly patupaiarehe behaviour, a beautiful young woman came forward and gave Ihenga a drink from a calabash. The curiosity and friendliness of Ngati Rua made Ihenga think that their real intention was to kill him and eat him, so seizing an opportunity when the patupaiarehe were not watching him, Ihenga escaped down the mountain to safety.

Later, however, Ihenga returned and became friendly with the people of Te Tuahuoteatua and eventually lived near the mountain on the banks of the Waiteti Stream. He also named the mountain Ngongotaha after the kindness of the beautiful fairy woman – ngongo meaning 'to drink', and taha, 'calabash'.

This track has recently been extended and upgraded. It begins through fine virgin forest and then gradually climbs to the summit through dense bush much favoured by the patupaiarehe. The grade is steady rather than steep. Near the top it joins Mountain Road for the short section to the summit. The summit is bush-covered and there are no views.

Grade: Medium
Time: 2 hours return
How to get there: The track begins from the Violet Bonnington Reserve, at the Rotorua end of Paradise Valley Road.

CENTRAL NORTH ISLAND

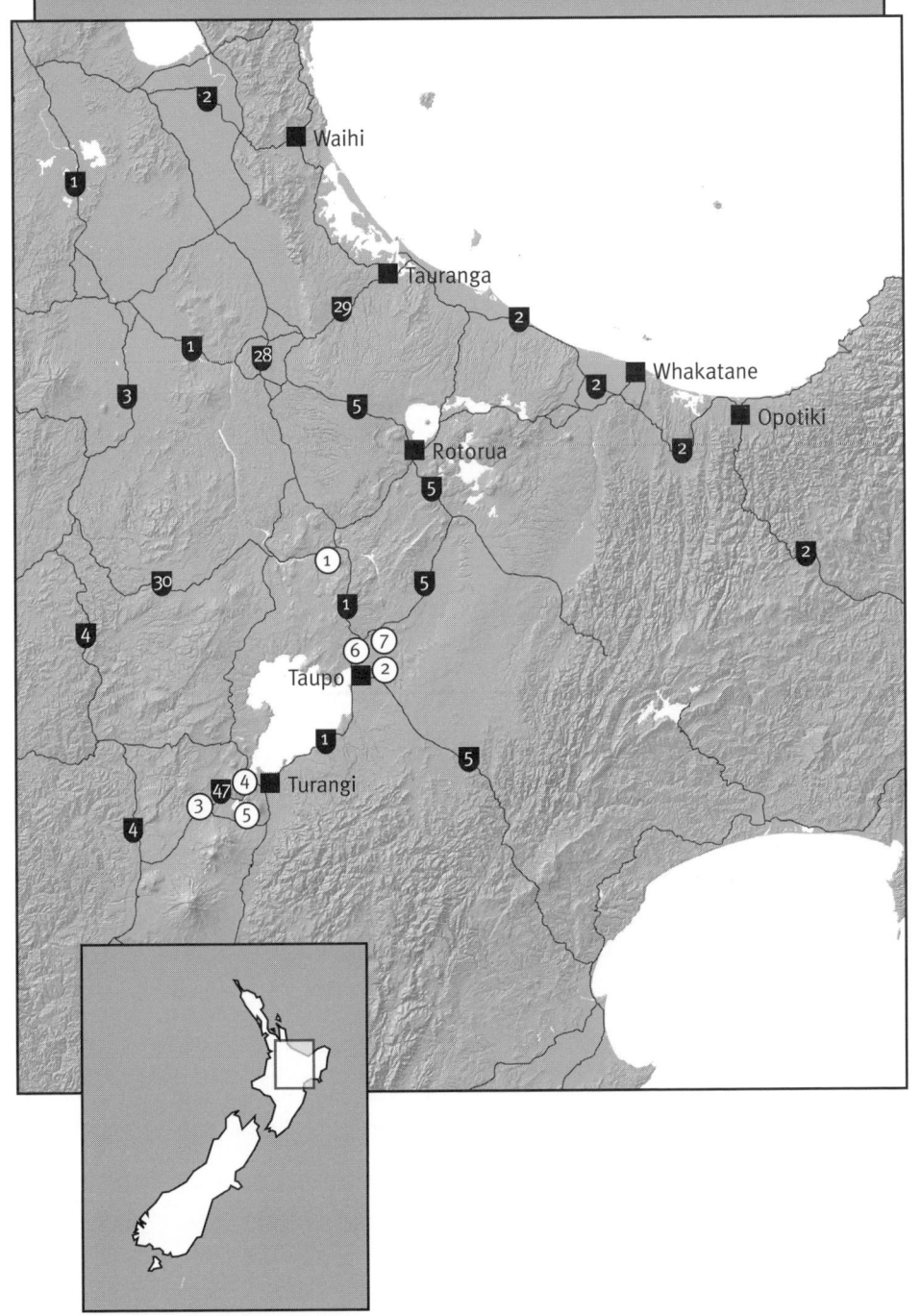

1 Pohaturoa

Just a single glance at Pohaturoa is all that is needed to know that this is the perfect place to build a pa, with the steep rocky cliffs encircling a summit that rises high above the swirling Waikato River.

In Maori legend Pohaturoa was the wife of Putauaki (Mt Edgecumbe), though this was only after he had been rejected by Pihanga.

Occupation goes back to Tia, a rangatira who arrived on the waka *Te Arawa* and who settled in the area, though it is likely that the area only ever supported a very small population. Ngati Hotu ousted an earlier people, the Kahupungapunga, and established a formidable pa on the summit of Pohaturoa. Despite the superb defences, the pa fell to a coalition of Ngati Raukawa seeking revenge for the death of a Raukawa woman married to the chief living at Pohaturoa.

When the missionary Henry Williams visited the pa in January 1840 he found a small group of people living on the summit though, not long after, the pa seems to have been abandoned. Palisades were still visible when the land was cleared to plant pines in 1927. In recent years the pines have been removed from the summit, though currently there is no public track to the top.

Pohaturoa is easy to distinguish as you whizz past in your car on SH1, but this short easy walk along the banks of the Waikato River will give you a much greater appreciation of just what a great citadel this pa really was. The walk is part of the 16-kilometre walk/mountain bike Snowsill to Atiamuri Trail, and the flat wide track meanders through regenerating scrub and fern to a magnificent viewpoint over the river to Pohaturoa. Here the river runs fast and clean, with numerous whirlpools and back-currents, and across the river the bulk of Pohaturoa appears impenetrable. Keep an eye out for friendly native bush robins along the track.

Grade: Easy
Time: 20 minutes return
How to get there: The track begins just 300 m from the intersection of SH30 and SH1, 25 km south of Tokoroa.

2 Opepe

After the defeat by militia and their Maori allies at Ngatapa in January 1869, Te Kooti escaped into the rugged Urewera country. However, the price his Tuhoe allies paid for sheltering Te Kooti became too much, with the government destroying Tuhoe villages and forcing their chiefs to surrender. When staying in the Urewera country was no longer tenable, Te Kooti sought the protection of Tawhiao in the King Country and started to make his way west in the direction of Lake Taupo.

On 7 June 1869 an advance party of Te Kooti's men came across the camp of the Bay of Plenty Cavalry. This unit was scouting the area for signs of Te Kooti, but despite this had failed to post sentries and was caught completely off guard by the attack. Nine men died at the camp and five others escaped, taking several days in bitterly cold weather to reach Fort Galatea.

The Opepe Reserve is cut in two by SH5 from Taupo to Napier. On the northern side of the road it is an easy 10-minute return walk through bush to the lonely graves of the soldiers, which later also became the burial place of local settlers. Across the road another 10-minute return walk will take you to the old redoubt, of which very little remains apart from an old well. Deep gullies on three sides made this an easily defended spot, though it saw no further action as Te Kooti had already moved further west.

Grade: Easy
Time: Allow 30 minutes
How to get there: Opepe Reserve is on SH5, 14 km from the junction with SH1 in Taupo.

3 Te Porere Redoubt

The government troops were desperate to capture Te Kooti Arikirangi Te Turuki as he was travelling west to seek the protection of the Maori King Tawhiao. However, Tawhiao was aware that Tuhoe had been severely punished for protecting Te Kooti and was reluctant to bring further bloodshed to his people, who had suffered badly at the hands of the British just a few years before.

With protection in the King Country denied him, Te Kooti had no choice but to make a stand, and he chose Te Porere, southwest of Turangi. He ordered two redoubts to be built. What makes these forts so interesting is that the old-style defensive pa was by this time redundant. These two redoubts externally resemble a British-style redoubt but the layout inside the fort is cleverly enhanced by lacing the interior with very deep trenches to protect the defenders from rifle and cannon fire.

Led by Lieutenant Colonel Thomas McDonnell, 500 government soldiers and their Maori allies, armed with rifles and cannon, attacked Te Kooti and his Tuwharetoa allies at Te Porere on 4 October 1869. The lower redoubt fell quickly and the defenders retreated to the upper redoubt, which was in turn easily overrun. Te Kooti just barely escaped with his life. Of the 41 casualties that day, 37 of Te Kooti's men died and just four government soldiers. Te Kooti's highly symbolic flag was also captured; it can now be seen on display at Te Papa.

Both redoubts are in an excellent state of preservation and are well worth the short detour off SH47. The walking is easy and the experience enhanced by excellent information boards and a lookout point over the upper redoubt.

Grade: Easy
Time: 45 minutes
How to get there: 26 km from Turangi on SH47

4 Tokaanu Thermal Walk

All through the Taupo and Rotorua thermal areas local Maori used the natural hot-water springs for bathing and cooking. Here at Tokaanu, behind the swimming pool is an active thermal area of pools with crystal-clear water bubbling up from deep in the earth, while in other places brilliant green/blue pools steam gently among the manuka. Small pots of boiling mud plop steadily, and everywhere hissing steam escapes from fissures in the ground. Much of the short loop track is on boardwalks and most of it is safely fenced.

Grade: Easy
Time: 20 minutes
How to get there: The walk begins over the bridge and immediately to the right of the Tokaanu Thermal Pools, off SH41 just north of Turangi.

5 Pihanga and Lake Rotopounamu

While the legend of the battle of the mountains is well known, Pihanga, the cause of all the trouble, is often overlooked and is in reality more a hill than a mountain.

Originally there were seven mountains in the area to the south of Lake Taupo, and all were passionately in love with gorgeous Pihanga. Eventually the rivalry erupted into an all-out fight and the seven mountains fought each other with fire, boiling water, and eruptions of smoke and lava, and by throwing searing hot rocks. For days earthquakes shook the land and the air was full of smoke and ash until a victor emerged. Tongariro had triumphed, but it had cost him the top half of the mountain, which he had pulled apart to throw at his rivals, and today Tongariro is not the tallest peak.

With defeat came banishment, and that very night, after the battle, the defeated mountains were forced to leave. Ngauruhoe and Ruapehu moved off just to the south, while Putauaki fled far to the east and now towers over the Kaingaroa plain. Hapless Tauhara, unable to bear the thought of being without Pihanga, moved slowly and when dawn came he remained forever looking across the lake to his lost love. The last mountain, Taranaki, was also the angriest and had fought the hardest and in his rage he stormed south, gouging out the Whanganui River, before turning west and settling by the sea.

Pihanga lies just southwest of Turangi, rising to a modest 1326 metres, with SH47 crossing just to the north. Within the folds of her bush-clad slopes lies a small lake, Rotopounamu, and this is the perfect place to experience first-hand hand the beauty that began all the fighting.

While the name means pounamu lake, the reference is to the colour of the water as no pounamu is found here (the water, however, is not always green). From the road it is a short but steady climb up to the lake. Untouched, the forest around the lake is mature red beech, kahikatea, rimu and matai. On the eastern side of the lake is Long Beach, an ideal picnic spot and a good place for a swim on a hot summer's day. The track follows the lake edge and is easy walking.

Grade: Easy
Time: 2 hours
How to get there: Travelling on SH47 from Turangi, the track is located on the left on the downhill side of Te Ponanga Saddle.

6 Taupo nui a Tia

Lake Taupo is closely linked to the great tohunga Ngatoroirangi, who arrived on the waka *Te Arawa*, which originally landed at Maketu on the Bay of Plenty coast. Legends about Ngatoroirangi vary considerably, but in one version he is actually responsible for creating the lake, though all agree that the lake's name is Taupo nui a Tia, 'the large cloak of Tia'. Tia was another tohunga on board the *Te Arawa*, and when the lake is rough, the whitecaps are said to be the white feathers that adorned Tia's cloak. At that time Taupo had no fish, and one day when he became hungry, Ngatoroirangi unravelled the threads of his cloak and threw them into the water, where they came alive as inanga and kokopu.

A walkway extends along the lake from the yacht club by the Waikato River all the way around to Wharewaka Point, a distance of around 7 km, and is easy walking all the way.

Grade: Easy

Time: 2 hours one way

How to get there: The walk begins on the corner of Ferry Road and Redoubt Street, where the Waikato River leaves the lake.

7 Huka Falls

In recent years extremely brave kayakers have attempted to negotiate the falls, and it appears that this bravado is not new. An early Maori chief narrowly escaped death by trying to negotiate the falls in a waka, giving rise to a proverb, 'A little water through the lashing hole wrecks the canoe'.

The best place to start this walk is to begin from Spa Park in Taupo, and you're better off not visiting Huka Falls beforehand. From Spa Park the track follows the river downstream through a variety of vegetation – not all of it exactly pristine, but with extensive planting of native trees along the track this can only improve.

The river as it leaves Lake Taupo is just plain stunning. The swirling waters are so clean and clear, and are a beautiful iridescent blue-green colour. The initially tranquil waters become increasingly swift as the falls near. The sheer volume of beautiful bright clear water that gushes through the narrow gap more than makes up for the modest drop of these falls. Over 200,000 litres of water per second roars over the 3-metre falls with a fury that is truly impressive.

The track is in excellent condition, though there are some steep parts. If you haven't organised someone to pick you up, you have to return the way you came.

 Grade: Easy
Time: 2 hours return
How to get there: Spa Park is off Spa Road, Taupo. You can also park at Huka Falls.

EAST CAPE, GISBORNE, AND WAIKAREMOANA

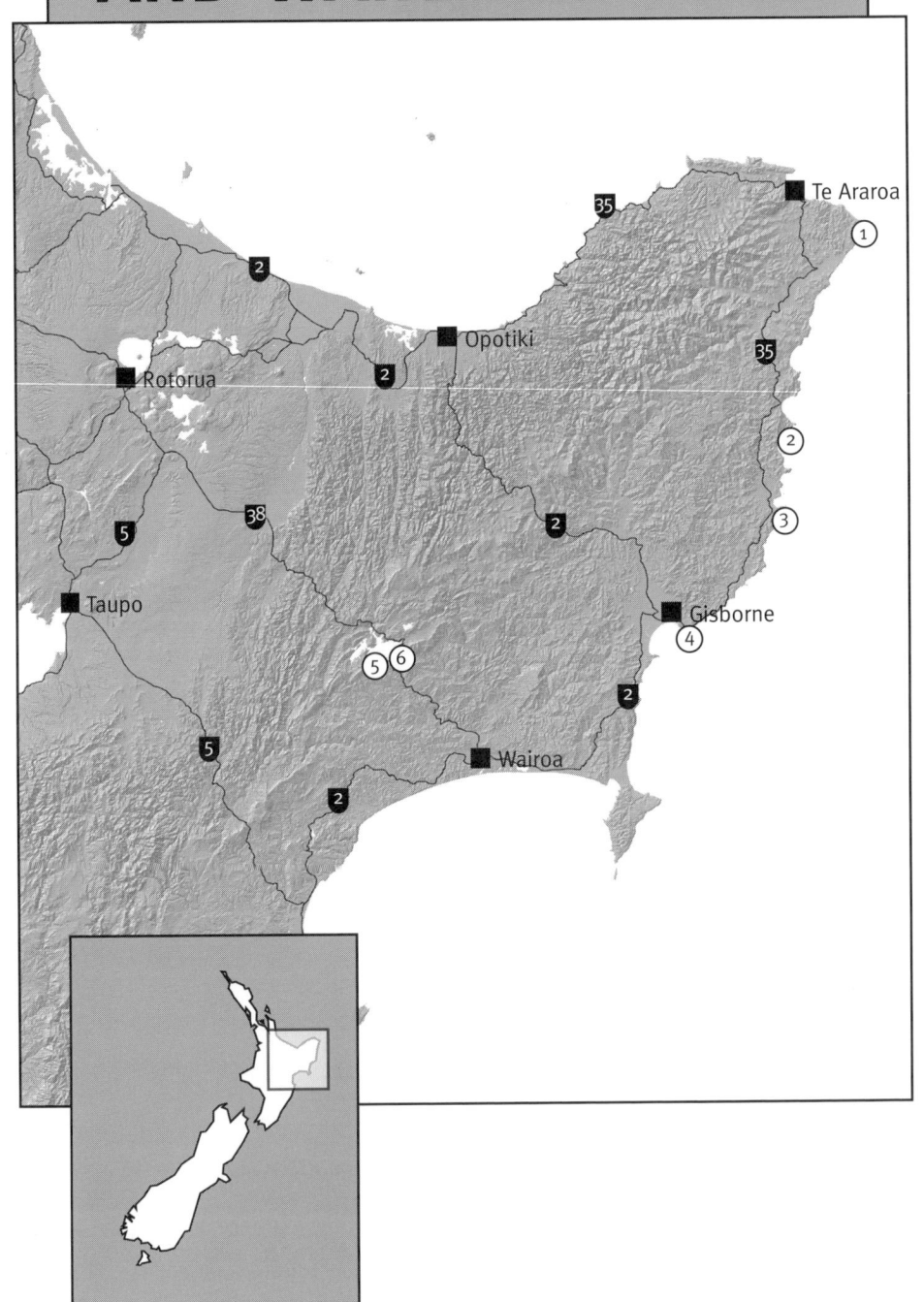

1 East Cape Lighthouse

Lighthouses were vital for local shipping, and as early as 1875 the East Cape was one of the areas where such a lighthouse was considered vital.

Authorities chose a small island lying 2 kilometres offshore, now called East Island, but known locally as Whangaokeno or Motu o Kaiawa. Despite warnings that the island was highly tapu, and despite the difficult access, work began in 1898. Four men drowned when the boat they were using to transport material to the island from the steamer *Hinemoa* overturned, and these men were buried on the tiny island. Just one month after the light first beamed out in August 1900, heavy rains washed away not only the winch and ropeway that hauled supplies up the cliff to the lighthouse, but also the small tramway that ran across the island.

Troubles on the island continued, and by 1906 three of the lighthouse keeper's children had died and were also interred on the island. In February the same year an earthquake hit the island, toppling the gravestones, and this was followed by a severe storm in July that not only cut the telephone link to the mainland, but washed the ketch *Sir Henry* onto the island's rocky shore, with the loss of three more lives.

When slips threatened the actual lighthouse in 1921, the decision was made to move the light to the mainland, where it is today; and once the lighthouse was removed, the slips and earthquakes stopped.

This is a beautiful location and you can see the island from the new lighthouse. The track climbs 150 metres to the lighthouse and includes a long flight of stairs. The road from Te Araroa is unsealed, winding and slow going.

Grade: Medium
Time: 45 minutes return
How to get there: 20 km from Te Araroa

2 Anaura Bay

One of the most beautiful beaches on the East Cape, Anaura Bay has the finest and largest remaining tract of coastal forest on the cape.

In the bay lies Motuoroi. This island was once inhabited and was famous for the skill of its people in working pounamu, transported at great effort from the West Coast of the South Island. Just a short distance to the north is a smaller island, Motuhina, never inhabited but famous for its population of muttonbirds.

Anaura Bay was visited by James Cook in October 1769. After being welcomed by local chiefs, Cook was able to replenish the *Endeavour* with fresh water. However, it is the record of the gardens at Anaura Bay that gives us one of the best glimpses of a Maori lifestyle that has long disappeared. Cook and his men were very impressed with not only the large area under cultivation but also the neatness of the gardens. One commentator recorded:

> *But the cultivations were truly astonishing . . . [They] surpass any idea we have formed of them. The ground is completely cleared of all weeds . . . with as much care as that of our best gardens. The sweet potatoes are set in distinct little molehills which are arranged in some straight lines.*

Today the bay supports only a small population, swelled over the summer by holidaymakers.

A track loops around the bush and up to a lookout over the bay that has a surprising number of native birds and a great view over the bay and Motuoroi. However, the beach is unsurpassed for a great walk.

 Grade: Medium
Time: Lookout 50 minutes return; Cooks Cove 3 hours return
How to get there: 15 km north of Tolaga Bay, turn off SH35 into Anaura Bay. At the beach turn left and follow the road to the camping ground. The track starts opposite the entrance to the camping ground.

3 Cooks Cove Walkway

Lieutenant James Cook first landed in Aotearoa at the Turanganui River at modern-day Gisborne, but the first contact with Maori was a disaster that left several dead. In desperate need of water and firewood, the *Endeavour* sailed north to this cove in October 1769.

The ever-observant Cook and his crew left us one of the few detailed descriptions of Maori life in the eighteenth century. Maori on this coast were expert fishermen and had large areas under cultivation, not just along the coast but in valleys stretching far inland. Surprisingly few, if any, of the pa were occupied, indicating that this was a period of peace, though the local people demonstrated haka for the men of the *Endeavour* and told stories of war and conflict.

Banks and Parkinson were impressed by the fine carvings that they observed on both a meeting house and a substantial waka. Tupaea, the Tahitian who acted as the expedition's translator, particularly impressed the local people and they renamed several localities after him, including the cave he slept in. The well dug by Cook's men was called Te Wai-keri-a-Tepaea, 'the well dug by Tepaea'.

The walkway to the cove takes 2.5 hours return and is through open farmland. Initially the track is an easy uphill walk to a wooden platform that looks down on Cooks Cove below; and from the lookout the track winds downhill to the cove itself. The track is closed for lambing from 1 August through to Labour Day weekend.

Tolaga Bay is a curious name, being neither Maori nor English. The area is known in Maori as Uawa nui a Ruamatua, which is usually shortened to Uawa. Where Cook acquired the name Tolaga is uncertain, though it may be that he confused the name of the bay with a wind from the north, 'te raki'.

Grade: Medium
Time: 50 minutes return to the lookout; 2.5 hours return to the cove
How to get there: Wharf Road, signposted off SH35 at the southern end of Tolaga Bay.

4 Kaiti Hill

The base of Kaiti Hill holds a special place in the story of Polynesian migration to Aotearoa, as it is here at the mouth of the Turanganui River that two voyaging waka arrived: *Horouta* and *Te Ikaroa a Rauru*. As with Cook, many centuries later, the *Horouta*'s first sight of land was the cliffs of the great headland across the bay, which the captain Paoa named after his dog, Te Kuri a Paoa. This headland later became known as Young Nicks Head.

However, Kaiti is also associated with a great love story. A young man living at Kaiti fell in love with a girl living at Opape, near Opotiki, but he had been unable to declare his love for her before she returned to her home. Confused about what he should do, he formed an idea while walking along the beach that by chance he might be able to send a message to his love by way of a shellfish. Picking up a live shellfish he whispered a message of passion and love and put the shell back in the water. Entrusted with such an important mission, the shellfish made the long and difficult journey around the coast to Opape.

After the long journey the valiant shellfish washed up on the beach at Opape. One day, while out gathering shellfish, the girl came upon the messenger of love, but quickly threw it back in favour of a bigger specimen. Undaunted, the plucky shell constantly contrived to place itself in the path of the girl until, one day, she realised that she had seen this one shellfish time and time again. This time she picked it up and with a length of flax hung the shellfish around her neck, where it came to rest on her heart. Finally the shellfish was able to convey the message entrusted to it on the faraway beach below Kaiti Hill. Now aware of her distant lover's true feelings, the girl set off alone to travel the difficult path through the Waioeka Gorge to be finally reunited with her true love on Kaiti Hill.

The walk uphill is in two stages. The first is a steady to steep uphill climb to the lookout Te Kuri a Paoa, which has views over Gisborne city, inland and across the Turanganui. A little further along is the Cook statue. From this point it will take another 10 minutes to reach the carpark lookout further uphill. There are two options to access the carpark lookout: a steep 'fitness trail' that is shorter but all steps to the top; and the Shady Oaks track, which is much more gradual.

Grade: Medium
Time: Te Kuri a Paoa lookout 45 minutes return; carpark lookout 1 hour return
How to get there: Follow the road to the port and the Cook memorial. The track starts opposite the memorial.

5 Waikaremoana

The creation of Waikaremoana began with an everyday dispute between the chief Mahu and his daughter Haumapuhia (though there are different versions and in one Haumapuhia is a son and Mahu is known as Manaia).

One day Mahu wanted water from a sacred spring, but Haumapuhia refused to collect it. Mahu went himself, but as he was very angry at his daughter's disobedience he didn't hurry and took a long time. In the meantime Haumapuhia had a change of heart and, now worried that her father had not returned, went to the spring to look for him.

Mahu's anger now reached such a height that he decided to drown his disobedient daughter in the spring and Haumapuhia, with her head underwater, desperately called on the gods to help. Leaving her lifeless body in the water, the gods responded by turning Haumapuhia into a taniwha with enormous strength. As she came slowly back to life she began to struggle. As Haumapuhia thrashed about in the small spring, it began to grow. First she pushed out to the north, then to the east, and the long inlets that she created filled with water. Finally with one great burst of strength Haumapuhia smashed through the rock at Onepoto and headed for the sea. However, the sun began to rise and turned the hapless Haumapuhia into stone. She became trapped at Waikaretaheke, where today she still lies in the bed of the river.

For those visiting Waikaremoana, and for whom the Lake Waikaremoana Great Walk (5–7 days) is not an option, this short walk will give a taste of one of the better-known sections of the great walk. The massive bulk of the Panekiri Bluff dominates the southern end of the lake, rising to over 1100 metres at the summit known as Puketapu. However, the more modest first trig can be reached after a steady uphill walk of one hour on a good track, and it has magnificent views over the lake.

The beginning of the walk is from the shelter at Onepoto, and the first short section is flat. This grassy area was once the parade ground for the Armed Constabulary, and a redoubt was built here in the early 1870s. Government forces clashed with the supporters of Te Kooti nearby in 1866, but by the time the redoubt was built Te Kooti was long gone. Very little remains apart from an old cemetery and a limestone rock carved with the names and dates of soldiers stationed here in the 1860s and 1870s.

Once you enter the bush, the track is uphill all the way.

Grade: Medium

Time: 2 hours return

How to get there: This is the first section of the Great Walk from Onepoto, 12 km south of the Aniwaniwa Visitor Centre.

6 Onepoto Caves

This complex of caves, rock overhangs, arches and tunnels was used by local Maori in time of trouble as a refuge or a pa punanga, and was known as Te Ana-o-Tawa. In one famous story, chief Tuwai protected the people sheltering there by standing at the narrow entrance to the cave and killing five attackers one by one as they tried to enter.

This walk is a great way to explore the jumble of rocks from the giant landslide that formed the lake, according to geologists, though the track is convoluted with numerous side tracks and caves. You will need to wear shoes with good tread as the rocks are often a bit slippery. You will also need a torch.

There is a good lookout point over the lake.

Grade: Medium

Time: 1 hour return

How to get there: Onepoto, 12 km south of the Aniwaniwa Visitor Centre.

HAWKE'S BAY

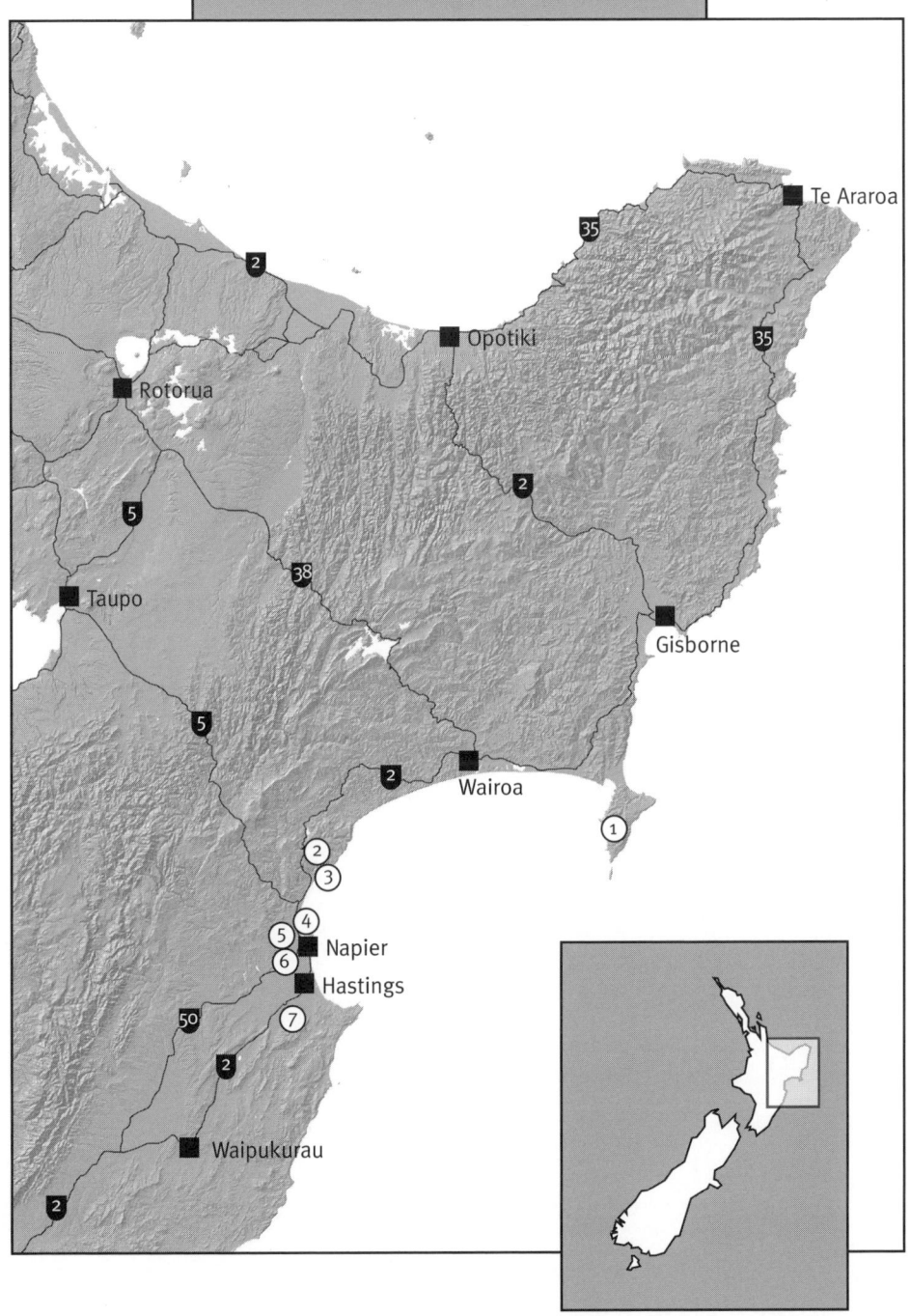

Te Araroa

35

Opotiki

35

2

Rotorua

5

38

Taupo

Gisborne

5

2

Wairoa

1

2

3

4

5

Napier

6

Hastings

50

7

2

Waipukurau

2

1 Mahia Peninsula

In the Maori legend of Maui hauling up his great fish (the North Island), Mahia is known as Te Matau a Maui, 'the fishhook of Maui'.

In the fourteenth century the great waka *Takitimu* landed here, and Ruawharo, the tohunga on the waka, decided to end his voyaging and he settled on the peninsula. Tradition also has it that Ruawharo brought whales to the bay, and the wharenui at Opoutama is named in his honour.

Later still, Kahungunu visited Mahia after hearing stories of a beautiful woman, Rongomaiwahine. Finding that the stories were indeed true, he married Rongomaiwahine – a union from which many local people are descended.

Coronation Reserve or Piko o Te Rangi on the eastern side of the peninsula is a natural rock basin that was once used by Bishop William Williams to baptise local Maori. A small cleft in the rocks is said to have been used to store bibles.

Most of the peninsula has been stripped of vegetation, but the Mahia Peninsula Scenic Reserve protects 374 hectares of coastal bush. Steep in places and with some stream crossings, the loop track has a lookout with great views to the south.

Grade: Medium
Time: 2 hours return
How to get there: The reserve is located 7 km south of Mahia Beach on
Kinikini Road, which is a narrow winding gravel road.

2 Lake Tutira

Lake Tutira is alive with waterfowl, including ducks, pukeko, swans, herons and teals, and numerous pa around the lake are testament to the appeal it held for early Maori.

The narrow strip of land that runs between Lakes Tutira and Waikopiro

was the site of a very unusual pa called Te Rewa. Taking advantage of
the location, the pa was built up with tree trunks and then protected by
a moat. Even in 1882 few signs of the pa remained, and today a raised
mound is the only trace. A number of other pa sites can be found on the
eastern side of the lake.

Adjoining Lake Tutira to the south is tiny Lake Waikopiro. The walk
around this lake takes about 30 minutes. The Kahikanui and Galbraith's
tracks together form a loop on the eastern side of the lake. This walk
begins at the far end of the picnic area, and the track passes through
regenerating native bush. There are views over the lake, and the remains
of an old pa can be seen on a headland.

 Grade: Easy
Time: Lake Waikopiro Walk, 20 minutes; Kahikanui and Galbraith's
Track Loop, 1.5 hours
How to get there: Tutira is on SH2, 44 km north of Napier.

3 Waipatiki Reserve

Part of the track within the bush was originally an old Maori trail that
linked the plains to the south with settlements around Wairoa. This trail
was developed into a bridle track in 1860, but by 1900 the inland road to
Wairoa had been opened and the track fell into disuse.

The initial part of the track is a steep uphill climb to a junction with a
sign referring to an upper and lower track, but it doesn't matter which
route you take as this part of the track is a loop. If you want to do the
steep bit first, take the upper track.

It is worthwhile taking some time to visit the very attractive, sandy
Waipatiki Beach, which is just a few kilometres down the road at the
bottom of the valley, and which in pre-European times was famous for its
good flounder fishing.

 Grade: Medium
Time: 1 hour 15 minutes
How to get there: From Napier, take SH2 for 20 km and then turn right
in Tangoio Road (follow the signposts to Waipatiki Beach). After 6 km
turn into Waipatiki Road and the reserve is clearly marked to the left.

4 Pania of the Reef

the tale of Pania is one of the most famous and tragic Maori legends. It is very close in sentiment to Hans Christian Andersen's 'The Little Mermaid' and while it is remotely possible that Andersen could have heard of Pania (he wrote the story in 1836), it is highly unlikely.

Pania lived in the sea, but she was fascinated by life on land. Every evening she swam to the shore to explore the world of humans, faithfully returning to sea at dawn. One evening a local chief, Karitoki, came down to a spring at the foot of the cliff and there he caught sight of Pania hiding in the flax. Immediately he fell in love with Pania and they secretly married that very night, though when dawn came Pania returned as usual to the sea.

So their married life began with Pania joining Karitoki in his whare every night and in the morning returning to the sea. Eventually Pania gave birth to a strange child, a son completely without hair who was named Moremore, 'the hairless one'. Karitoki was now even more anxious that he might lose both his wife and son to the sea. He consulted a tohunga for help. The tohunga told him that if Pania and his son were to touch cooked food they would never be able to return to the sea. That night Karitoki went ahead with the plan. However, as he was about to place the food on them as they slept, Ruru the morepork cried out a warning which woke Pania. Horrified, she fled back to the sea where her own people greeted her and took her down to the depths, never to return.

Pania was turned into a reef, where she lies with her arms outstretched, though no one is sure if she is pleading with Karitoki to explain his actions or if she is still expressing her love. Her son Moremore was transformed into a taniwha in the shape of a shark and acts as a kaitiaki of the bay.

The statue of Pania was unveiled in 1954 and is a firm favourite with both locals and visitors. When the statue was stolen in October 2005, the uproar was such that the thieves abandoned the statue and it was restored the following month. The motivation for the theft was never made clear.

The reef itself lies about 500 metres north of the port, is 1600 metres long running in a northeast direction, and is marked by two large buoys at either end. Walking from the statue on Marine Parade to the point overlooking the reef is an easy stroll of about 30 minutes.

Grade: Easy

Time: 30 minutes

How to get there: The statue is located in the gardens on the Marine Parade next to the Tom Parker fountain.

5 Whakamaharatanga Walkway

Rorookuri Hill was once an island in the Ahuriri Lagoon, which originally occupied the vast area between the hill and Napier. The violent 1931 earthquake lifted the ground level by over a metre, substantially reducing the size of the lagoon; subsequent drainage for farming and airport development reduced the wetland further still. Now only a small tidal lagoon remains just south of the airfield.

One pa occupied the summit of the hill, and another occupied a headland. The pa were key to controlling the important food resource of the lagoon, and their strategic location is obvious, with views along the bay both north and south. Otiere pa sits on a narrow headland at the bottom of the hill and would originally have been surrounded by water on three sides, while a deep defensive trench protected the land access. The wide terraces and defensive ditches are still very clear today.

These were not only the only pa around the Ahuriri Lagoon. At Bay View was Heipipi; Park Island was occupied by Umuroimata pa; Te Iho o Terei was on Quarantine Island; and at the other end of the lagoon was the enormous complex of Otatara (see below).

The walkway is across farmland and is easy walking, though the tracks are closed for lambing during July, August and September.

Grade: Easy
Time: Rorookuri Hill summit 25 minutes return; Otiere pa and hill summit 45 minutes; circular track 1 hour
How to get there: Take SH22 from Napier north and just before Bay View turn left into Onehunga Road. The walk begins 1 km down this road on the left.

6 Otatara Pa Historic Reserve

The location alone of Otatara would indicate its importance. Situated high above the Tutaekuri River, the views from Hikurangi pa at the top of the hill are superb and encompass all of the Heretaunga plain and far inland.

Both pa were established around 1400 AD, and over time various iwi have occupied this site, including Te Tini o Awa, Ngati Koaupari, Ngati Mamoe and Ngati Ira, until the pa came under attack in the seventeenth century by Ngati Kahungunu under the leadership of Taraia. While Hikurangi fell, Taraia was unable to take Otatara and built a new pa at Pakowhai. A short time later he again began a siege of Otatara and finally captured the pa by tricking the defenders, after which it was abandoned.

The pa are perfectly situated to take advantage of the vast resources of the shallow lagoons between them and the ocean, while the river gave access to the forest resources further inland. The site is huge, covering almost 100 hectares, and everywhere there are terraces, house sites, kumara pits and defensive earthworks. Hikurangi occupies the summit while Otatara is more in the style of a headland pa and has been partially destroyed by quarrying.

A large tidal lagoon, Te Whanganui a Orotu, an extension of the enormous Ahuriri Lagoon, originally came right up to the foot of the pa, but the 1931 earthquake effectively drained the land.

The recent addition of a carved gateway, palisades and tall pou give this reserve an ancient air, and the open grassy site allows a clear view of terraces, defensive ditches, house sites and kumara pits.

Grade: Medium
Time: 1 hour
How to get there: Springfield Road where Gloucester Street crosses the Tutaekuri River

7 Te Mata Peak, Havelock North

The legend of Te Mata begins with a lingering conflict between the people of Waimarama on the coast and those living on the Heretaunga plain. To find a solution, the Heretaunga people gathered at Pakipaki and, with the help of an old kuia, came up with a plan to make Te Mata, the chief of the Waimarama people, fall in love with Hinerakau, the beautiful daughter of a Heretaunga chief.

The plan worked and Te Mata was required to prove his love for Hinerakau by completing a series of Herculean tasks, one of which was to eat his way through the hills that separated the coast and the plain, thereby creating a path to make travel between the two peoples easier. On his very last bite, Te Mata choked and died; his body now forms the hills and the gap he created with his final mouthful is known as Pari Karangaranga or 'the echoing cliffs'.

However, the story ends tragically as Hinerakau had also fallen in love with Te Mata and, consumed with grief, she covered her dead husband with a blue cloak before leaping to her death from the peak; the gully at the base of the cliff was formed by her falling body.

The rugged barren peak of Te Mata, rising 399 metres above the Tukituki valley, has the most spectacular view in every direction, from Mahia to the north through to Ruapehu on a particularly fine day. While a road goes to the peak and it is easy to drive to the top, it is worth spending some time walking here in order to gain a better appreciation of this wonderful countryside. The hills are laced with a network of tracks, so it pays to check out the information board at the entrance to the park.

An easy walk begins at the second carpark just past the restaurant. This steady uphill track follows the rocky escarpment overlooking the Tukituki River to Te Mata Peak. From this point you can return down the road or continue on past the main carpark and along the ridge to the Redwood Grove and then return via the Te Mata Walk.

Grade: Medium
Time: Allow 1 hour
How to get there: Te Mata Peak Road, Havelock North

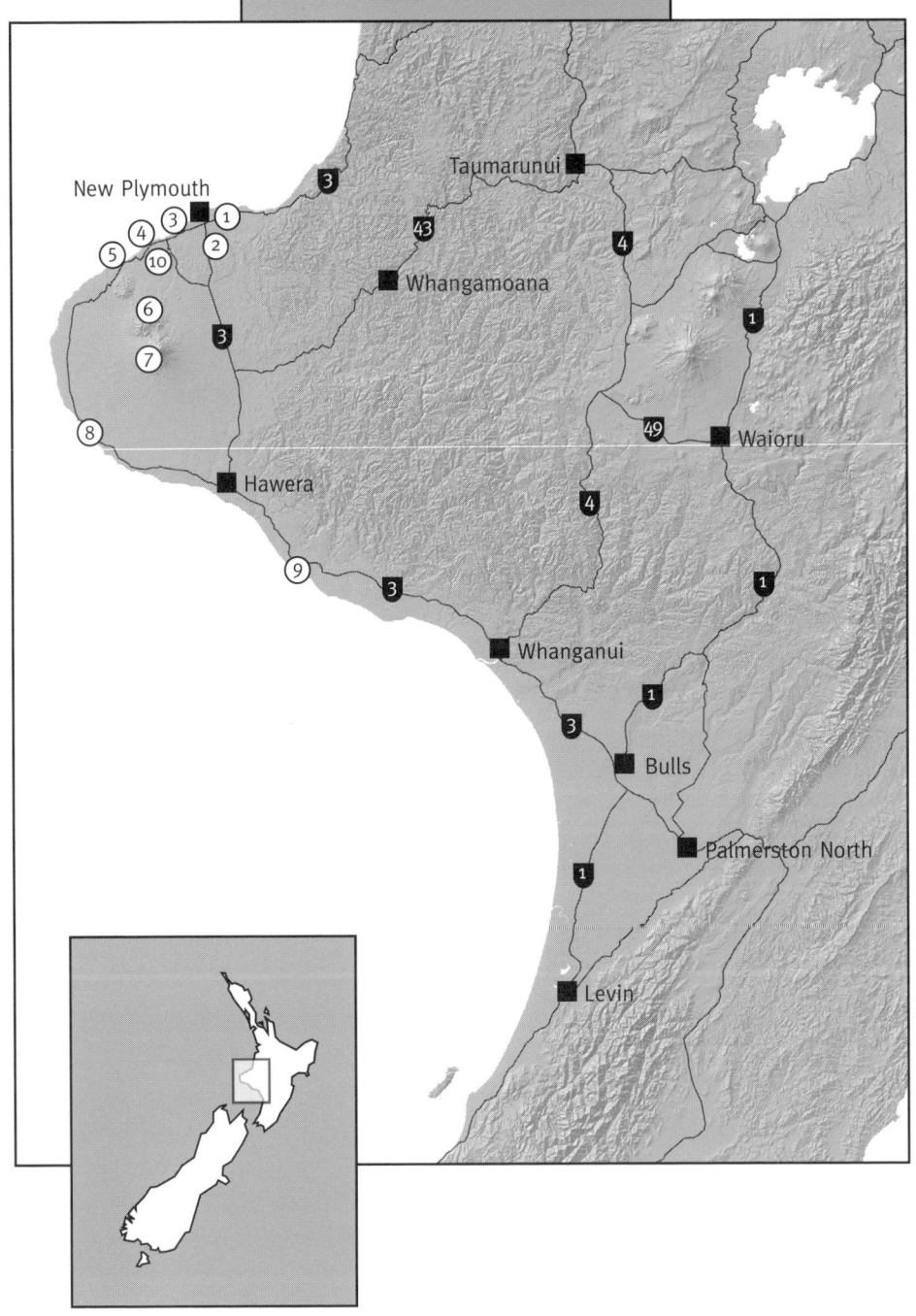

TARANAKI

New Plymouth

Taumarunui

Whangamoana

Waioru

Hawera

Whanganui

Bulls

Palmerston North

Levin

1 Awatetake Pa

Located on a cliff high above the Waitara River, this pa is ringed on three sides by a single defensive ditch that is one of the most impressive of any in the country. The description 'ditch' does these earthworks a great injustice, as even now they are still very deep and broad, much more moat-like and still very difficult to scale. Once they would have been topped by a bank and palisading, making a very impressive and, to enemies, formidable sight. Rua or food pits are still visible throughout the pa, though today the site is covered in trees that include many old karaka and a very old totara that would date back to when the pa was occupied.

The track begins over a stile at the back of the gravel yard (and not down the farm track). From there it crosses farmland, marked by orange triangles, and is easy walking, but expect electric fences and gates and boisterous stock.

 Grade: Easy

Allow 45 minutes

How to get there: From SH3 at Waitara take Princess Street, which eventually becomes Ngatimaru Road. The track begins on the corner where Ngatimaru Road meets Tikorangi Road West.

2 Pukerangiora Pa

A major pa on a high bluff overlooking the Waitara River, Pukerangiora saw bitter fighting during the Musket Wars period of the 1820s and 1830s. At one stage the pa fell to invaders, forcing many of the defenders, including women and children, to try to escape by leaping from the cliffs above the river.

During the New Zealand Wars of the 1860s, the pa was the centre of a campaign led by the elderly Major General Pratt, who adopted slow siege tactics including a series of redoubts and a long sap, which are still clearly visible. Pratt's technique, described as 'a mile a month', drew criticism from the colonists; one report said, 'The war in Taranaki maintains its peaceful course.' However, the British were not slow to adapt to Maori fighting techniques developed in response to the use of guns and cannon. Pa were built to withstand cannon fire and engineered to ensure that a full frontal assault was near-suicidal. Moreover, Maori defenders would use a pa to slow down the attack and then quickly abandon the position to avoid heavy casualties in the face of an attacking force that had greater numbers and was better armed. In reality Major General Pratt knew that a drawn-out fight with careful advances was one tactic that would wear down his enemy, and when the sap eventually reached the palisading, a truce was agreed and the defenders abandoned the pa to Pratt.

The site is not well maintained and the signage is minimal and confusing, but don't be put off by that. The main carpark is about 200 metres past the first sign and is easy to miss. The military sap to the pa is behind the trees to the left of the first sign. The road from the turnoff is also signposted with the location of the redoubts built as part of the attack on the pa. From the point where the pa overlooks the river there are wide views back to the coast.

Grade: Easy
Time: 20 minutes
How to get there: From SH3 east of Waitara, turn into Waitara Road and then continue for 7 km to the pa on the left.

3 Pukewarangi and Parihamore Pa

Virtually all the pa in Taranaki were within 5 kilometres of the sea, and these two pa in the heart of modern-day New Plymouth are typical. Pukewarangi is not large, but this small hilltop pa still retains the terraces and earthworks. Very little is known of the history of Pukewarangi, though a local newspaper reported in 1908 that the pa was used for training the Taranaki Rifles – a reflection that, even at that late stage, the prospect of war had not entirely disappeared.

In the eighteenth century the beautiful Urukinaki, the daughter of Kahutaia, the chief of Parihamore, attracted attention from men all over Taranaki, including the powerful chief Potaka. However, Urukinaki was not the least bit interested in Potaka, who she thought was not only too old, but ugly as well. Angry and insulted, Potaka was not one to take rejection lightly. Gathering up his warriors, he laid siege to Parihamore.

The siege dragged on for months and, with her people facing starvation, Urukinaki was left with little choice: she went out to Potaka and agreed to be his wife.

Both pa are accessible via the Te Henui Walkway, which runs from the Coastal Walkway and cuts inland following the course of Te Henui Stream. As you walk upstream, the first pa, Pukewarangi, is on the hill to the left and is recognisable by a group of tall pine trees that crowns the summit on which the old pa stands. Parihamore is further upstream where the walkway finishes, and is located at the end of Bell Street behind the Western Institute of Technology.

Grade: Easy
Time: 45 minutes one way
How to get there: There are numerous entry points to Te Henui Walkway, but it is such a pleasant track that is worth starting from the Coastal Walkway.

4 Paritutu Rock

Looming over the modern-day port of Taranaki is the sharp rocky pinnacle of Paritutu. The flat area at the top is not very large, but anyone who has climbed the rock will know how difficult it would have been for any invading force to capture this pa.

Used by Te Atiawa right up until the 1830s, the pa held out against attack from Waikato in 1832 while other pa in the area fell to the invaders. Try as they might, nothing that the Waikato warriors offered could induce the defenders to come down from their eyrie. Paritutu was well stocked with food, but water was the greatest problem as the only source was halfway down the western face. This difficulty was solved by lowering a person down the cliff at night with calabashes, which were then hauled back to the summit. Any attempt by the enemy to disrupt this process drew musket fire from the offshore island pa of Mataora and Motu o Tamatea. The pa survived the siege.

While the climb is steep and not for those afraid of heights, the rocky scramble to the summit is made easier by numerous steps and wire railings near the top. The views are spectacular, south along the coast, southeast to the mountain and north over the port and city.

 **Grade:** Hard
Time: 40 minutes return
How to get there: Centennial Drive, New Plymouth, near the port.

5 Ratapihipihi

This small reserve of rare lowland bush takes its name from a traditional method of hunting birds. By blowing through a leaf, a hunter perched high in a tree would attract birds such as kaka to come very close, where they were easily killed by a blow from a short club.

Ratapihipihi was also the name of a nearby kainga that was destroyed during the Taranaki wars of the 1860s by the Taranaki Rifle Volunteers. Today the kaka, kainga and the lowland forest of Taranaki are all long gone, but this beautiful reserve is a rare view of what the bush wilderness around Taranaki was like before the coming of people. There are two loop tracks on excellent paths and the walking is easy, with just some steps to climb.

 Grade: Easy
Time: Two loops: one 20 minutes return; the other 30 minutes return
How to get there: At the end of Ratapihi Road off Cowling Road on the south side of New Plymouth

6 Te Koru Pa, Oakura

Occupied from around 1000 AD until 1826, this is one of New Zealand's most ancient pa sites. Overlooking the Oakura River, Te Koru pa is unusual in that stone has been used extensively. This is very rare for pa in Aotearoa, where wood was much more readily available. Occupied by Nga Mahanga a Tairi for many centuries, the pa fell to an overwhelming force of Te Atiawa in the early nineteenth century, and was finally abandoned in the face of the Waikato invasion in the 1820s. One of the finest examples of Taranaki carving was found at Te Koru in 1898 and is now held at Puke Ariki museum in New Plymouth.

The pa is well preserved, with terraces, food pits and defensive ditches all clearly outlined. The stones from the river below were used extensively on the outer facings of the defensive ditches and for kumara pits. The pa is bush-covered, which makes exploration more intriguing, though there is a good view of the river from a lookout point. The use of stone is an indication to some theorists that Aotearoa was inhabited by an ancient stone-using culture long before 1000 AD.

The walk to the pa is through a grassy open paddock and then through bush on the pa itself. Do not climb on the steep banks as the stonework is fragile and easily damaged.

Grade: Easy

Time: 30 minutes return

How to get there: At Oakura turn left into Wairau Road and follow the signposts 4 km down this road.

7 Taranaki Mountain

There is no mountain in this country more imposing or dramatic than Taranaki, standing alone and surrounded by some of the most fertile land in the country. The splendour of this peak wins the hearts of Maori and Pakeha alike.

Many New Zealanders know the story of the fight between Tongariro and Taranaki over the beautiful Pihanga, with the loser, Taranaki, heading off towards the setting sun. However, there is another version of this story. In this case Taranaki was originally married to the majestic Ruapehu, but Tongariro secretly admired and lusted after Taranaki's beautiful wife. While Taranaki was out hunting, Tongariro made his move and Ruapehu fell under his charm and into his arms, but the pair were discovered together when Taranaki returned at the end of the day. In the almighty stoush that followed, Taranaki was defeated, gouging out the Whanganui River as he moved away, and creating the vast Ngaere swamp when he rested for a while and his great weight caused the ground beneath him to sink. Ruapehu has lived to regret her infidelity, and when the wind blows from the east, a fog drifts from the summit of Ruapehu across to her lost love Taranaki.

The summit of Taranaki is a demanding full-day hike that needs a high degree of fitness, good equipment and tramping experience. For those wanting something less demanding but still satisfying, a number of good short walks begin at the North Egmont Visitor Centre. Among these walks, the lookout on the Holly Hut Track will take you beyond the forest to the subalpine region just below the mountain.

From the Visitor Centre follow the Veronica Loop Track uphill to the junction of the Holly Hut Track and continue for another 10 minutes along the Holly Hut track to a lookout with a seat. There are broad views over the Taranaki lowlands, while the mountain looms high above the track. Even within this short distance the vegetation changes markedly from alpine forest to more open subalpine shrubs and tussock. While this walk is all uphill, the track is well formed and the grade more steady than steep.

Grade: Medium
Time: 1 hour return
How to get there: 12km from New Plymouth, turn off SH3 at Egmont Village and follow Egmont Road to the North Egmont Visitor Centre.

8 Te Rere o Noke/Dawson Falls

These falls were named after a warrior, Noke, who had a reputation for mischief and, as with most mischief-makers, one day just went too far. Pursued by a group intent on killing him, Noke fled through the dense forest on the lower slopes of Taranaki. Unable to shake off the men following him, Noke came to the falls and hid behind the torrent of water, keeping stock still while his pursuers ran past him. Outwitting his would-be killers, Noke made good his escape by travelling far to the east. Thereafter the cascade became known as 'the falls of Noke'.

The short track to the falls is well signposted just below the carpark. Leading through moss- and fern-encrusted forest, it goes down steep steps, which can be slippery because of the constant wetness. The 18-metre falls drop over an ancient lava flow, throwing up a continuous spray, adding to the normally high rainfall that keeps the vegetation wet throughout the year.

Grade: Medium
Time: 30 minutes return
How to get there: Turn off from the centre of Stratford and follow the signs for 19 km.

9 Te Namu Pa

This small but superbly sited pa was the scene of one of the most important battles fought in Taranaki when, in 1833, a huge force of Waikato warriors invaded from the north. Pa after pa fell to the Waikato warriors, who were heavily armed with muskets. At Te Namu pa at Opunake, Wiremu Kingi Te Matakatea faced the formidable foe of 800 trained warriors with just 400 people, including women and children, and just one musket.

Wave after wave of Waikato surged at the pa, but this small fortress was perfectly situated for defence. At first glance it is hard to believe Te Namu is natural, but on all sides a rock face protects the pa from enemies. The natural defences were further enhanced by earthworks and palisading. In the end the Waikato invaders, after suffering heavy losses, were forced to retreat and eventually withdrew from Taranaki.

Later, in 1834, the kainga and defensive works were destroyed by men from HMS *Alligator*; but even today Te Namu is impressive. The pa is on private property but is accessible to the public. However it is a urupa so please treat the area with respect. It is not possible to get up onto the pa itself.

The best access is via the track that begins at the Opunake Cemetery and crosses farmland and then over the Otahi Stream to the pa.

Grade: Easy
Time: 30 minutes return
How to get there: The start of the walk is at Opunake Cemetery at the end of Wilson Road off SH45.

10 Patea

Turi was one of the great early navigators who journeyed from Hawaiki to Aotearoa to settle. He was later acknowledged as Turi-he-patea-paipo-moana or 'Turi who drinks the ocean'.

Captaining the great waka *Aotea*, Turi first landed at Aotea Harbour just north of Kawhia. After spending some time to establish the kumara plants they had brought aboard the waka, he travelled with his hapu overland to the mouth of the Patea River. Today the marae at Patea still bears his name, Wai o Turi.

On a spectacular rocky bluff overlooking the river and the sea, a formidable pa was established, a pa that even Te Rauparaha on his journey south in 1822 chose to avoid. This pa was the subject of a painting executed by Charles Heaphy in 1839 and simply called *Patea*, depicting a dramatic rock face topped by palisading overlooking the river. Edward Wakefield visited the pa in the same year, though Wakefield called the pa Haere Hau and the other pa at the river mouth Tihoi. Wakefield noted that the pa was very impressive and protected by steep cliffs and 'an assault would have been sheer madness'.

The river side of the pa was considerably damaged when the cliff face was dynamited in order to lay the tracks for the railway line to Hawera in 1881.

This walk follows the tidal Patea River along sandy bluffs to the pleasant and tidy picnic area near the old breakwater. The old pa site is plainly visible and still impressive across the river.

In the centre of Patea is a highly stylised garden featuring upright replica whale bones. The garden commemorates the story of Tutunui, a whale that was the pet of the famous chief Tinirau. When Tinirau's son was born, the birth rites were performed by the tohunga Kae, and as part of the ceremony the priest was fed a tiny piece of the flesh of the whale, Tutunui.

Some time later, after much persuasion, Tinirau allowed Tutunui to take Kae to his home on another island; but this was a mere trick, as Kae had never forgotten the delicious taste of whale meat. Engineering the death of Tutunui by stranding, Kae then cooked his flesh and wrapped it in koromiko leaves to hold the fat and flavour. However, Tinirau discovered the true cause of the death of his pet and, in revenge, had the deceitful Kae put to death. That, unfortunately, is not the end of the story, as Kae's family avenged his death by killing Tinirau's young son.

This legend gave rise to a saying, 'Tena te kakara a Tutunui', 'there rises the savoury smell of Tutunui', which is used when someone's guilty actions are exposed.

Grade: Easy

Time: 40 minutes return

How to get there: The track begins at the end of the road that leads along the western side of the Patea River right by the bridge; or from the carpark at the river mouth.

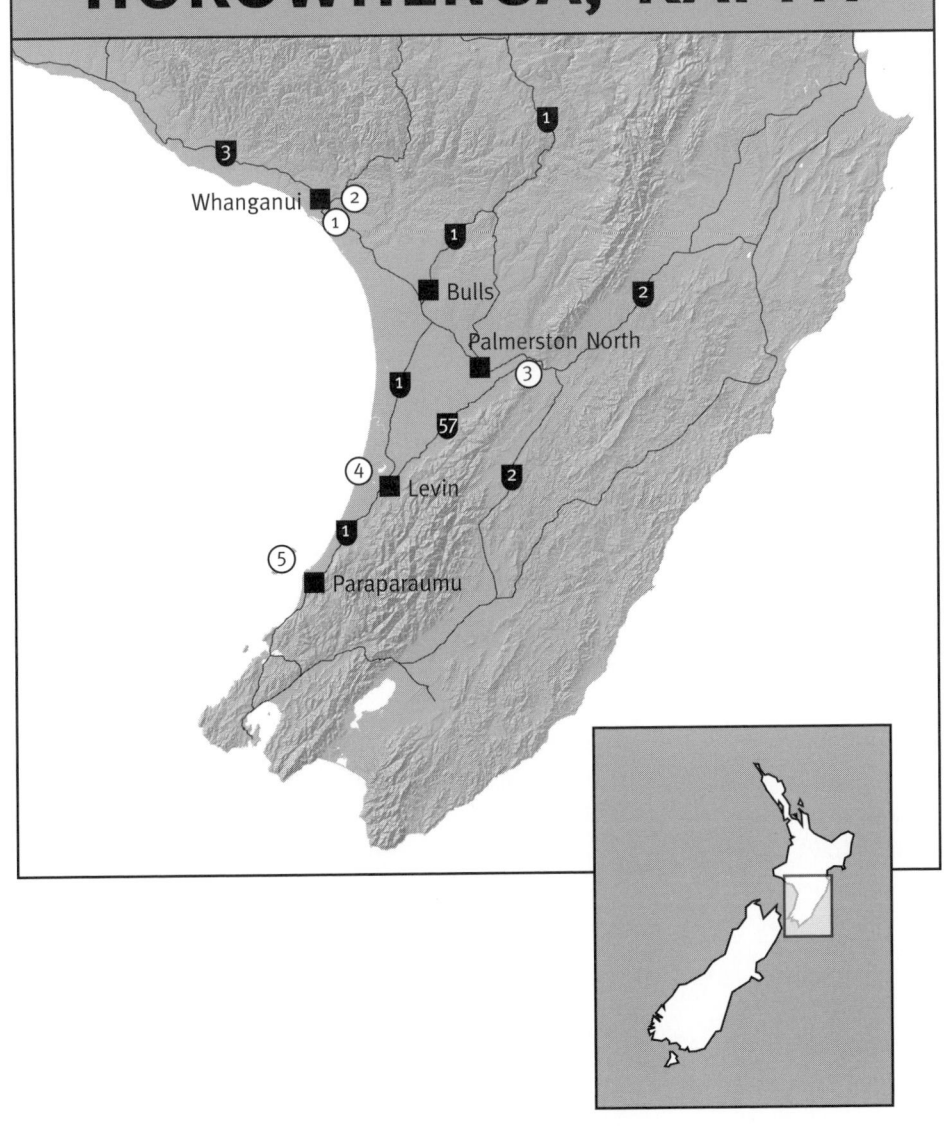

1 Whanganui

This walk covers just a short distance and, in the briefest fashion, covers almost the entire Maori history of Whanganui.

In legend the Whanganui River was created by Taranaki as he was driven from his home in the centre of the island after his epic battle with Tongariro over the love of Pihanga. As he left he first headed south and carved out the course of the river then, on reaching the coast, turned west and travelled to where he is today. Behind him the deep valley filled with his tears.

Kupe was said to have discovered the mouth of the river, but it was the people of the *Takitimu*, captained by Tamatea, who first explored the river itself, closely followed by the waka *Aotea*, whose people later settled in the area.

There has been much, and often bitter, discussion over the spelling of the name of both the river and the city. In the local Maori dialect the 'h' is silent, replaced by a short glottal stop as is common in other Polynesian languages. Ideally the word should be written 'W'anganui' to indicate the silent letter, but it came to be written as 'Wanganui', reflecting the local pronunciation. However, in written form the word makes no sense as the name means 'large harbour', and therefore should be written 'Whanganui'.

Following the wishes of the local iwi, the New Zealand Geographic Board changed the name of the river to Whanganui, but in a referendum the vote strongly favoured the retention of the spelling Wanganui; the mayor, Michael Laws, stated that the city over the years had developed 'its own identity, its own history, its own pride, its own mana'. Ironically with the change of the river's name to Whanganui, it is now pronounced by many people incorrectly with the 'wh' fully sounded as a soft 'f'.

Above the river is Queens Park, the site of the pa Pukenamu ('sandfly hill'), which in 1832 was attacked by Te Atiawa from Taranaki. The pa withstood three days of ferocious fighting, with Te Atiawa finally retreating after suffering heavy losses.

In 1846 during tensions over land the pa was occupied by the British

Army's 58th Rutlandshire Regiment, who replaced the pa with a fort which they named the Rutland Stockade. This in turn was demolished in 1882 and the hill was turned into a park, renamed Queens Park in honour of Queen Victoria.

Between Queens Park and the river lie the Moutoa Gardens – a small, pleasant park with formal gardens and old trees, which in February 1995 was occupied by Te Runanga Pakaitore. In pre-European times, this area was the site of Pakaitore pa and a trading place for people living along the river. Te Runanga Pakaitore asserted that this area was never included in the purchase of land for the city – a claim the city council rejected. Moreover, local Maori saw the park as a monument to colonialism, as it included a statue of Premier John Ballance and a statue dedicated to Te Rangihiwinui Kepa (Major Kemp), who actively supported the British throughout the New Zealand Wars. During the occupation of Motua Gardens, the head of John Ballance was replaced by a pumpkin and today only the base of the statue remains and the issue of ownership has never been satisfactorily resolved.

To begin this short walk, start by the Moutoa Gardens, walk along the river (Somme Parade) and then turn left into Church Place, right into Bell Street and then left into Ingestre Street and walk up the hill to Queens Park and then return down the other side and back to the gardens. A trip to the Whanganui Regional Museum, adjacent to the gardens, is really worthwhile, as the museum has an extensive collection of paintings of rangatira by Gottfried Lindauer, commissioned by Sir Walter Butler for a London exhibition, and a superb waka taua built around 1810.

 Grade: Easy
Time: 20 minutes
How to get there: Moutoa Gardens are on the corner of Taupo Quay and Somme Parade.

2 Waitaha Pa, Whanganui

Overlooking a long stretch of the river, this superbly constructed pa took full advantage of a long and very narrow ridge with double defensive ditches at both ends of the pa complementing the naturally defensive site. As with most pa, time has eroded the depth of the ditches and smoothed off the steeper slopes so that some of the impact is lost. The deep kumara pits are still visible. The pa runs for about 300 metres along the ridge and, though it was occupied only 200 years ago, the identity of the iwi that built and lived in this fine ridge pa is now long forgotten.

The walk to the pa is uphill on a rough grassy track.

Grade: Medium

Time: 20 minutes return

How to get there: 5 km north of Whanganui on SH4

3 Manawatu Gorge

As with many natural features, the creation of the Manawatu Gorge is steeped in Maori mythology.

On the heights of the Puketoi Range (east of Pahiatua) grew a giant totara tree that had a deep passion to reach the sea. That passion grew until finally the tree stirred with great energy and came down from the hills. At first the mighty tree turned northwest, gouging out the valley where the Mangatainoka River now runs, but found its way to the east was blocked by the high peaks of the Tararua Range. The desire to reach the sea was so great that the tree smashed its way through the hills, creating the Manawatu Gorge and the lower reaches of the river, and finally reached the coast at modern-day Foxton.

In the heart of the gorge is a large red-tinted rock called Hinepotae. According to legend the rock is said to deepen in colour on the death of an important member of the local Rangitane iwi. In the past, karakia were recited at the rock to ensure the safety of those travelling through the gorge by waka. On the Ruahine side of the gorge is another rock, Te Ahu a Turanga, and this rock marks the sacred place of Turanga, a great Rangitane ancestor.

The gorge was also known to Maori as Te Apiti, 'the narrow passage', and Te Au-rere-a-te-tonga, 'the rushing current of the south'.

A track runs the length of the southern side of the gorge, though for the most part it does not follow the gorge but runs slightly inland. There are good views of the gorge along the way. The grades are comfortable, though steep in places, and the track is excellent so it is not difficult to walk.

Grade: Medium

Time: 3 hours one way

How to get there: At the Palmerston North end of the track there is a carpark on the left, just before the road enters the gorge; while at the Woodville end the track entrance is located on Ballance Gorge Road just across the Ballance Bridge.

4 Lake Papaitonga

Lake Papaitonga is a small lake surrounded by the finest lowland bush remnant. It was once the scene of a bloody massacre of the local Muaupoko iwi by the invading Te Rauparaha.

Early in the nineteenth century the area was settled by the Muaupoko people. There are are two small islands in the lake, Motukiwi and Motungarara. The smaller of the two islands was artificially constructed, and both were occupied by pa protected by the lake.

In the early 1820s Ngati Toa chief Te Rauparaha visited the area with his family. They were hosted by Muaupoko at Te Wi near Papaitonga. Suspecting that Te Rauparaha's real intention was to settle in the area long-term, Muaupoko decided to kill the visitors. Unfortunately for Muaupoko, Te Rauparaha narrowly escaped, though his son and daughter and many of his relatives died. Biding his time, Te Rauparaha finally sought revenge on both Muaupoko and their allies Ngati Apa, based on Kapiti Island, whom Te Rauparaha suspected of being behind the earlier ambush.

In 1823 Te Rauparaha attacked the two pa in the lake, and one after the other the pa fell to Ngati Toa warriors. Only a handful managed to escape the fearful slaughter that followed. In the same year Te Rauparaha conquered Kapiti Island and Ngati Apa met the same fate.

However, Te Rauparaha remained unforgiving of the massacre of his family at Te Wi and was not yet finished with Muaupoko. After the 1823 attack, the few survivors returned to their lake pa. In 1827–28 they were again attacked by Ngati Toa and this time almost entirely annihilated, with just a few survivors fleeing into the mountains or finding refuge with other tribes. The lake pa were never reoccupied.

The track is in excellent condition and winds through fine lowland forest, with boardwalks through the swampy sections, to two lookout points over the lake.

Grade: Easy
Time: 40 minutes return to the Otomuri Lookout
How to get there: 4 km south of Levin, turn off SH1 into Hokio Beach Road. Lake Papaitonga is signposted to the left.

5 Kapiti Island

For most people Kapiti Island is closely associated with the famous fighting chief Te Rauparaha, but the Maori history of the island goes back much further.

According to tradition both Kapiti and Mana Island, just to the south, were created by Kupe with one strong blow from his patu. Several tribes occupied Kapiti, appreciating its natural qualities as a fortress and cultivating the sheltered and more accessible eastern side of the island. Kapiti became known as motu rongonui or 'famous island' and whoever held Kapiti effectively controlled Raukawa Moana/Cook Strait.

Kapiti is a contraction of Te Waewae-kapiti-o-Tara-raua-ko-Rangitane, which acknowledges the island as marking a boundary between Ngati Tara and Rangitane, a boundary that was swept away with the arrival of Te Rauparaha and Ngati Toa.

After first settling in Otaki in 1823, Ngati Toa under Te Rauparaha decided to take the island. They were met with fierce resistance from Ngati Apa, who were well aware of the fate that had befallen their allies Muaupoko, but gradually pa after pa fell to the invaders and Te Rauparaha finally completed his conquest of the island with the capture of Waiorua, the last Ngati Apa stronghold. At the same time Te Rauparaha took Mana Island, which then became the home of Te Rangihaeata, a nephew of Te Rauparaha.

From his island base Te Rauparaha launched his conquest of Wellington and the South Island. While he was uncompromising in respect of his defeated enemies, he not only shared the island with Pakeha whalers, but actively encouraged them to set up a whaling station on the island.

In 1840 the local Kapiti chiefs signed the Treaty of Waitangi on the island as it travelled around the country.

One of the best day walks in the Wellington area is a tramp to Tuteremoana, the summit of the island (521 metres). There is an option of two tracks to the top. The Wilkinson Track is better formed, has the easier grade, but is longer (3.8 kilometres) than the steeper and rougher Trig Track (2 kilometres). Covering both tracks as a loop is a popular option with the fitter (up the Trig and down the Wilkinson) as the tracks meet a short distance from the top.

There are also several shorter walks on the flat for those who wish to visit the island but are less keen on the hike to the summit.

Above left: Motuoroi Island off Anaura Bay was famous for its skilled greenstone carvers.

Left: Lake Waikaremoana was created by the taniwha Haumapuhia.

Above: Pou and pallisading mark the entrance to Otatara and Hikurangi pa near Napier.

Below: Pania's passionate love for Karitoki ended badly.

Above: Te Mata Peak marks the place where the giant Te Mata finally met his match.

Left: Te Rere o Noke, now known as Dawson Falls, on the southern slopes of Taranaki.

Below: Spectacular defensive ditches encircle Awatetake pa near Waitara.

Left: There is a great view of the Whanganui River from the Waitaha pa site.

Below: Kapiti, Te Rauparaha's island stronghold, is just 5km off the coast north of Wellington.

Left: Lake Papaitonga, near Levin, was the scene of bloody clashes in the 1820s.

Middle left: Explorer Kupe disturbed a giant octopus that lived in a cave at Rangiwhakaoma/ Castle Point on the Wairarapa coast.

Below: Te Pa o Kapo was the strongest and best fortified pa in the Porirua area.

Right: Well preserved house sites and kumara pits are features of Te Pae o Te Karaka pa near Picton.

Middle right: Te Pokohiwi/Wairau Lagoons was the scene of New Zealand's great archaeological discovery by 16-year-old Jim Eyles in 1942.

Below: Te Taero o Kereopa/Boulder Bank, Nelson, was created by Kereopa in his dramatic escape from Kupe.

Top: This stepped pa is one of several that dot the Kaikoura Peninsula.

Far left: Maui strains as he hauls up the North Island. Kaikoura Walkway, South Bay.

Left: A monument marks the remains of the most important Ngai Tahu pa, Kaiapohia, north of Christchurch.

Below: This narrow isthmus, despite being heavily fortified, failed to protect Onawe pa on the Banks Peninsula from Te Rauparaha.

Top: Rakaia Gorge was created by a taniwha in his bid to capture the troublesome northwest wind.

Above left and right: This fantastic Maori rock drawing of a taniwha is a highlight of a visit to Opihi, west of Timaru.

Right: The Moeraki Boulders are, in Maori legend, the flotsam of an ancient waka that sank off the Otago coast.

Top: Puketapu Hill in North Otago was once the stronghold of the mysterious patupaiarehe.

Middle: Te Puka a Takitimu or Monkey Island is the anchor stone of the waka *Takitimu*.

Right: Huriawa pa, north of Dunedin, held out in a dramatic siege in the seventeenth century.

Grade: Medium

Time: 3 hours return

How to get there: To visit the island you must have a permit. These are available from DOC online, the DOC Wellington Visitor Centre and the i-SITEs in Paraparaumu, Otaki, Levin and Porirua. For the permit you will need the date of your visit, what part of the island you want to visit and the name, age group, gender and nationality of every person travelling to the island.

Once you have your permit you have two boat operations to choose from: Kapiti Tours www.kapititours.co.nz or Kapiti Marine Charter www.kapitimarinecharter.co.nz

WAIRARAPA

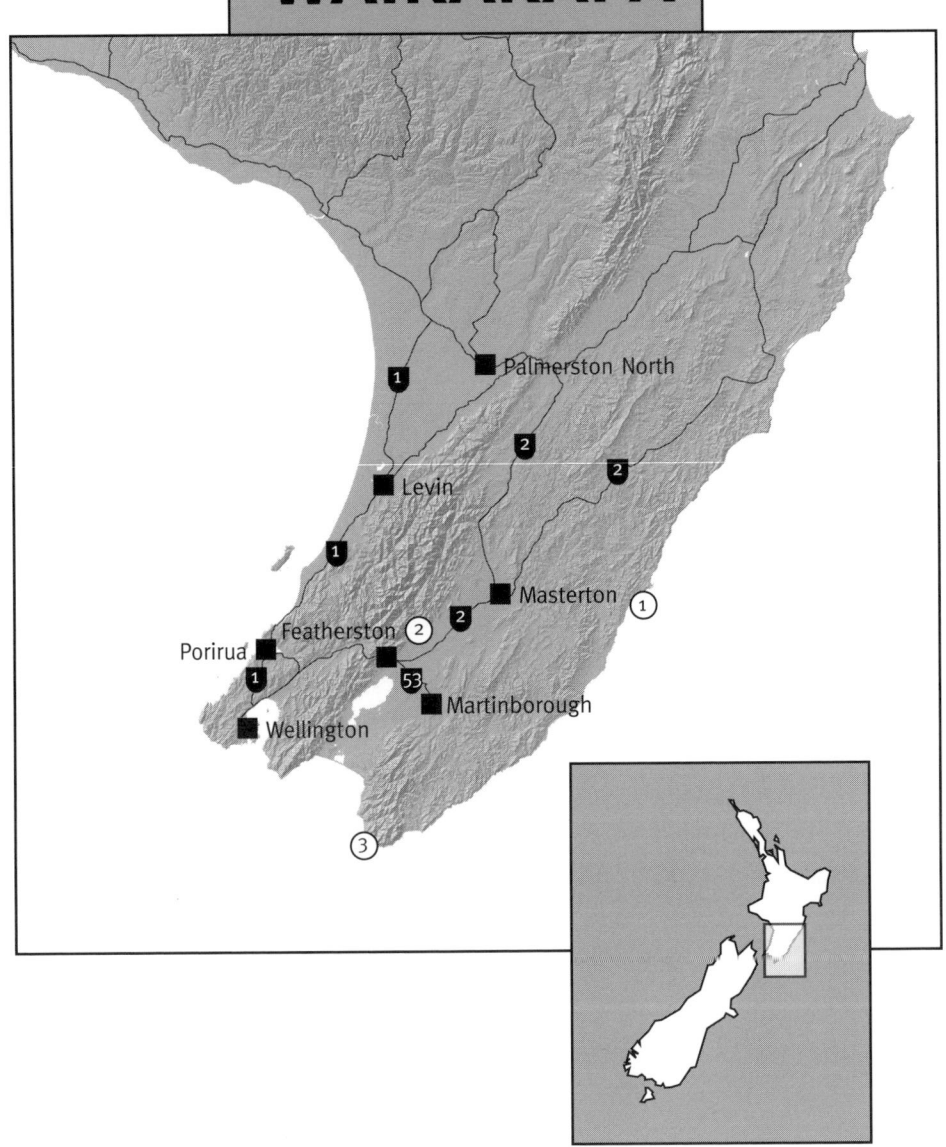

1 Rangiwhakaoma/Castle Point

It is appropriate that the dramatic landscape of Rangiwhakaoma/Castle Point was also the location of one of Kupe's most lively escapades. While sailing along this coast in the great waka *Matahourua*, Kupe disturbed a giant octopus that lived in a cave in the cliffs. Taking fright, the huge creature fled from the waka, heading first south and then north through Cook Strait with Kupe in hot pursuit. Finally the octopus had no choice but to turn and fight, attacking the waka with great fury, wrapping its enormous tentacles around *Matahourua*. Kupe had to act fast as the waka was in danger of being pulled apart. He flung a gourd far into the sea and the octopus, thinking a man had fallen overboard, released the waka and grabbed the gourd. Kupe seized his chance and killed the octopus with a blow to the head with his adze.

The name Rangi-whaka-oma means 'where the sky runs'. Although this coast was too inhospitable to support a permanent Maori population, it is clear from middens in the sand dunes that this was a favourite spot for gathering shellfish, especially paua.

The wild coast here is spectacular, and the walk up to the lighthouse is especially dramatic when a southerly swell is running. The walk initially crosses a sandy spit on a raised boardwalk, then gradually climbs up to the lighthouse. From the lighthouse the track drops down to a lookout point, and it is possible to clamber around the rocks back to a point just above the boardwalk. Take some time to climb up the rocks overlooking the reef and lagoon, a very popular spot for fishing.

Grade: Easy
Time: 40 minutes
How to get there: 65 km northeast of Masterton.

2 Punganga Pa, Mt Holdsworth Lookout

A punganga pa acted as a last refuge in times of serious trouble, and was likely to be located in a cave, an island or, in this case, in deep and inaccessible bush. Construction was rudimentary as they were designed to provide temporary shelter, and all that remains at this site are basic earthworks, but they are not easy to miss.

This is a solid uphill trudge, not actually up Mt Holdsworth itself but instead up to a lookout point with a view of Mt Holdsworth deep in the Tararua Range across the valley. The pa is about halfway up to the lookout. The track begins to the left just over the swingbridge.

Grade: Hard

Time: 40 minutes return to the pa; 1 hour 15 minutes return to the lookout

How to get there: From Masterton take SH2 to 1 km south of the Waingawa River bridge, turn right into Norfolk Road and travel a further 16 km to the parking area.

3 Te Kawakawa/Cape Palliser

As with much of this coast, the area around Cape Palliser has close associations with Kupe. The name of the cape refers to a garland that Kupe's daughter fashioned from the leaves of a kawakawa tree that she found growing here. Just to the west of Te Kawakawa is an area of cliff face notable for its lighter shade of rocks, called Nga Ra o Kupe, 'the sails of Kupe'. On the shore below is a large flat rock where Kupe stood to view the snow-capped Kaikoura mountains across the strait; this is called Matakitaki a Kupe, 'the watching place of Kupe'.

A great place to view the coastland is from the Cape Palliser lighthouse. The 258 steps lead to the lighthouse located 78 metres above the sea. It will make you puff, but it is worth the effort for the fantastic view along the coast.

Grade: Medium

Time: 20 minutes return

How to get there: From Martinborough, take the road south towards Lake Ferry and then turn left on the road to Ngawi. The lighthouse is 5 kilometres past Ngawi. The road to Ngawi is excellent – sealed, mainly straight, it follows the coast with just one or two rough patches through the unstable terrain; though the last section from Ngawi is unsealed gravel road.

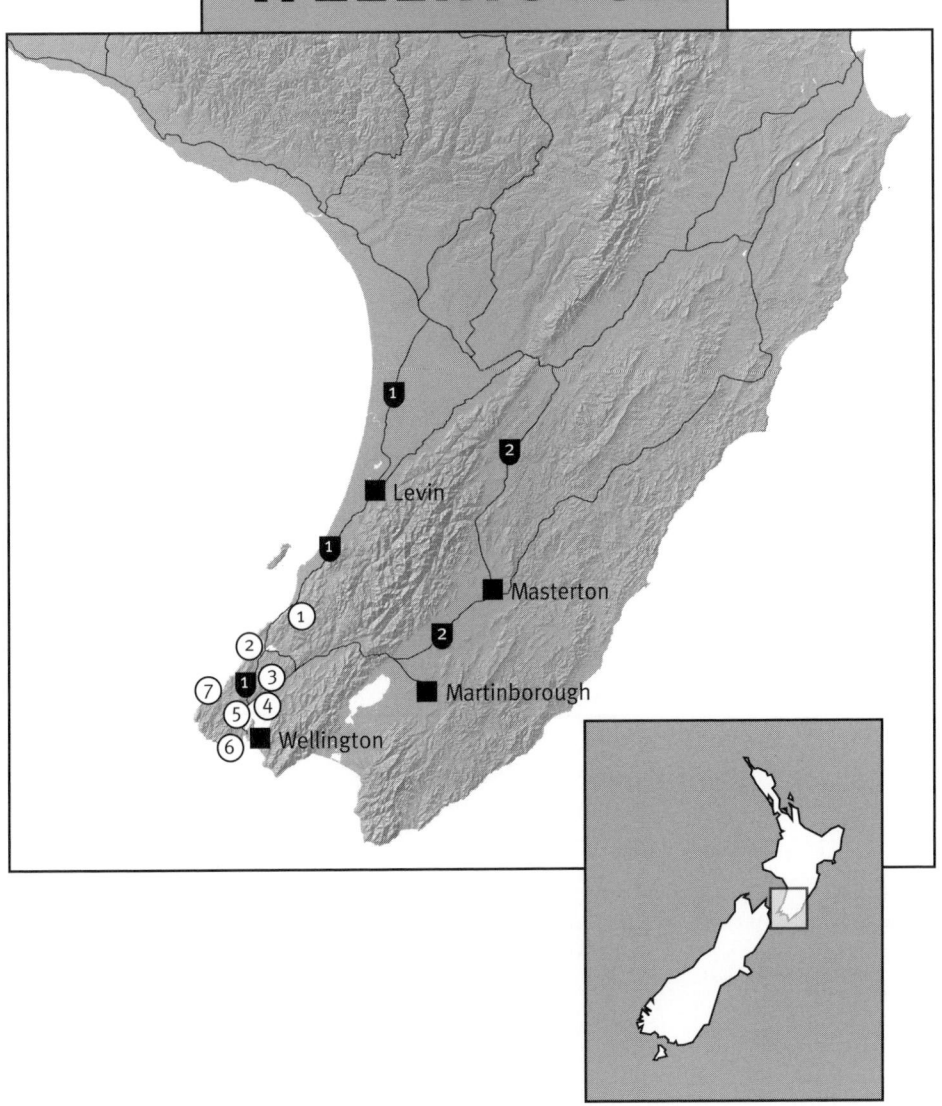

WELLINGTON

Levin

Masterton

Martinborough

Wellington

1 Battle Hill

Even today the site of the last engagement of the New Zealand Wars around Wellington is relatively remote, but in 1846 this area was covered in dense bush; it was difficult to travel through at the best of times and in winter almost impossible.

After clashing with troops at Pauatahanui, Ngati Toa under the leadership of Te Rangihaeata (Te Rauparaha's nephew) drew back 6 kilometres to a position in steep and rugged hill country. They quickly but effectively fortified a hilltop clad in dense bush. The British troops, though heavily outnumbering the Maori, realised that a direct attack would be suicidal.

The first action against Te Rangihaeata began on 6 August in bitterly cold weather, with heavy gunfire from the 250 British soldiers as well as 150 Maori, mainly Te Atiawa but also including some Ngati Toa men opposed to Te Rangihaeata. The musket fire made little impression, and after the death of three British soldiers, the attacking forces withdrew down the hill. (Te Rangihaeata lost nine men on the same day.)

On 8 August two mortars were hauled up the steep hillside, through bush and mud, and were fired at the hilltop fort: 80 mortar rounds pounded the Maori positions. But still the British refused to move forward and eventually they withdrew completely on 10 August, leaving their Maori allies to continue the fight.

Over the next few days, the two sides skirmished inconclusively and finally Te Rangihaeata, realising that in the long run it was impossible to hold the fort, slipped away under cover of the rain and dark, leaving his enemies to find an empty shell on the morning of 13 August.

Today Battle Hill is farmland, the bush mostly gone, replaced by grass and grazing sheep. The uphill walk is a good solid climb, and it can only be imagined what it was like pulling heavy iron mortars up the hill while under fire. Only some minor earthworks remain of the Maori and British positions, but extensive interpretive panels help to make this a very worthwhile excursion.

A number of tracks start by the farm buildings. The best one to take is the Summit Loop Track (the first part of which is also the Farm Loop Track). This is all uphill, though it follows a farm track so the grade is steady rather than steep. Once you reach the top, enjoy the atmosphere and the view before taking the return track via the bush reserve. This starts with a very steep downhill walk and then follows the stream along a bushy valley, emerging into the camping area not far from the start. On a blustery day you will be grateful to be out of the wind on the return trip.

Grade: Medium

Time: 1.5 hours

How to get there: Battle Hill Farm Forest Park is on Paekakariki Hill Road, 6 km from the intersection with SH58 at Pauatahanui.

2 Te Pa o Kapo

Regarded as the strongest and best fortified of the Ngati Ira pa in the Porirua area, Te Pa o Kapo may have been occupied for as long as 400 years. However, when Te Rauparaha invaded the area in 1819–20, of the three pa in the Porirua area only Waimapihi was inhabited. Te Pa o Kapo had already been abandoned and was never reoccupied.

In 1901 the ethnographer Elsdon Best (who was born in Tawa) visited the pa and was impressed by the superb defences. He noted that at that time the stumps of the totara palisading were still visible.

Today the pa retains the key elements of the defences that made it so famous. The already narrow access to the small headland was accentuated by a deep trench and by steepening the cliffs on either side. Even today, it is still a bit of a scramble onto the main part of the pa. Wide terraces still remain and of course the view along the coast and across the strait is undiminished by time.

Grade: Easy

Time: 15 minutes return

How to get there: The small reserve is clearly marked on Terrace Road, Titahi Bay.

3 Korokoro

The name Korokoro is closely related to the Maori name for the North Island, Te Ika a Maui or 'the great fish of Maui'. In Maori legend the whole island is the fish, Wellington Harbour is the mouth and the Korokoro valley is the throat of the fish.

This walk to the Korokoro dam will take you into the very throat of Maui's great fish. The loop walk drops down steeply through mature nikau, rimu, rata, tawa and kohekohe to the Korokoro Stream at the bottom of the valley, where an old water supply dam is located. The return walk is longer, but on a much gentler grade.

Grade: Medium

Time: 50 minutes

How to get there: Follow Dowse Drive up from the Western Hutt motorway just north of the Petone turnoff. From Dowse Drive follow the signs to Oakleigh Street carpark.

4 Te Whanganui a Tara/Wellington Harbour

The harbour itself takes its name from Tara, who lived at Mahia and, with his brother Tautoki, journeyed down to the area we now know as Wellington. So impressed were Tara and Tautoki that they convinced their father, the great chief Whatonga, that the harbour was an excellent place for a new settlement. Known as Ngai Tara, they built several pa in the area, including Te Whetu Kairangi and Rangitatau on the Miramar Peninsula. Later Ngai Tara intermarried with Ngati Ira, also from Hawke's Bay, and the iwi around Wellington eventually became known as Ngati Ira. Despite the abundance of kai moana, the cool summer climate restricted the growth of crops, and it is estimated that the pre-European population was well under 1000.

One of the best places to view the 'great harbour of Tara' is Matiu or Somes Island, which as it happens has links with Kupe: the two main islands in the harbour are named after Kupe's daughters, Matiu (Somes) and Makaro (Ward). Maori never permanently occupied either island as they lacked a consistent source of fresh water; they used the islands only for seasonal food gathering and as refuges in time of conflict.

Purchased by the New Zealand Company and renamed Somes after the deputy governor of the company, Joseph Somes, the island was used as a quarantine station first for people and later for animals, and also as a detention centre during both world wars.

Now the island is an important wildlife sanctuary and with extensive replanting is home to endangered birds and tuatara.

On arriving on the island a good option is to head uphill to the Visitor Centre and spend a few minutes bringing yourself up to speed with the island's history. From there head uphill to the gun emplacements, which not only have a great view over the harbour but also give a clear outline of the island. From that point you can access the island circuit track, which is well formed, offers easy walking and for the most part is high above the shore and therefore has excellent views all the way around.

Grade: Easy

Time: 2 hours

How to get there: East by West stop at the island on their cross-harbour ferry route (www.eastbywest.co.nz, phone 04 499 1282).

5 Matairangi/Mt Victoria

The most accessible of Wellington's numerous hills, Matairangi rises 196 metres and has fantastic views over the city, Cook Strait, Hutt Valley and the Tararua mountains. The summit itself is called Tangi Te Keo; the name is closely associated with the creation of the harbour itself.

Once there were two taniwha, Ngake and Whataitai, who long ago lived in the harbour when it was still a lake. Ngake was a restless and energetic taniwha who resented his confinement in the lake and hungered for the open sea just a short distance away. Finally Ngake devised an escape plan. He launched himself from the shallow northeast corner of the harbour directly at the rocks to the south. His full force smashed through the land and he made his escape to the sea and in the process created the entrance to the harbour.

Whataitai took another course and pushed from the western side of the lake – where his long tail created the Ngauranga Gorge – and headed down the western side of what is now the Miramar Peninsula. However Whataitai, after living in a lake, had not calculated the effect of the tide created by Ngake's escape and became stranded by the outgoing tide. Whataitai was trapped and died, and his body formed the isthmus that links Miramar to the mainland.

As Whataitai breathed his last, his soul took the form of a bird that flew off, crying *keo keo keo*, and landed on the top of the hill to tangi for Whataitai. The suburb of Hataitai takes its name from the taniwha Whataitai.

There is a maze of tracks up and down the city flank of Mt Victoria, and the signage is not that clear or consistent. However, you can't get lost if you apply this simple rule: walk uphill on the way there, and downhill on the way back.

Grade: Medium
Time: 1 hour return
How to get there: The track begins in Charles Plimmer Park off Hawker Street, Mt Victoria.

6 Pariwhero/Red Rocks

It is not exactly certain when Kupe, the great Polynesian explorer and the discoverer of Aotearoa, first landed in this country. Some put his arrival before 1000 AD, while others put it much later. All around the country there are many place names associated with Kupe's voyages – and in particular around the Wellington area, which suggests Kupe spent considerable time there. Kupe first came ashore near Seatoun, which is known as Te Turanga o Kupe, the great standing place of Kupe.

There are two stories associated with Kupe and the Red Rocks. One story has Kupe gathering paua, and when he accidentally gashed his hands on the rocks, they became stained with his blood. The other story involves Kupe's daughters – and there are variations here as well. When Kupe set off to explore the South Island, he was away for such a long time that his daughters (or just one daughter) feared for his safety. One version has it that his daughter, overcome with grief, threw herself off the cliff, and her blood covered the rocks. A variation on that theme is that his daughters cut themselves as a traditional sign of mourning, and it is their blood that now gives the rocks their name Pariwhero (red rocks).

There is no need for signage at Red Rocks Point as the striking red colour of pillow lava, formed underwater over 200 million years ago, is obvious. A flat 4WD track follows the wild exposed coast where bull kelp swirls in the brutal tides and oystercatchers scuttle along the stony beaches. The only thing that spoils this scene is the 4WD vehicles that frequently use this track, and not all drivers are considerate to walkers. This is not such a problem during the week when few people are about, or on Sunday when the track is closed to vehicles, but the busy 4WD traffic can be very unpleasant on a Saturday.

Grade: Easy
Time: 1.5 hours
How to get there: At Owhiro Bay, follow the Owhiro Bay Parade west to the carpark at the end.

7 Makara

Exposed to both northerly and southerly winds, the sheer wildness of Makara is its essential appeal. This hasn't always been the case and several Maori pa sites in the area are testament to the richness of both sea and forest. Even James Cook remarked on the din of the dawn chorus of bird song from the coastal forest although he was anchored almost a kilometre offshore. This Ngati Ira pa is clearly visible from the beach, occupying a low headland just to the south.

The walk begins at the southern end of the beach and traverses farmland as the track climbs solidly uphill. A rough unmarked track goes off to the right and follows a sharp ridge to the headland pa. Not particularly large, the pa was well protected by the steep cliffs on three sides and by a deep ditch across a very narrow neck on the land side. Small terraces and kumara pits are still visible all along the ridge.

The strategic value of the site is immediately obvious – the whole of Cook Strait is in clear view, with Mana and Kapiti islands to the north, the Marlborough Sounds to the west, and the Kaikoura mountains away to the south.

The walk to the pa site takes around 50 minutes return and if the uphill walk does appeal, then a stroll along the coast to the point below the pa will take about 25 minutes return.

Grade: Medium
Time: 50 minutes return
How to get there: From the western end of Karori take the Makara Road to the beach.

SOUTH ISLAND/
TE WAI POUNAMU

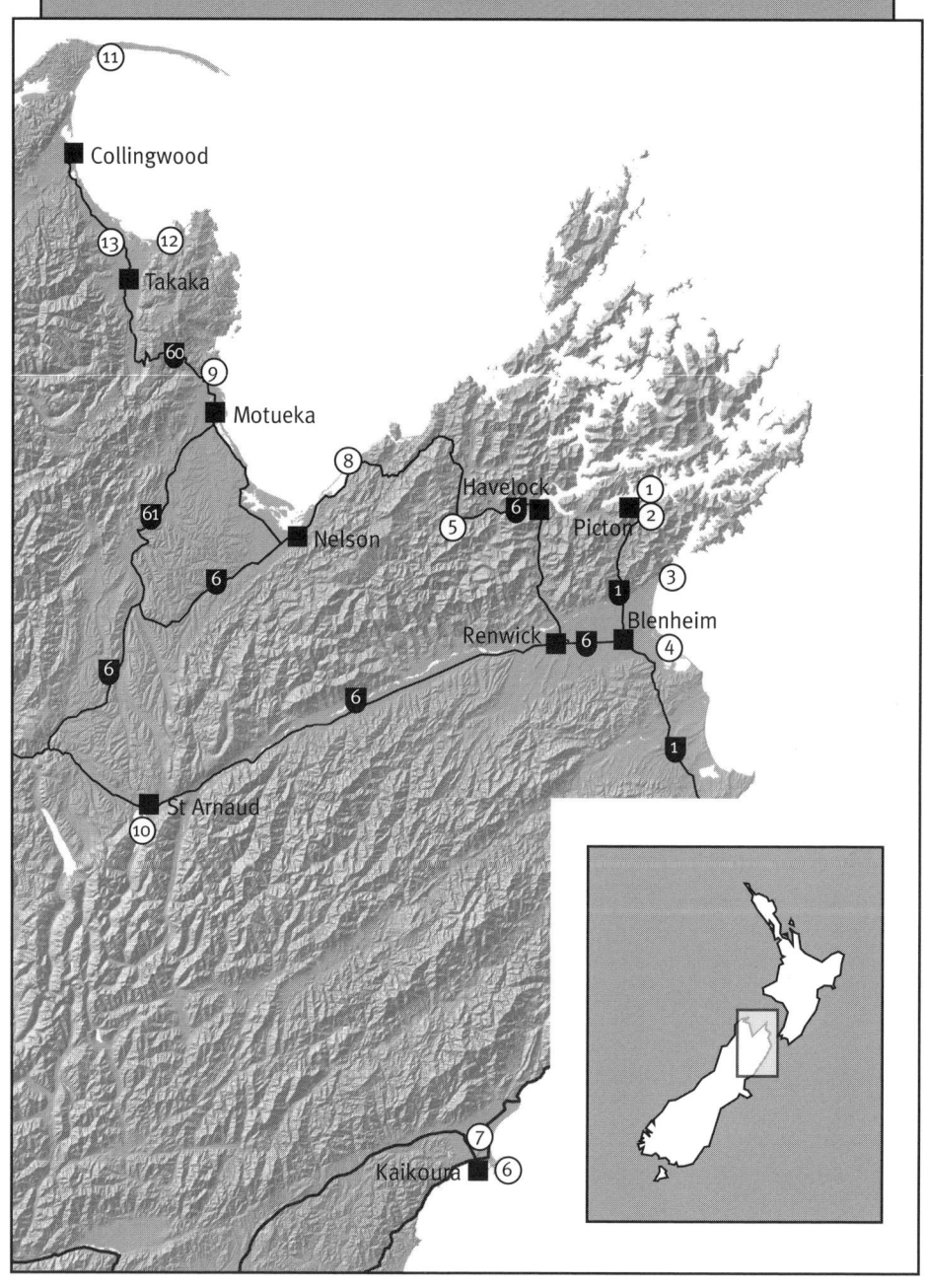

MARLBOROUGH, KAIKOURA AND NELSON

1 Karaka Pa, Picton

Te Pae o Te Karaka Pa was named after the Ngati Mamoe chief Te Karaka, who settled here around 1700 AD. Te Karaka was killed when Ngai Tahu led by Tu Ahuriri captured the pa in 1720 AD, and the pa in turn became a Ngai Tahu stronghold.

In the 1820s musket-wielding Te Atiawa invaded the Sounds and, after capturing several pa nearby, made their move on Te Karaka. The defenders had been warned by others fleeing from the invaders to escape, but they decided to make a stand, believing that they were safe in their strongly fortified pa. Approaching from the sea in waka, Te Atiawa launched an assault with heavy musket fire. Now realising that escape was the only option, the occupants fled through the land gates, but ran straight into a trap. Te Atiawa warriors had hidden in the bush and few escaped the deadly ambush. The pa was burnt, abandoned and never reoccupied.

In addition to having great views over Queen Charlotte Sound, this pa is particularly well preserved with defensive ditches, house sites and kumara pits clearly outlined. Tracks from the pa lead down to two shingle beaches.

 Grade: Easy
Time: 20 minutes return
How to get there: From Picton take the Waikawa Road to Waikawa Bay and then continue along the narrow road towards Port Underwood. The walk is well marked on the left-hand side of the road.

2 Ihumoeoni/The Snout

Totaranui or Queen Charlotte Sound was long a favourite location for Maori. Kupe visited the area on his legendary voyage. The calm waters were ideal for fishing and rich in shellfish and the lush bush was alive with bird life. The sheltered bays, good rainfall and sunshine made this area one of the most favourable in the South Island for growing crops.

Today the end of this long peninsula is known by both its English name, The Snout, and its Maori name Ihumoeoni, 'the nose of the sand worm'.

The first section of this track is a 10-minute walk along an unattractive wide access road flanked by gorse. The track then narrows and enters regenerating bush with expansive views that unfold as you walk along the peninsula. From Queen Charlotte View there are excellent views far to the north, on both sides of the peninsula numerous bays and bush-clad ridges line the sound, and the town of Picton is behind you. Ihumoeoni at the end of the peninsula is a further 40 minutes from Queen Charlotte View.

Grade: Medium

Time: 2.5 hours

How to get there: From Picton take the Waikawa Road, then turn left into Loop Drive, which is clearly marked and is one-way. Continue along the drive to the carpark just before the road turns sharply downhill to the right. The track begins from the northern side of this carpark.

3 Te Pukatea, Whites Bay

The small, sandy, bush-clad Whites Bay is in direct contrast to the dry open country south of the Wairau River. Whites Bay was known to Maori as Te Pukatea; this was also the name of a pa overlooking the bay. The pa stood in the area where the road to the bay meets the Port Underwood Road, though now not a trace of the pa remains. This was not the main pa of the area – that was Wairau pa, located to the southwest of Whites Bay on the banks of the Wairau River.

The Treaty of Waitangi, on its journey around the South Island, was signed northeast of Whites Bay on Horahora Kakahu Island in Port Underwood.

Pukatea Loop Walk is a short walk that follows the stream up from the bay through the bush and eventually emerges on the road to Whites Bay in the area where the pa was located.

Grade: Easy
Time: 25 minutes return
How to get there: From Blenheim, take the road to Rarangi Beach and Port Underwood. Where the road starts climbing uphill at Rarangi, drive a further 4 km to Whites Bay.

4 Te Pokohiwi/Wairau Lagoons

The Wairau Bar is one of New Zealand's most important archaeological sites. Its cultural treasures were first discovered in March 1942 when Jim Eyles, then 16 years old, was digging an air-raid shelter near the family home. Among the shingle Jim was sharp-eyed enough to notice unusual bones, shells and blackened stones – and he kept on digging.

What Jim unearthed proved to be one of the oldest occupied sites in New Zealand, dating back to at least the thirteenth century and, as subsequent excavations uncovered, closely linked to the initial settlement by settlers from Eastern Polynesia.

The middens along the bar have yielded evidence that the early Maori had a wide diet that included fish, seals, kiore, tuatara, porpoise, shellfish, kuri and birds – some of which are now extinct. Of the extinct birds, bones have been found of at least six species of moa, the flightless New Zealand swan, the New Zealand crow and the gigantic Haast eagle. Evidence suggests that over 8000 moa were slaughtered and over 2000 moa eggs consumed.

Along with the evidence of food, there were also distinctly Eastern Polynesian-style fishhooks, chisels, adzes and harpoon points. More important were necklaces consisting of cotton reel-shaped pieces held together by cord in a style common in the Marquesas Islands, east of Tahiti. This has led archaeologists to surmise that the origins of the legendary homeland of Hawaiki was somewhere in Eastern Polynesia. In all 50 burial sites have been excavated.

This track through the Wairau lagoons to a point overlooking the Wairau Bar unfortunately begins by going through the middle of Blenheim's sewerage treatment plant, but it quickly emerges onto a vast saltmarsh of interlacing lagoons and languid tidal creeks that are home to some unique salt-tolerant plants and alive with aquatic bird life. Open and windswept, the track meanders across the saltmarsh. While generally it is well maintained and flat, it is boggy and very wet in places, so you will need waterproof footwear – or even gumboots.

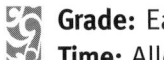 **Grade:** Easy
Time: Allow up to 2 hours
How to get there: The track begins at the end of Hardings Road, 5.5 km south of Blenheim off SH1.

5 Titiraukawa/Pelorus Bridge

The junction of the Pelorus/Te Hoiere and Rai rivers was part of an old Maori trail that passed over the Maungatapu Saddle and linked Tasman Bay to the Sounds. This was also the location of a small kainga called Titiraukawa, though the bitter fighting during the Musket Wars saw the village abandoned, and by the time Europeans arrived the area was largely uninhabited.

Today the area around Pelorus Bridge has some of the best mature lowland forest in the Marlborough region. In addition to black, red, hard and silver beech, there are miro, tawa, totara and kahikatea; some of these trees, such as miro, are not found further south.

The prolific birdlife includes bellbirds, tui, kereru and the occasional kaka and kakariki. This is also home to the long-tailed bat, which can be seen on summer evenings flitting over the river. Known as pekapeka, the bat is the herald of the mythical hokioi, a night-flying bird with a terrible scream that was never seen, but that warned of death and disaster. The saying 'Pekapeka rere ahiahi, hokioi rere po', 'The bat flies at twilight, the hokioi in the dark of night', urges the traveller to hurry home when bats are sighted. It also means that those going about unseen in the dead of night are up to no good – a sentiment that holds true even today.

The Circle Walk begins just across the road bridge and immediately to the right. It is dead flat to the substantial suspension bridge over the Rai River where it joins the Pelorus River. Beyond the bridge the track is undulating and forms a loop, part of which follows the high bank of the Pelorus River with views over the water and Totara Flat.

Grade: Easy
Time: 30 minutes return
How to get there: On SH6, 18 km west of Havelock.

6 Kaikoura

The Kaikoura Peninsula and mountains have a long and vital Maori history beginning with the creation of the very land itself. This is where the mighty demigod Maui braced his foot on a seat of his giant waka in his titanic struggle to haul up his great fish Te Ika a Maui (the North Island). In this ancient story, the Kaikoura Peninsula is known as Te Taumanu o te Waka a Maui.

Like many place names in the South Island, Kaikoura is also closely connected with the great explorer Rakaihautu and his son Rakihouia. What we now call the Kaikoura ranges were originally called Ka Whata-tu-o-Rakihouia, a name that celebrates the abundance of food in the area when Rakaihautu and Rakihouia were exploring.

The name Kaikoura, though, relates to another chief, Tama ki te Raki, and is a shortened version of Te Ahi-kaikoura-o-Tama-ki-te-Raki – 'the fire that cooked the crayfish of Tama ki Te Raki', and was given to the area when this chief was travelling down the coast in pursuit of his three runaway wives. He continued to pursue his wives down the coast and around Foveaux Strait until he found one of them turned to pounamu near Milford Sound. Continuing on, he found his other two wives and their waka also turned to pounamu. Today his wives give their names to the principal types of pounamu: Tangiwai, Kahurangi and Kawakawa.

First occupied by Waitaha people, then by Ngati Mamoe and in turn by Ngati Kuri, an iwi of Ngai Tahu, the peninsula has at least 11 pa. Disaster struck the area in 1828 when Te Rauparaha attacked the peninsula to avenge an insult by the chief Rerewhaka, who taunted Te Rauparaha by telling him that if he ever came to Kaikoura then Rerewhaka would rip open his belly with a barracouta tooth.

While the pa were well defended, luck favoured the Ngati Toa invaders as the locals were expecting a party of relatives to arrive from the south. Seeing the waka offshore, the unarmed defenders left their pa to greet the arrivals. They were too late in realising their mistake, and Te Rauparaha had an easy victory, quickly taking all three pa on the peninsula. As many as 1000 people died or were taken as slaves, with the remaining population fleeing south. Many years later, Ngai Tahu drove the Ngati Toa invaders back north and recovered their lands around Kaikoura.

The Kaikoura Walkway is a three-hour trip around the peninsula, though in reality the most interesting section is at the end of the peninsula and can be covered in much less time.

The seal colony at Point Kean attracts the crowds, but the entrance at

South Bay is a better place to start this walk. The track begins through two magnificent carved gateways depicting Maui hauling up his great fish. Just to the left up on the cliff top is the site of an old pa.

The lookout has a great view of the narrow rocky promontory that was also an old pa site. Now called the Sharks Tooth, it was named Te Rae-o-Atiu by an early explorer, Tamatea, after the legendary homeland Hawaiki; Point Kean, also a pa site, was named Te Rae-o-Tawhiti.

From the lookout follow the cliff tops to Point Kean, where there is a good view of a stepped pa to the west. Drop down to the carpark and return along the rocky coastline. This section can be difficult at high tide, but the section affected by the tide is close to the Point Kean carpark, so if the tide is not right and you need to turn back, you are not missing too much.

Grade: Easy
Time: 1.5 hours return
How to get there: Turn off SH1 onto South Bay Parade, south of Kaikoura. Continue along South Bay Parade to the carpark at the end.

7 Takahanga Pa

Today the pa on the open farmland of the peninsula are the more visible ones, but the main pa in the area was Takahanga, which is right above the main street of Kaikoura. Once occupied by Ngati Mamoe, the pa became a Ngai Tahu stronghold until Ngati Toa, led by Te Rauparaha, launched a surprise attack in 1828, heavily armed with muskets. Led by rangatira Rerewaka, the Ngai Tahu defenders were forced to retreat south, though eventually they regained the pa under the leadership of Taiaroa, Tuhawaiki and Karetai.

There are no traces of the old pa and the site is now occupied by a small urupa with commanding views to the north.

Grade: Easy
Time: 10 minutes return
How to get there: The pa is right by the centre of Kaikoura but not so easy to find. At the southern end of the main street are two small parks where West End becomes The Esplanade. On the right-hand side are old whale trypots. The track up the hill is to the left of these.

8 Te Taero a Kereopa/Boulder Bank, Nelson

Like many of the place names around Aotearoa, Te Taero a Kereopa has a close connection with the exploration of Kupe. When two of Kupe's men, Kereopa and Pani, decided to settle rather than continue voyaging, they deserted in two waka and headed towards Waimea (Tasman Bay). Setting off in hot pursuit in his waka *Matahourua*, Kupe started gaining on the fugitives. In their panic to slow Kupe down, they threw Kupe's daughter overboard. Plucking her from the water, Kupe now redoubled his efforts to catch Pani and Kereopa and eventually started to catch up with them as they entered the wide bay.

Kereopa now called on the gods with a powerful karakia to create a barrier between his waka and the *Matahourua*. The gods answered with boulders from Horoirangi (Mackay Bluff) collapsing into the sea and forming a long line, with Kereopa on the inside and Kupe out to sea. Kereopa won the day, keeping ahead of Kupe and finally making it to shore where he disappeared into the deep bush. Today several tribes descend from Kereopa, most notably Ngati Kuia.

Kupe's attention then turned to Pani in his waka *Takaporewa*, who likewise called on the gods and pleaded with local taniwha to delay Kupe, but had much less success. In his haste, Pani's waka overturned in the very rips he had invoked near Rangitoto Island and all aboard were drowned.

At first glance the Boulder Bank looks tempting for a good long walk, but in reality the loose stones and boulders make walking along the bank surprisingly hard work. A short section at the beginning is, however, a smooth level path and an easy short stroll. How far you want to go after that is up to you.

Grade: Easy
Time: 20 minutes return
How to get there: Boulder Bank Drive off SH6, 7 km north of Nelson

9 Tokongawha/Split Apple Rock

This curious split rock sits just off a narrow beach in Towers Bay just north of Kaiteriteri. The name Tokongawha means 'burst open rock' and refers to a legend where either two brothers or two chiefs (depending on the version) fought over this particular rock and, rather than continue the argument, decided to cut the rock in half. Quite why they were fighting over this rock is anyone's guess.

A short walk down steps and through regenerating bush leads to a long beach of golden sand. The rock sits just off the beach.

 Grade: Easy
Time: 30 minutes return
How to get there: From Kaiteriteri Beach take the Sandy Bay Road north for 4 km and then turn into Tokongawa Drive. After 2 km turn right into Moonraker Way, where the parking area is located.

10 Lakes Rotoiti and Rotoroa

Like most of the lakes in the South Island, the two that form the heart of Nelson Lakes National Park are connected with the early explorer Rakaihautu. While over the years Rakaihautu has acquired supernatural powers, this embellishment is a common way of showing respect to an exceptional ancestor, in much the same way as biblical figures lived exceptionally long lives and performed superhuman deeds. Stripping back the mythological aspects, it is clear that Rakaihautu explored much of the South Island in his waka *Uruao* and is a central figure in many tribal whakapapa.

Rakaihautu is said to have at first followed the coastline, but when he landed near the modern-day city of Nelson he decided to journey deep into the interior. Working his way inland, he began digging deep trenches with a gigantic ko or digging stick, heaping up the earth on either side. The trenches eventually filled with water and became Lake Rotoiti ('small lake') and Lake Rotoroa ('long lake'), while the soil heaped to one side became the mountains.

Continuing south, Rakaihautu created all the major inland lakes as well as the mountains we know as the Southern Alps/Ka Tiritiri o te Moana ('the ripples of the sea'). Rakaihautu eventually reached Te Ara a Kiwa (Foveaux Strait), where he finally settled.

Maori never settled permanently around Rotoiti and Rotoroa, but the lakes were a resting point for those on the pounamu trail from the West Coast to Tasman Bay and the Wairau valley, and were also used as a seasonal hunting ground for fish and birds.

While Rotoroa is larger and deeper, Lake Rotoiti is more accessible and has a wider range of facilities. Water taxis are a convenient way to access more remote parts of the lake, including the track that follows the entire shoreline. Other longer tramps include Mt Roberts Circuit, the St Arnaud

Range Track and the Lakeside Track to Whisky Falls.

Three short walks begin from the eastern side of Kerr Bay and are essentially loop walks, each progressively longer than the other, so it is very easy to find one here to suit all abilities. The forest is part of a 'mainland island' scheme, where predators are eradicated and permanently excluded from a section of forest, allowing native birds to recover and flourish.

The Bellbird Walk is an easy walk along the lake and through a short section of forest. The Honeydew Walk continues further along the shore and then has a slight uphill section before looping back through bush. The longest track is the Loop Walk, which follows the shoreline past several small beaches and then becomes a steady uphill trek as it follows a ridge through open beech forest. This track can be rough underfoot and muddy in parts, and the open nature of the forest means you need to check regularly that you are following the orange triangle markers.

 Bellbird Walk
Grade: Easy
Time: 10 minutes

 Honeydew Walk
Grade: Easy
Time: 30 minutes

 Loop Walk
Grade: Medium
Time: 1.5 hours

How to get there: The walks start from Kerr Bay in the St Arnaud township on SH63 between Blenheim and Murchison.

11 Onetahua/Farewell Spit

Whale strandings in the shallow waters along the eastern shore of Onetahua are a common occurrence, but Maori legend has quite a different take on these events.

The story begins with a fight at Onetahua between kuku (mussels) and pipi for supremacy on the sandy beach. The battle was won by the pipi, who drove the mussels in retreat to the rocks where they cling to this day.

The noisy fight drew the attention of Takaakho (a shark) and Te Pu (a whale), who quickly decided that while the fight held no interest for them, the victorious pipi with their large tasty tongues would make good food for their hungry families. Gathering their children about them, Te Pu and Takaakho rushed the pipi, which turned out to be far too quick for the great sea creatures and pulled their heads back into the sand. Finding the pipi gone, the whales ended up with only a mouthful of sand and stranded in the shallow water. This David and Goliath defeat by the pipi of the whales and the sharks became known as the battle of Waimapihi.

Only 2.5 kilometres of the spit is accessible to the public. This loop walk is located within the Puponga Farm Park – a working farm at the base of the spit that acts as a buffer to preserve the delicate ecosystem of the spit and is an area of outstanding beauty in its own right. The walk follows the 'inside' beach (Golden Bay) and the 'outside' beach (Tasman Sea).

From the carpark walk north along the inside beach to the end of the row of pine trees. It is on this section of the walk that you are most likely to see wading birds. At the end of the pine trees turn left and cut across the spit through farmland and swamp to the outside beach. In contrast to Golden Bay, this beach is a huge stretch of white sand pummelled by relentless surf. At the beach turn left and walk to a red disk that marks the return to the carpark via a narrow gully of nikau palms and farmland.

Grade: Easy

Time: 1.5 hours

How to get there: At Puponga turn right and follow the road to the beach just beyond the information centre; or you can park at the information centre and take the short walk down to the beach.

12 Abel Tasman Memorial

In December 1640, Dutch explorer Abel Janszoon Tasman arrived off the coast near Wainui in two ships, the *Heemskerck* and the *Zeehaen*. Unfortunately, the stay was both short and unpleasant when his sailors clashed with local Maori, resulting in the death of four men. Naming the area Moordenaars (Murderers) Bay and the country Staten Landt (later changed by a Dutch cartographer to New Zealand), Tasman never set foot on land and departed from the country in early January.

Prior to Tasman's arrival, Maori had lived in the area known as Mohua for around 400 years, and the warriors who confronted Tasman were most likely from the iwi Ngati Tumatakokiri, who had a pa at Taupo Point. There is some conjecture that Tasman may have entered either a tapu site or an area that had a rahui placed on it. It is also likely that the strange ship and oddly dressed white people were perceived as harmful spirits.

There is a short walk up to the memorial set high on a bluff overlooking Golden Bay. You can return to the road by the narrow concrete path to the left that leads to a further lookout with views far to the west.

Grade: Easy

Time: 15 minutes

How to get there: On the seaward side of Abel Tasman Drive, between Pohara Beach and Ligar Bay.

13 Te Waikoropupu (Pupu) Springs

Claimed to produce the clearest spring water in the world, the springs are a series of eight interconnected vents that discharge up to 14,000 litres per second. The water is a mixture of salt and fresh water as the huge underground water system encompasses an area twice the size of Lake Rotorua and extends out under the sea.

The springs are home to one of the three most important taniwha in Aotearoa — Huriawa, who was brought to this place by the legendary Rakaihautu. Today Huriawa and her children still guard the prow of Rakaihautu's waka *Uruao* at the mouth of the Waitapu River (a contraction of Nga Waitapu-o-Uruao).

Known as a kaitiaki taniwha, Huriawa uses this spring as a resting place when she is not performing the vital function of clearing waterways both above and below ground, especially after flooding. Underground caves and rock formations are all the work of Huriawa, and she travels throughout the North Island and as far south as Lake Pukaki.

For Maori, the waters of the springs were used for healing; today the area is still a wahi tapu.

The walk to the springs is on an excellent track through bush that includes some fine old totara and rimu trees. The short loop walk is only a few minutes extra, and you may well see native birds on the loop section.

Grade: Easy

Time: 25 minutes return to the springs; 40 minutes for the loop walk

How to get there: Follow SH60 north of Takaka for about 4 km and, after crossing the Takaka River, turn left onto Pupu Valley road and go a further 2.5 km.

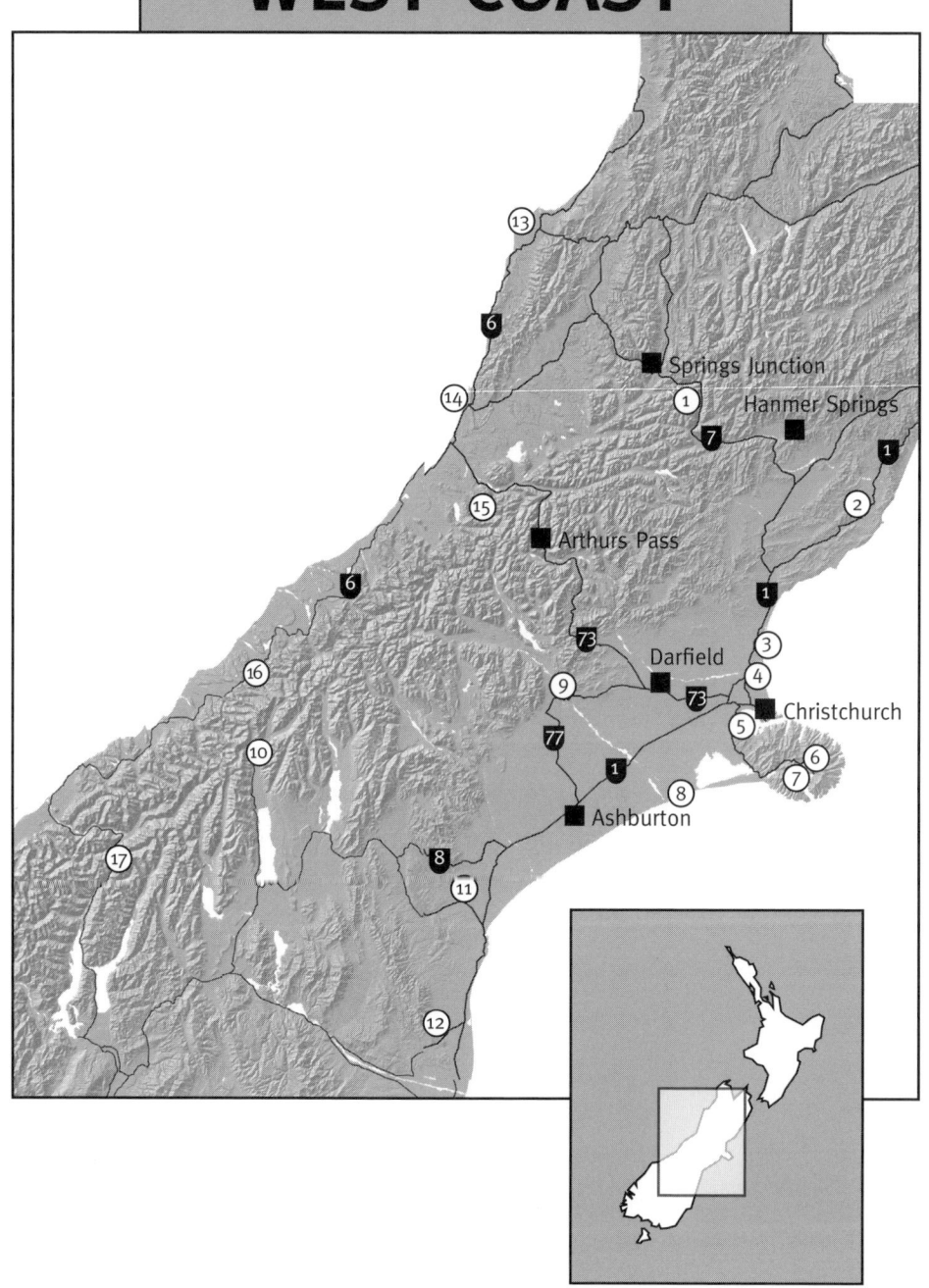

CANTERBURY AND WEST COAST

Springs Junction

Hanmer Springs

Arthurs Pass

Darfield

Christchurch

Ashburton

1 Kopi o Kaitangata/Lewis Pass

Much lower than Arthurs Pass, the Lewis Pass at 864 metres is an old Maori pounamu trail that follows the Lewis River south of the pass and the Maruia River to the north.

The Maori name has a rather grisly origin. Slaves were often used to transport food and in times of scarcity a slave might be killed and eaten. This journey across the mountains was particularly difficult and it was common at the pass itself to stop and eat. The Maori name Kapai-o-kai-tangata means 'a good meal of human flesh' and today that name is reflected in the naming of Cannibal Gorge.

Lewis Pass lookout is right at the high point of the Lewis Pass and is reached by a short but steep climb through bush and tussock to a marvellous vantage point with views of the Maruia River, Cannibal Gorge, Gloriana Peak and the Freyberg Range. The track is not marked but is easily found, though take care to park carefully off the road on the bend.

For something gentler, just a few hundred metres on is the Tarn Nature Walk, which is a flat, easy loop walk through subalpine vegetation with views to the mountains to the north.

 Lookout Walk
Grade: Hard
Time: 30 minutes return

 Tarn Walk
Grade: Easy
Time: 20 minutes return

How to get there: Both walks are 22 km east of Springs Junction. The walks are just 200 m apart.

2 Mata Kopae/St Annes Lagoon

This small lake provided early Maori with vital food sources in the normally dry landscape of North Canterbury. Even today the lake is packed with bird life, and in the past it was a great place for catching eels. Though not permanently settled, the lake area was both a seasonal hunting ground and a stopping point for those travelling between Kaikoura and the main Ngai Tahu settlement at Kaiapoi. It is a good spot to take a break and stretch your legs on the road between Christchurch and Picton.

Grade: Easy
Time: 30 minutes
How to get there: On SH1, 3 km north of Cheviot

3 Kaiapoi Pa

Kaiapoi or Kaiapohia was the main Ngai Tahu pa in the Canterbury area, built around 1700 AD when Ngai Tahu first migrated to the area. It was built by Moki for his brother Tu Rakautaki. The pa was initially called Te Kohanga-o-kaikai-a-waro, which was later changed to Kaiapohia.

The pa was sited on a peninsula surrounded by deep swamp. A maze of waterways and lagoons protected the pa on three sides, and this was enhanced by deep ditches and stout palisading. A feature of the pa was a number of defended gates; the main entrance was located to the left of where the monument now stands. The pa had a population of around 1000 people and was considered unassailable – but all that was about to change with the coming of Te Rauparaha.

Te Rauparaha visited Kaiapoi in 1828 on the pretext of trading pounamu, when in fact he was busily ascertaining the strength and defences of Ngai Tahu. Acutely aware of his real intentions, Ngai Tahu claimed that Ngati Toa had insulted them by dragging the corpse of a local woman through the swamp, and they used this insult as a reason to attack the visitors. In the ensuring mêlée, eight Ngati Toa were killed and eaten but – fatally for Ngai Tahu – Te Rauparaha escaped.

In the summer of 1831–32 Te Rauparaha returned to take revenge. During a three-month period of inconclusive skirmishes, Ngati Toa built a series of covered trenches up to the palisades, against which they piled dry manuka with the intention of setting fire to the wooden fencing. Realising their plan, the defenders within the pa decided to take advantage of a strong northwest wind blowing away from the pa and set fire to the manuka. As luck would have it, the wind suddenly switched to the south and the wooden walls burnt, allowing Te Rauparaha and his warriors into the pa. The slaughter that followed was fearful, and fewer than 200 of the 1000 inhabitants escaped to Onawe pa on Banks Peninsula.

Kaiapoi was never reoccupied, and even 20 years later the Reverend James Stack removed large piles of bones for burial. However, Ngai Tahu later reversed their losses and later still peace was made when Te Rauparaha returned many of those captured at Kaiapoi and Onawe.

Today little remains of this formidable pa. The swamps have been drained and the site is surrounded by farm paddocks, while the defences and gates have been reduced to grassy mounds. Near the road a towering white monument emblazoned with the simple words *Ngai Tahu* was built in 1898, but in the interests of reconciliation there is no reference to the fall of the pa. A wooden lookout point designed to give the visitor an overview of the site has unfortunately fallen into disrepair. However, the old pa holds an air of the past and, with a bit of imagination, a walk around the old pa briefly takes the visitor back to times long gone.

Grade: Easy
Time: 20 minutes
How to get there: 27 km north of Christchurch, 500 metres down Preeces Road off SH1

4 Brooklands Lagoon and the Ihutai/Avon-Heathcote Estuary

The great estuaries at the mouths of the Waimakariri, Avon and Heathcote rivers were a vast food larder for early Maori. These sheltered waters provided shellfish, eels and waterfowl, and even today over 70 bird species have been recorded at the Brooklands Lagoon south of the Waimakariri River. Right up to the 1880s the Brooklands Lagoon was an important food-gathering area for local Maori, until game fishing legislation introduced at that time banned everyone from taking fish from the river.

Further south, in the sand dunes between the Waikari River and the mouth of the Heathcote and Avon rivers, thousands of campsites have been found. The Maori name for the area, Kaiaua ('to eat yellow-eyed mullet') reflects the importance of the area to early Maori. Like elsewhere in the country, the long stretches of beach made for easy walking and were busy trails for those on the move. The Maori name for the Avon is

Otakaro or 'the place of a game' and the Heathcote is Opawaho, a name that lingers in the suburb of Opawa.

Spencer Park is part of a wider complex of parks that encompasses a large area of beach, lagoon, saltmarsh and dune country south of the mouth of the Waimakariri River and includes the Brooklands Lagoon. Attracting a wide range of wading birds, the area around the lagoon has a number of easy tracks that vary in length. There is also a raised viewing platform that gives a good view over the tidal flats, and a bird hide situated on top of a small dune that is ideal for bird watching.

On the northern side of the Avon-Heathcote estuary at the end of Southshore Spit is a wilderness area of dunes and stunted vegetation through which a short track links coastal scrub, beach and tidal mudflats. It is here that godwits gather in the summer. The walk is best done at low tide, when more of the estuary shoreline is accessible.

Brooklands Lagoon Walk
Grade: Easy
Time: 30 minutes
How to get there: The track begins at the information board at the entrance to Spencer Park on Heyders Road, off Lower Styx Road.

Ihutai/Avon-Heathcote Estuary Walk
Grade: Easy
Time: 20 minutes return

How to get there: End of Rockinghorse Road, Southshore Spit, but take care not to park in the turnaround area.

5 Omahu Bush Reserve

This small bush remnant on the Summit Road just below Coopers Knob harks back to a time of bitter conflict between Ngati Mamoe and Ngai Tahu. Te Rakiwhakaputa, a Ngai Tahu chief, had captured all the Ngati Mamoe pa around Whakaraupo (Lyttelton Harbour), but was still in pursuit of fugitives who had hidden deep in the forest in the rugged hills. When Ngati Mamoe chief Mawete and his followers were ambushed by Ngai Tahu, they were finally caught and killed at the peak, and the area became known as Omawete, 'the place of Mawete' (now Coopers Knob). Some of Mawete's men escaped and hid in the dense bush below the peak, which then took the name Omahu, a blended meaning of 'running silently' and 'a place of healing'.

While the large trees have gone, the bush is surprisingly dense, though there is some open country with great views of Lake Ellesmere. There are three interconnecting tracks that loop down the hillside, so it is easy to choose a walk to suit. However, while the track is well formed, it is steep and muddy in parts.

Grade: Medium
Time: 40 minutes return
How to get there: On the Summit Road, 9 km south of the Sign of the Kiwi at the top of Dyers Pass Road. The track information and track entrance is 300 m from the Gibraltar Rock carpark.

6 Otepatotu

Throughout Aotearoa, the dense bush-covered peaks were the favoured refuge of the elusive patupaiarehe. One South Island tradition has it that the patupaiarehe were descendants of the mysterious Hawea tribe, who came from a land far to the north. Elsewhere on Banks Peninsula, other landmarks are also connected with the fairy people, including The Monument, which was known to Maori as a patupaiarehe pa named Te Pohue.

To capture the appeal of these peaks to the patupaiarehe, the best time to visit Otepatotu is when there is low cloud smothering the peaks. Through the mists, the great ancient totara hung with mosses and the dense ferns that cloak the bush floor take on the atmosphere that the shy and retiring patupaiarehe favoured.

The track to the peak is steady rather than steep, but it is slippery and uneven in parts and poorly signposted. Initially the path winds through bush. At the junction, not long after starting, take the track to the left. It quickly emerges into a flax field from where a short detour to the top of a rocky bluff in fine weather gives great views over Akaroa Harbour.

The track then enters dense bush dominated by fine old totara, before again emerging into low scrub that crowns the summit known as Lavericks (755 metres). From the summit take the track to the right along the fenceline, and at the next junction (unmarked) take the wide track to the right which eventually emerges not far from the carpark.

Grade: Medium
Time: 45 minutes return
How to get there: Otepatotu Reserve on the Summit Road, 4 km southeast of the Okains Bay/Summit Road junction.

7 Onawe Pa

Onawe Peninsula, shaped like a giant teardrop, juts out into waters of the upper Akaroa Harbour and rises to a height of over 100 metres. Linked to the mainland by a narrow strip of land and virtually cut off at high tide, at first glance this was an ideal position for a fortified pa – in fact, the early French settlers called it Mt Gibraltar.

After the fall of Kaiapohia, Te Rauparaha turned his attention to Onawe, the only remaining Ngai Tahu pa in the area and the refuge for many of the survivors. There he cut off the pa by dividing his forces to cover both sides of the narrow isthmus linking the pa to the mainland. The pa had some disadvantages: the terrain allowed for the attacking force to take a position on the hills above the pa where they could easily observe both the defenders and the defences within the pa; the peninsula was large, with no steep cliffs to protect it; and, more importantly, with the isthmus sealed there was no escape route. Te Rauparaha found the pa difficult to capture, but once the opportunity arose, he was very quick to take it.

Seeing Te Rauparaha's frustration during the long siege, Ngai Tahu forces under Tangatahara decided to press their advantage and harry Ngati Toa. However, the attack went wrong and Ngai Tahu retreated back to the pa. Ngati Toa warriors quickly followed, using captives from Kaiapohia as a screen. Reluctant to fire on the attackers for fear of hitting their relatives, the defenders left the gates open too long and Ngati Toa poured into the pa. The well-defended pa now became a trap and few inhabitants escaped the terrible massacre, which was followed by a cannibal feast at Barrys Bay.

When peace was finally established in 1839, Ngai Tahu returned to the peninsula, but they were a shadow of their former force and never recovered from the deadly raids in 1831–32.

The track starts to the right of the carpark and skirts around the beach (not over the bluff); it is difficult right on high tide. From there it is an easy walk through open grassland to the top. Today, details of the pa are hard to discern. The rocky outcrop at the summit is called Te Pa Nui o Hau.

Grade: Easy

Time: 1 hour return

How to get there: At Barrys Bay turn into Onawe Flat Road. The walk starts from the carpark at the end.

8 Taumutu, Kaitorete Spit

Running over 20 kilometres between Lake Ellesmere (Te Waihora) and the sea, the Kaitorete Spit was known to Maori as Ka Poupou-a-Te-Rakihouia, or 'the great eel weir of Te Rakihouia' (another name for the lake was Te Kete-ika-o-Rakaihautu, or 'the food basket of Rakaihautu'). In pre-European times, the main settlements centred on two pa on the southern shore, near the lake entrance at Taumutu where, as the Maori name suggests, the lake's outlet acted as a giant eel trap. While the outlet is frequently closed completely, early Maori constructed special narrow channels to trap migrating eels. Nowadays the lake is considerably degraded, but back then it was a vital source of not only eels, but aquatic birds as well. Taumutu was also well placed on the main trail down the east coast, between the settlements around Banks Peninsula and those along the Otago coast.

Taumutu pa was the centre of a bitter inter-iwi conflict that became known as the Kai Huanga, or 'eat relation' feud. The feud so weakened Ngai Tahu in the area that it in effect paved the way for defeat by Ngati Toa.

The conflict began simply enough when a woman at Waikakahi on the eastern shore of Lake Ellesmere put on a dogskin cloak belonging to Tamaiharanui, the principal chief of Ngai Tahu. For such an insulting act, utu was expected and exacted, but instead of taking revenge on the woman herself, Tamaiharanui's family killed a slave belonging to the woman. This in turn led to a further revenge killing and the conflict began to spiral out of control.

Returning from Kaikoura, Tamaiharanui stopped off at Kaiapohia with advice to those there to stay out of the fight. Gathering his forces, Tamaiharanui attacked Taumutu and in the ensuing fight several Kaiapohia women living there were killed. Now the people of Kaiapohia sought revenge, and from a simple impetuous act, the fighting now embroiled all of Ngai Tahu. More and more groups were pulled into the ugly vortex until the people of Taumutu abandoned their pa and fled south to seek the protection of their relatives in Otago.

Later, under false assurances from Tamaiharanui that it was safe to return to Taumutu, the people returned, but were attacked on the way by Tamaiharanui and the entire Taumutu hapu was slaughtered. The pa was never reoccupied. Only the invasion of Te Rauparaha put an end to the conflict, but the much weakened Ngai Tahu were now unable to resist the invaders from the north.

The pa at Taumutu is no longer discernible, but it is a wild and beautiful place to visit. The best way to approach the area is along the beach, where you can walk as far as you like.

Grade: Easy

Time: Allow at least 1 hour

How to get there: There are two beach access points off Pohau Road, Taumutu. One is on Gullivers Road, where there is a bridge over the small stream. The second is on an unmarked road on the right after Gullivers Road, where there is a shallow ford. You will get your feet wet.

9 Rakaia Gorge Walkway

Fierce nor'westers are a dominant feature of Canterbury weather and naturally there is a Maori legend to explain this occurrence.

Long ago in the foothills of the mountains lived a taniwha. If left well alone and undisturbed, this taniwha was trouble to no one. He was particularly industrious and tidy and took great pride in his gardens and possessions. During a spell of very cold weather, the taniwha journeyed away from home to find a hot spring to warm himself. Out of the mountains came a bad spirit in the form of the wild northwest wind and tore up the taniwha's gardens, flattened his fences and tossed around all his belongings.

When the taniwha returned he was furious and, after putting his property back in order, he was determined to outsmart the evil wind. Hauling rocks and boulders down from the mountain, the taniwha created a narrow gap along the Rakaia River with the intention of trapping or at least slowing down the wind. However, the plan nearly backfired as the narrow gap made the wind blow stronger and, heating up as it went, it made the taniwha so hot that his body blistered and his sweat fell on rocks and boulders.

Today the wind and the taniwha have an uneasy truce, occasionally tussling when the wind blows warm out of the mountains, but usually the wind doesn't blow too hot or too strong across the plain and ruin the taniwha's garden. The barrier that the taniwha built is still there as the Rakaia Gorge and, if you look closely, you wll see the small crystals in the rocks that are the beads of sweat that fell from his brow. Fighting Hill above Windwhistle is named to commemorate this eternal tussle between the taniwha and the wind.

The Rakaia Walkway begins at the narrowest part of the gorge by the bridge and then follows the river through forest remnants and up onto old terraces to a lookout point. With snow on the mountains, the views are endless and spectacular. For the most part the track is easy walking, though there are some uphill sections, but these are more steady climbs than steep and the track is well formed and well maintained.

A shorter walk that follows the gorge to a wide grassy terrace will take about one hour return.

Grade: Medium
Time: 3.5 hours return; short walk, 1 hour return
How to get there: The walk begins at the carpark below the bridge on the north bank of the Rakaia River on SH77.

10 Aoraki/Mt Cook

Very few of the peaks of the Southern Alps were given names by Maori, whereas almost every stream and lake, no matter how small, has a Maori name. Possibly this reflects the fact that, to Maori, streams and lakes were important sources of food, whereas the bleak snow-capped peaks were of no food value and therefore of less interest. One peak that not only has a name but a legend attached is Aoraki/Mt Cook.

Aoraki was one of three brothers, the sons of Rakinui, the Sky Father, by his second wife (Papatuanuku, the earth mother, was his first wife). However, Rakinui decided he was in love with Papatuanuku after all and subsequently divorced again in order to remarry her.

The brothers, however, had other ideas and decided to journey from the heavens to the earth in a magical waka to create a rift between Papa and Rakinui. Once on earth, the brothers witnessed the strength of the love between the sky and the earth, and decided to return to their mother to break the sad news and to console her. Once they were under way, however, the waka met a terrible storm, struck a reef and overturned, forcing the brothers to clamber onto the upturned hull to await rescue. No rescuers came and instead a cold southerly wind sprang up, and within a short time the brothers and all their crew froze to death and turned into stone.

Aoraki was the tallest and oldest brother and became our highest peak, while his brothers and crew became the lesser mountains. The mountainous chain we know as the Southern Alps became Te Waka-o-Aoraki, the upturned canoe of Aoraki.

New Zealand's highest mountain Aoraki, at 3754 metres, is at the heart of Aoraki/Mount Cook National Park, a park that covers an area of over 70,000 hectares and contains all but one of New Zealand's peaks over 3000 metres.

One of the best views of Aoraki, accessible by a short walk, is from the Kea Point Lookout. Meandering through matagouri and mountain totara, the track skirts the glacier debris of the Mueller Glacier to a spectacular lookout point in an alpine basin surrounded by mountains, with Aoraki standing proud at the head of the Hooker valley.

 Grade: Easy
Time: 1 hour return
How to get there: Just before Aoraki/Mount Cook village turn right into Hooker Valley Road and drive to the White Horse Hill campground carpark at the end of this road. The track starts from this carpark.

11 Opihi Rock Drawings

While Maori rock drawings are not unusual throughout Aotearoa, they are especially prolific in the limestone country north and south of the Waitaki River. These drawings have often been dismissed as the mere doodling of the bored, trapped in rock shelters by bad weather. To be fair, many of the drawings are in fact very simple sketches of the outlines of birds, plants and people. The problem of the drawings as art is further compounded by the deterioration over time of both the limestone and the materials used (usually charcoal), so that what remains is often difficult to see, let alone to appreciate the original intention and impact.

However, the iconic taniwha at Opihi is in a league of its own and can, without a doubt, be seen in the context of art. Several factors make this drawing exceptional, beginning with the location on the roof of a rocky overhang, which is just the perfect height for someone to draw comfortably for a long period of time. The surface of the rock is also consistently smooth, which may explain the size of the drawing, at around 1.5 metres long and 0.5 metres wide. Drawn with considerable technical skill, the taniwha is clearly not the work of someone just idling away a rainy day.

What makes this drawing so appealing is the taniwha's incredibly 'modern' lines; it is executed with an aesthetic that seems contemporary, simple and stylish. This is one piece of art that has not gone out of fashion. What is more, it is out there on its own. There is little resemblance to other taniwha carved in wood in the more traditional and complex style. This very simplicity raises speculation that the drawings date back a considerable period, and there are links in style to art from Eastern Polynesia. While there are many other drawings in this small valley, none is as large as this taniwha.

Little is known about the origins or date of the drawings in the region, but it appears they were drawn over a considerable period of time including right up to the end of the nineteenth century, when Maori names were added further along the valley, and near Duntroon the rock drawings include European sailing ships.

The walk in this shallow valley is marked by orange marker posts and takes in a number of small caves and rocky overhangs, many of which contain drawings. The taniwha's location is easily recognised, as it is protected by a wire grille.

Grade: Easy

Time: 25 minutes return

How to get there: Take Tanawai road, then Opihi Road towards Hanging Rock off SH8 from Pleasant Point township. Before you cross the river turn left into Gays Pass Road and then, shortly after, right into Gould Road. Go to the end of this gravel road (about 1.5 km) where the road forks into two tracks. The beginning of the walk is over the stile to the right, though the entrance to the track has no signage.

12 Hunters Hills

The English name Hunters Hills actually has a Maori connection. When surveyor Charles Torlesse visited the area in 1849, the local chief Te Huruhuru told the surveyor that he frequently hunted in the hills. Back in Akaroa, Torlesse related the story to mapmaker Captain John Stokes, who subsequently labelled the range the Hunters Hills on his 1851 map.

The original Maori name of the Hunters Hills also relates to hunting, but with an unhappy ending. The elderly chief Te Kaumira was hunting with other men in the hills when a sudden storm separated the chief from his men. Although he found shelter in a cave near the source of the Pareora River, the weather was too cold and the chief froze to death. The hills became known as Te Tari-a-Te Kaumira, and Mt Nimrod was Te Tahu-a-Te Kaumira.

There are several short walks in the Hunters Hills near Waimate. One of the most pleasant is through Gunns Bush, a bush-clad river valley that includes several old totara. The loop track is mostly easy walking, though muddy when wet.

 Grade: Easy/medium
Time: 1.5 hours return
How to get there: The entrance is off Lower Hook Road, at Gunns Bush Camp, 13 km northwest of Waimate township.

13 Tauranga/Cape Foulwind

Te Tai Poutini (Westland) was never an attractive place for early Maori, with one exception: pounamu. A wet cool climate meant very little in the way of crops could be grown, the coast was rugged and dangerous for fishing, there were few lagoons and only the narrow coastal plain was suitable for habitation. A sealer, John Boultbee, in 1826 estimated the entire population was around 500, and even that had dropped to less than 200 by 1857. The largest settlements in Te Tai Poutini were around the mouth of the Kawatiri (Buller River), Mawhera at the mouth of the Grey River, and Okahu or Jackson Bay.

Cape Foulwind, appropriately known as Tauranga, 'sheltering anchorage', broke the worst of the southerly winds to protect waka out fishing and sheltered the small plain around the mouth of the Kawatiri ('deep and swift'). Omau and Tauranga Bay were also sheltered for fishing and important for gathering shellfish, especially mussels. Most important of all was the abundance of kekeno or fur seals; it is estimated that as much as 80 percent of food energy for local Maori came from seals.

Legend has it that the waka *Tahirirangi* arrived in the area around 950 AD under the guidance of the great rangatira Ngahue.

The fragile population around Kawatiri was devastated by the invasion by Ngati Rarua under the leadership of Niho and Takere, who defeated Poutini Ngai Tahu in 1831–32, though the invaders withdrew in 1837.

The walkway at Cape Foulwind takes around 1.5 hours return if you start the walk at Tauranga Bay and walk to the lighthouse and back. The track follows the cliff top and is easy walking with great coastal views. Just 10 minutes from Tauranga Bay is the seal colony, which is a great spot to watch fur seals as the lookout points are directly above the colony. The number of seals varies with the season, though the best time to see seal pups is between December and March. However, keep a sharp eye out as seals are hard to see and they are not confined to the colony: there may be more seals here than you first think. A heavy swell makes this walk even more dramatic.

Grade: Easy

Time: 1.5 hours return

How to get there: From Westport, head south then just over the Buller River, turn right into Cape Foulwind Road. It is 12 km to the lighthouse and a further 5 km to the seal colony at Tauranga Bay. If you are heading south from the seal colony you can take Watsons Lead Road, which joins SH6, 16 km north of Charleston.

14 Mawhera/Greymouth

One of the main settlements on the coast was at Mawhera, at the mouth of Mawheranui (Grey River); the principal pa was on the hill just above the centre of modern-day Greymouth and was also called Mawhera ('widespread river mouth'). This pa was a focal point of the pounamu trade with the great Ngai Tahu pa at Kaiapoi in Canterbury.

In Maori legend, the Mawhera Gap, where the river breaks through the low coastal range, was one side of a great canoe that was gradually filling with water, threatening to inundate the entire South Island. Tu Te Rakiwhanoa, a powerful ancestor, smashed through the canoe and saved the island from drowning. Another story says that the narrow coastal ranges are two giant tuatara and their heads meet to drink at the river mouth. The lagoon near Cobden was known as Te Akaaka-o-Poutini, 'the place where Poutini anchored', after an early Polynesian explorer.

Grade: Easy

Time: 1 hour return

How to get there: The Grey River walk starts at Mawhera Quay, on the river by the town centre, and continues along the river to the entrance of the small fishing harbour.

15 Pounamu and the Arahura River

In Maori legend there were originally two stones: Poutini (pounamu) belonging to Ngahue; and Whaiapu (flint), which belonged to Hinetuahoanga. Jealous of Ngahue's stone, Hinetuahoanga drove Ngahue out of Hawaiki to Aotearoa on the waka *Tahirirangi*, where Ngahue hid his pounamu near Arahura. Still hidden under the protection of a taniwha, also named Poutini, the pounamu occasionally breaks into small pieces and is washed down the river.

The importance of pounamu within Maori culture cannot be overestimated; the very name of the South Island, Te Wai Pounamu, relates directly to this stone. Found only in the South Island, in pre-European times pounamu was highly valued both for ornamentation and for weapons – in particular, patu or handheld clubs. Unlike many other stones, pounamu keeps a very good edge, and many of the patu were so highly valued that they were given individual names. Even today these pounamu patu and mere carry so much mana that, if found, they are quickly returned to their rightful owners, for to keep them would bring very bad luck. Traditionally pounamu is given as a gift and is not acquired for oneself.

The Arahura River near Hokitika is the primary source of pounamu, and there are several outlets in the town where it is sold and visitors can see it being carved into a variety of objects. However, be aware that much of the jade sold in this country is from Canada and China, and if you are keen to purchase pounamu then ask specifically if the stone comes from New Zealand. Even the label 'New Zealand made' can disguise the fact that the stone comes from elsewhere and is only carved in New Zealand.

There are four main types of pounamu found in New Zealand, each with different properties and names: inanga – pearly, grey-green in colour; kawakawa – a rich dark green, often with small flecks; kahurangi – very rare, translucent and flawless; and tangiwai – olive to blue-green and softer than the three other types.

There are very few accessible points to the Arahura River for walking. A public walkway runs along the river near Milltown and follows the river to the Cesspool, a picturesque spot despite the name. The track is not formed or even marked, but it begins just over the Arahura bridge near Milltown and follows the river. Please note that all pounamu in the river is owned and managed by Ngai Tahu, and cannot be taken away.

Grade: Medium
Time: 1 hour return
How to get there: To get to Milltown (despite its name, Milltown now consists of just one house), take the road from Hokitika to Lake Kaniere. At the lake, take Milltown Road to the left. Follow this narrow gravel road through the bush past the one house until you reach the bridge over the Arahura River. The track is immediately to the right.

16 Ka Roimata o Hine Hukatere/Franz Josef Glacier and Te Moeka o Tuawe/Fox Glacier

According to legend, Hine Hukatere and her lover Tuawe were exploring the glacier country when Tuawe was swept away by an avalanche and killed. In her grief, Hine Hukatere shed so many tears that they froze and formed the glacier Ka Roimata-o-Hine-Hukatere, 'the tears of Hine Hukatere'. The body of Tuawe now occupies the next valley, which is now known as Te Moeka-o-Tuawe, 'the final resting place of Tuawe'.

Both glaciers have walks to the glacier terminal points, and guiding companies offer various walks up onto the glaciers. The distance of the walk to the glaciers varies considerably depending on the conditions in the valley and the position of the glacier. However, since both glaciers attract huge numbers of visitors, the tracks are also in very good condition and easy walking.

Franz Josef Glacier
Grade: Easy
Time: 1.5 hour return
How to get there: Franz Josef Glacier is 135 km south of Hokitika on SH6. The glacier walk is signposted from the bridge.

Fox Glacier
Grade: Easy
Time: 1.5 hour return
How to get there: Fox Glacier is 24 km south of Franz Joseph Glacier on SH6. The glacier is signposted from the highway south of the village.

17 Tiorapatea/Haast Pass

The road through the Haast Pass follows an ancient Maori path called Tiora-patea ('the way is clear'). This trail linked the substantial settlement at Okahu (Jackson Bay) with the people living on the Otago coast.

It was through this pass that the Ngati Toa chief Te Puoho led his war party in a surprise attack on Ngai Tahu, encamped for the summer at Wanaka in 1836.

At 563 metres, this is the lowest pass through the mountains. At the pass itself there is a short walk to a lookout point. This new track zigzags up through beech forest that gradually thins as you climb, and finally reaches a lookout over the pass. The view is down the bush-lined pass both east and west, and all around are snow-capped mountains. It is a bit of a slog but the track is well formed so take your time as the dramatic views are worth the effort.

Grade: Hard
Time: 40 minutes return
How to get there: On SH6, 61 km from Haast

OTAGO AND CENTRAL OTAGO

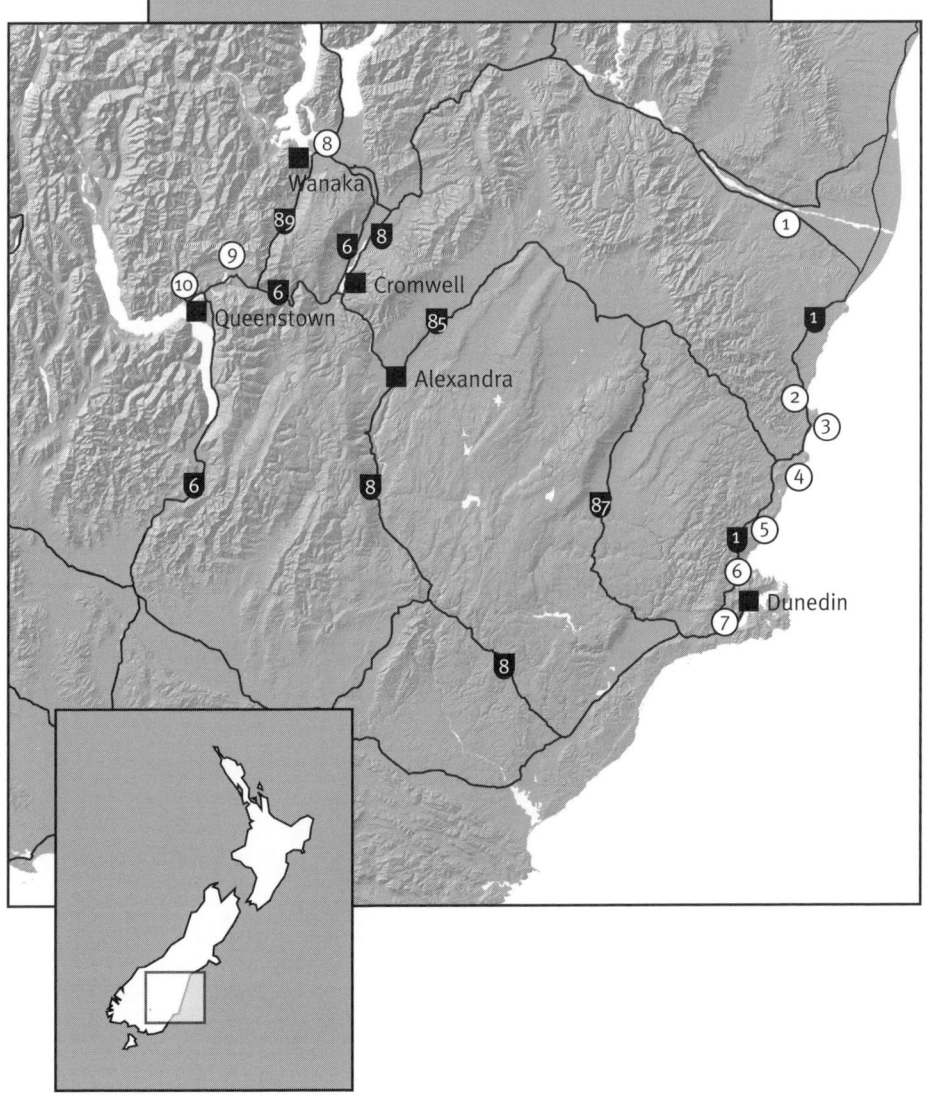

1 Maerewhenua Rock Drawings, Duntroon

Over 500 Maori rock-drawing sites have been found in the South Island, and just over 100 in the North Island. It is possible that the art form was common throughout Aotearoa and that more drawings have survived in the Waitaki area because of the relatively dry climate and the location of the drawings in dry sheltered caves and overhangs. Rock art can be either scratched into the surface or drawn and painted on. The paint was usually made from animal fat mixed with various other media such as soot or charcoal, kokowai and yellow ochre.

Over 20 Maori rock art sites have been found in the Waitaki valley, but most have since disappeared. Of the three remaining sites, Maerewhenua and Takiroa near Duntroon are the most accessible.

Maerewhenua is a substantial rock shelter lined with simple drawings. This shelter was utilised over hundreds of years, but is unlikely to have been permanently occupied – this would have been a seasonal food-gathering area. In addition to the drawings, there is evidence of cooking fires, bird bones and fishhooks. It appears that the drawings were added to, altered and improved over the years, and the subjects range from extinct birds such as moa and pouakai (Haast eagle), through to nineteenth-century sailing ships and names.

The location is a long shallow cave stretching over 30 metres. Many of the drawings are initially difficult to make out, but spend some time and gradually the scale of them is revealed. To reach the site there is a short steep walk uphill from the road.

Grade: Easy
Time: 15 minutes return
How to get there: 500 m east of Duntroon on the Livingstone–Duntroon road off SH83

2 Moeraki Boulders Walk

These unusual boulders are just part of the wreck of a giant legendary waka *Araiteuru*. The hull of the waka has now turned into the rocky reefs that lie off Matakaea/Shag Point, and the body of the captain is a small promontory. On Moeraki Beach lies the flotsam from the wreck – the gourds, fishing floats and nets.

While most people stop by the beach, go for a quick walk and then move on, an attractive alternative is to drive to the small picturesque fishing village of Moeraki and park at the beginning of the Millennium Track on Haven Street. From here it is one hour return to the boulders on the beach. The boulders are best seen at mid to low tide, as at high tide they are underwater. If you stop by the café just off SH1 and use their track to the boulders, there is a small fee.

 Grade: Easy
Time: 20 minutes return from the public carpark; 1 hour return from Moeraki village
How to get there: The public car park is on Moeraki Boulders road, off SH1 just north of the turnoff to Moeraki village. The Millennium walkway starts in Moeraki at the southern end of the beach.

3 Katiki Point Walk

Though little of this pa now remains, it is a superb site located on a narrow spur of land almost surrounded by sea, and well worth the short walk. The pa, known as Te Raka-a-Hineatea, was established in the eighteenth century as the principal base for the Ngai Tahu invasion of Ngati Mamoe territory. The pa was built by Taoka, the son of Ruahikihiki, who had his main pa at Taumutu. Taoka became embroiled in a bitter feud with his nephew Te Wera at Huriawa, a conflict that led to the famous siege of Huriawa and the destruction of Mapoutahi near Waitati (see below). The pa resisted many attempts to capture it and once the conquest was completed, it fell into disuse.

From the historic Katiki lighthouse the track wanders downhill over open grass to a narrow rocky point, and it will involve some rock hopping to get over to the pa site. The views down the coast are superb and, as a bonus, penguins and seals are common along the rocky shore.

Grade: Easy

Time: 45 minutes return

How to get there: Turn off SH1 to Moeraki. At the village, turn right into Tenby Street, which becomes Lighthouse Road. Drive 3 km to the end of this gravel road.

4 Puketapu

Puketapu is the very distinctive-shaped hill topped by a tower just to the north of Palmerston township. It is special to both Maori and Pakeha. The hill is named after a woman who was a survivor of the great waka *Araiteuru* that sank off Matakaea/Shag Point (of Moeraki Boulders fame); many other hills along the Otago coast are named after others from the same waka.

Once covered in dense bush, Puketapu was also a favoured haunt of the patupaiarehe and, according to Maori tradition, the heavy mists that often shroud the summit allow the patupaiarehe to reclaim the hill and play music undetected.

There are basically two tracks to the top of the hill, and either way involves a good climb. From the road, the track steadily works its way uphill across farmland. When you reach the water tank, you see the most obvious track going straight up the hill. This is a steep and slippery climb that will have you panting at the top. However, if you go immediately to your right, a much longer but more gently sloping track will take you to the top, but will add another 20 minutes. If you are up for the steep climb, go up that way, then down the easy slope.

Grade: Medium/hard

Time: 1 hour 15 minutes return

How to get there: From SH1 just north of the Palmerston shops, turn into Stour Street, cross the railway line and go 500 m. The track begins on the left.

5 Huriawa Pa, Karitane Beach

Huriawa peninsula was the perfect location for a fortified pa – volcanic in origin, with steep cliffs and sea on three sides. Defenders of the pa had uninterrupted views both north and south along the coast and over the estuarine marshes to the east. A Ngai Tahu stronghold, Huriawa was the scene of an epic siege in the eighteenth century.

The rangatira of Huriawa was Te Wera, who became embroiled in a family feud with his nephew Taoka, though the cause of the conflict has long been forgotten. Tension escalated between the two and finally Taoka decided to attack Huriawa. Te Wera had anticipated the attack and had vastly improved the defences of Huriawa and had the pa well stocked with food. Even under siege the defenders could go out fishing from a small cove on the north side of the pa called Te Awamokihi (Raft Cove). Usually the weak point in any pa was the lack of water, and here Huriawa was fortunate to have a small spring that provided the pa with just enough water. After the siege this spring became known as Te Punawai-a-Te-Wera ('Te Wera's well').

Taoka camped on the sandspit just to the north of the main land gate, Te Kutu-o-Toretore. His forces assaulted the pa and raided the surrounding countryside; any hapless stragglers were immediately consigned to the hangi pits.

In order to demoralise and weaken the defenders, Taoka devised a daring plan to steal the wooden carving of Kahukura, the god of war, who also appeared in the form of a rainbow and whose image was under the close guard of the tohunga Hatu. In the dead of night two warriors entered the pa at low tide through the sea caves on the southeastern corner and stole the precious carving.

In the morning Hatu discovered the theft and, while pandemonium swept through Huriawa, outside Taoka's men performed haka, called insults about the poor protection of the pa and waved Kahukura above their heads. However, their bravado was not to last long. Hatu, invoking all the gods, pulled together his considerable powers and stretched out his arms towards the enemy, crying out, 'Return to us, O Kahukura.' The carving flew through the air and came to rest at the feet of Hatu.

Now it was the turn of those within Huriawa to celebrate; to Taoka's men, the signs were clear that the gods favoured Te Wera. Thoroughly discouraged, Taoka gave up the siege of Huriawa, which had by that time lasted six months, and turned his fury towards Mapoutahi just a little way to the south.

The entrance to the pa is through a beautifully carved gateway and the track meanders gently to the end of the peninsula, with great views along the coast in both directions. The convoluted nature of Huriawa is such that specific evidence of terraces and defences is not so easy to spot, but Te Wera's well is still visible, and the great blowholes through which the thieves stole into the pa can be found on the south side of the pa.

Grade: Easy
Time: 45 minutes
How to get there: From SH1 turn off towards Karitane and take the road right to the beach. At the beach turn left along Sulisker Street and continue 500 m uphill to the entrance.

6 Mapoutahi Pa

Like Huriawa pa to the north (see above), Mapoutahi was located on an inaccessible peninsula, protected by steep cliffs and superbly fortified. Taoka could make no impression on the impregnable fortress. However, the attack took place in the middle of winter and, on one particularly cold night, the sentries of Mapoutahi set up dummies at the entrance to the pa and then retreated to the warmth of the fires in the huts. Alerted to the ruse, Taoka attacked, quickly seized the pa and then proceeded to massacre the inhabitants. The pa was never reoccupied and the peninsula became known as Mata-awheawhe, 'the dead gathered in a heap'.

While today the fortified ditches and terraces have largely disappeared, the site of the pa is nothing short of perfect. Steep cliffs and a very narrow access point made it easy to protect, while the sea and wide lagoons to both north and south provided an excellent food resource. In either direction the views are extensive, Orokonui lagoon and the Otago Peninsula to the south, and Purakaunui Inlet immediately to the north, with Huriawa pa glimpsed in the distance.

There are two ways of getting to the pa; the most picturesque involves walking along the beach and around Doctors Point. From the carpark, walk down the beach and head south right around Doctors Point, passing through sea caves on the way. This walk can only be undertaken at mid to low tide, and even on those tides there is a short scramble over rocks that have tumbled down from the coastal cliffs. If the tide is not right, the northern access to the pa is via Osborne Road and from there a short walk through the sand dunes to the pa.

Doctors Point
Grade: Easy
Time: 1 hour return
How to get there: Turn off SH1 at Waitati and turn left into Doctors Point Road. Follow this road to the end and park by the beach.

Osborne Road
Grade: Easy
Time: 25 minutes return

How to get there: Turn off SH1 at Waitati and then take the road
to the Orokonui Ecosanctuary. Turn left into Purakanui Road and
then left again into Osborne Road and drive to the carpark at
the end.

7 Kapukataumahaka/Mt Cargill

Maori settlement in the bays around the sheltered waters of Otakou/Otago
Harbour dates back to the very early days of Polynesian immigration to
Aotearoa. One of the most populated areas in the South Island, with a
pre-European population estimated to be around 3000, Taiaroa Head was
the location of the main pa on the peninsula. This pa was named after the
famous fighting chief Te Matenga Taiaroa, who stopped Te Rauparaha's
invasion of Ngai Tahu land in the 1830s. A fort built in the nineteenth
century obliterated all signs of the old pa, and very few traces of Maori
occupation can be found around the harbour.

Mt Cargill is known in Maori as Kapukataumahaka, and is said to
represent (depending on the version) the body of a warrior or of a princess,
with Buttars Peak the head and Mt Cargill the body. The mountain was a
favoured hunting ground of the chief Poho, who lived alongside the Water
of Leith, or Owheo (named after the whio or blue duck, which has long
disappeared from this stream).

You can drive to the top of Mt Cargill, but this walk through
regenerating bush and past the Organ Pipes is much more rewarding.
However, the summit is very exposed and often shrouded in cloud, so if
the weather is not good, don't bother with the hike as you will not see
a thing.

All the hard climbing on this walk is in the first 15 minutes, as the track
goes solidly uphill with quite a few steps in this first section; then it levels
off. From there it is a surprising easy walk to Mt Cargill, well within the
capabilities of anyone with reasonable fitness, and with just another
short uphill stretch at the very top. The early part of the walk is through
fine bush, ferns and mosses. What look like carefully shaped steps are in
fact natural and are broken rock from the formation known as the
Organ Pipes.

From the Organ Pipes the track leads through more subalpine vegetation to the top of Mt Cargill, where a cairn indicates all the key geographical features. The 360-degree views over Dunedin and the coast north and south from this 676-metre peak are spectacular.

Grade: Medium
Time: 2 hours return to the top of Mt Cargill
How to get there: From North East Valley follow North Road. After the point where North Road eventually morphs into Mt Cargill Road, the carpark is 3 km on the left, but there is very limited parking space.

8 Mt Iron Walk, Wanaka

There are two meanings of Wanaka: one version has Wanaka as a form of O-Anaka, 'the place of Anaka' – an early chief; or it can be interpreted as 'a place of renewal'. Either way, the lakes of Wanaka and Hawea were two of the lakes created by the legendary Rakaihautu when he journeyed the length of the island from north to south, digging out the lakes and heaping up the mountains with his magical ko.

Too cold in winter to sustain a permanent population, the area around Wanaka was a favoured seasonal hunting ground and was occupied over the summer months for fishing and hunting birds. The lakes were also a stopping point on the poumanu trading route from the West Coast to Otago through Tiorapatea/Haast Pass.

First occupied by the Waitaha people and later by Ngati Mamoe, the area became Ngai Tahu territory in the seventeenth century. However, all this came to an end in 1836 when Ngati Toa under Te Puoho swept down the West Coast and through the pass to launch a surprise attack on the lake settlements, from which they never recovered.

The walk up Mt Iron has great views of both lakes and is neither too long nor too demanding. Mt Iron, at 548 metres, stands isolated from the surrounding mountains and therefore offers excellent views in every direction. To take advantage of the easier grade, it is best to walk this loop track clockwise, up the gentler western slope and down the steep eastern side. The open nature of the low vegetation ensures endless views all the way.

At the top the views are in all directions – south along the Cardrona valley, east to the broad terraces of the Clutha River, north over Lake Hawea and west across Lake Wanaka and beyond to the Southern Alps.

Grade: Medium
Time: 1.5 hours
How to get there: 1 km east of Wanaka on SH6.

9 Waiwhakaata/Lake Hayes

Now called Lake Hayes, this small shallow lake is very favoured by photographers for the spectacular autumn colours and the reflection of mountains in the tranquil waters. The lake held exactly the same appeal to early Maori (minus the cameras), who named the lake Wai-whaka-ata or 'the water that reflects'.

Following the shoreline, this walk meanders beside the lake under the shade of old willows and poplars and with tranquil views over the lake and the mountains. The reserve at the northern end of the lake is particularly popular in summer, as Lake Hayes is much shallower than the deep mountain lakes and the water is not as cold for swimming. This is a great spot on a hot summer's day and is especially appealing in autumn with the trees turning vivid yellow and gold.

This easy flat track is not hard to find as it follows the shoreline. At the northern end, the track begins where the access road to the picnic ground meets the main road, while at the showgrounds it is down by the shore. The walk around the lake will take around two and a half hours, and a shorter walk from the showgrounds to the Lake Hayes Reserve picnic ground will take 30 minutes.

Grade: Easy
Time: Around the lake 2.5 hours; from the showgrounds to the picnic area 30 minutes
How to get there: Begin at either the showgrounds on SH6 from Queenstown to Cromwell, just before the turn-off to Arrowtown, or at the large picnic ground at the northern end of the lake.

10 Te Tapunui/Queenstown Hill

Te Tapunui rises steeply behind busy Queenstown and affords a spectacular view of Lake Wakatipu and the surrounding mountains.

A time long ago, the area now occupied by the lake was the favoured resting place of an ogre, sometimes called Kopuwai. All was well until the ogre kidnapped the wife of a local Maori chief. Unable to tackle the giant ogre, the chief bided his time until the ogre went to sleep between the mountains. Seizing his chance, the chief rescued his wife and, to prevent revenge, he heaped wood over the giant and burnt him to death. The gigantic hole left by the ogre filled with water, creating the lake; and all that remains of the ogre is his beating heart, which still causes the lake to mysteriously rise and fall.

As with most of the inland areas of Central Otago, the area around Queenstown was not permanently occupied but was used for seasonal hunting, with settlements at the junction of the Kawarau and Kimiakau (Shotover) rivers, another near Kawarau Falls (Te Rotu), and the main pa on the flat where Queenstown is today. First occupied by Waitaha and later by Ngati Mamoe, the area became Ngai Tahu territory in the seventeenth century.

This track is a solid uphill slog. The loop section is known as the Time Walk. Beginning through a beautiful wrought-iron gate, a series of illustrated panels takes the walker from the past to the present and finally the future, represented at the top by Caroline Robinson's simple sculpture *Basket of Dreams*. To follow the panels in the correct sequence, turn right at the junction where the track becomes a loop. This direction is also the gentler grade to the top.

Most of the walk is through pine and Douglas fir, with the occasional view glimpsed through the branches. However, near the top the vegetation is open and a grand view of the lake, mountains and town is laid out before you. At the small pond on top of the ridge, veer left to the *Basket of Dreams* and the track downhill; or, if you are feeling energetic having got this far, the track to the right will take you to the top of Queenstown Hill (907 metres), which is just 15 minutes' walk away. This is a steep walk that climbs up 500 metres from the carpark to the top, but it is an excellent track so take your time.

Grade: Hard
Time: 2 hours return, plus 30 minutes if walking up from the town
How to get there: Kerry Drive, Queenstown.

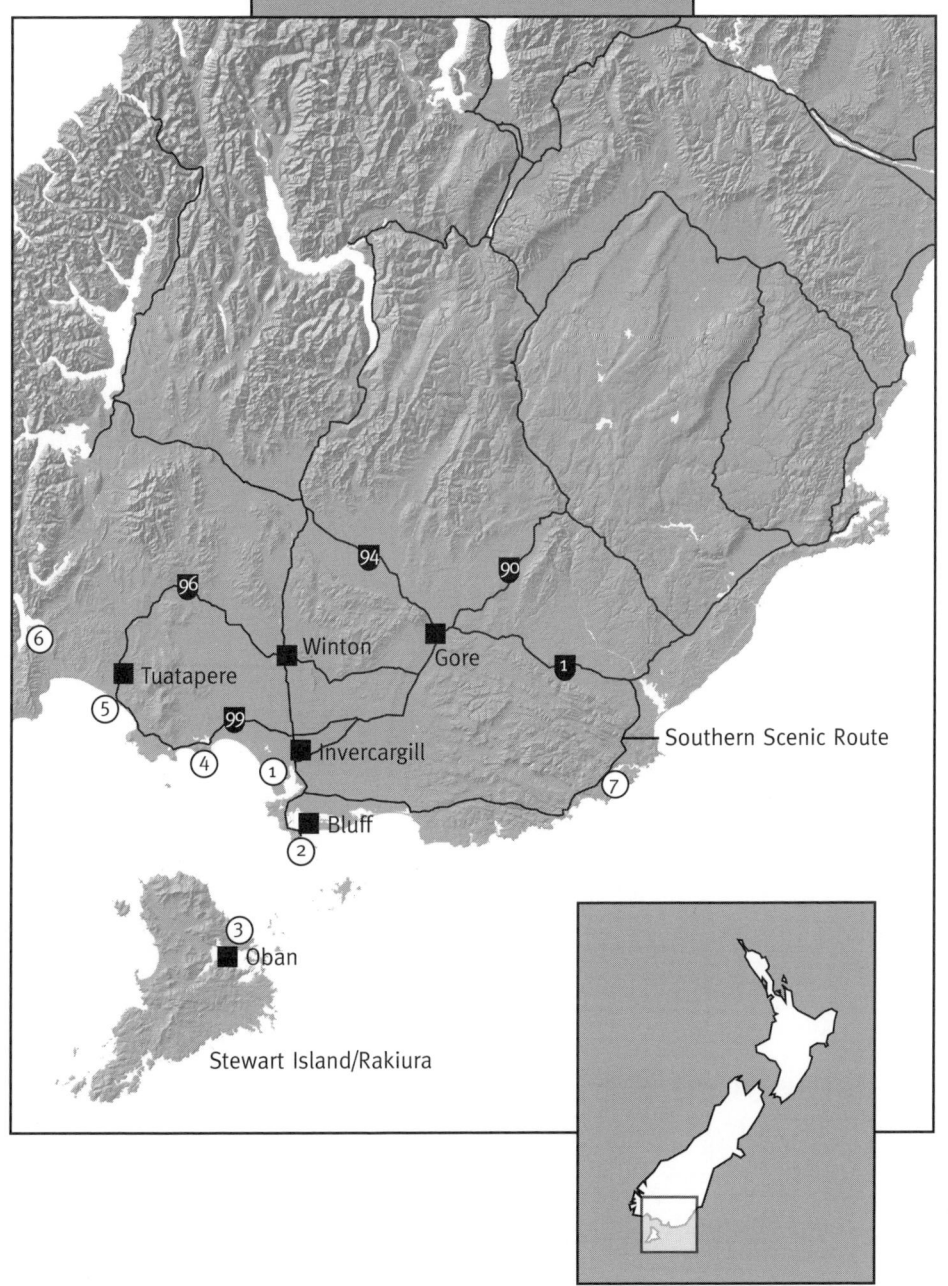

FAR SOUTH

Winton

94

90

96

6

Tuatapere

5

99

4

1

Invercargill

Gore

1

Southern Scenic Route

7

Bluff

2

3

Oban

Stewart Island/Rakiura

1 Noki Kaik, Sandy Point

Sandy Point is a large sand peninsula between the Oreti River and the open ocean at Oreti Beach. Although today much of the area is highly modified, a few patches of bush remain along the estuary. This area was a rich source of food for early Maori who maintained small settlements here, taking advantage of the sheltered mouth of Oreti River which, at this point, is a very wide shallow estuary. The main Maori settlement in this area was called Oue, though the pre-European population would never have been more than a few hundred people.

From the carpark, a short uphill walk leads to Hatchs Hill lookout, with views over the wide tidal New River Estuary (which is essentially the estuary for the Oreti River), Invercargill city and, beyond that, to Bluff. This is particularly picturesque at sunset. The track then leads downhill to the small sandy Noki Kaik Beach, where once was a small kaik (kainga or settlement), though no evidence is now visible.

Grade: Easy
Time: Beach 20 minutes return
How to get there: From Invercargill take Stead Street and drive towards Oreti Beach (Otatara). After 7 km turn left into Sandy Point Road and continue down this road for 6 km. Just past the end of the tarseal is a parking area on the left.

2 Motupohue/Bluff Hill

Motupohue or Bluff Hill (265 metres) is visible from most parts of the flat plain of Murihiku (the tail end of the land), which is now known as Southland. The first part of the name, motu meaning 'island', refers to the way the hill appears like an island; pohue refers to the native convolvulus that grows on the hill. Tradition tells that the summit is the possible burial place of two Ngati Mamoe chiefs; the hill, then as now, was an important landmark for both land and sea travellers.

The area around Bluff was only used for seasonal hunting and gathering, with the main pa actually occupying Ruapuke Island, which is said to have had seven pa and was the home of Tuhawaiki, also known as the King of Bluff or Bloody Jack. Bluff was also a source of argillite, an ancient and tough stone that was worked into adzes.

From the summit the views are superb, with the Takitimu mountains and the plain to the north, the Longwood Range and distant Fiordland to the west, Stewart Island and the islands of Foveaux Strait to the south, and Ruapuke Island lying 15 kilometres to the southeast. In Maori, Foveaux Strait is Te Ara a Kiwa.

There are two ways of walking up to the summit of Motupohue. The first track, Topuni Track, branches off to the right immediately after the beginning of the Foveaux Walkway. This is a solid uphill walk. The longer but more picturesque walk follows the flat, easy Foveaux Walkway to the lookout and then turns uphill along the Millennium Track to the summit. By returning down the Topuni Track, this walk becomes a loop that will take around two hours.

 Topuni Track
Grade: Medium/hard
Time: 50 minutes return

 Foveaux Walkway/Millennium Track/Topuni Track loop
Grade: Medium/hard
Time: 2 hours

How to get there: Both walks start from Stirling Point at the very end of SH1.

3 Rakiura/Stewart Island

Stewart Island was known to Maori as both Rakiura, 'heavenly glow' (which some say is a reference to the spectacular sunsets over the island), and Te Punga-o-te-waka-o-Maui, or 'the anchor stone of Maui's waka'.

Maori history on the island is sketchy; it is likely that it was used primarily as a place of refuge for vanquished tribes. One famous chief to move to the island was Te Wera, who led the successful six-month siege of Huriawa at Karitane. On the island at Paterson Inlet, Te Wera clashed with Ngati Mamoe in a battle named Kaitangata and, after causing strife elsewhere on the island, he moved back across the strait to the mainland to Matariki pa on the small island near Cosy Nook. Paterson Inlet is known in Maori as Te Waka a Te Wera.

Today a very popular destination within Paterson Inlet is Ulva Island, now a wildlife sanctuary and a short water-taxi ride from Golden Bay, just out of Oban. The island is small (you can't really get lost) and relatively flat, with a network of excellent tracks, all well marked and linking a number of very attractive beaches.

For a great view, a short hike up to Observation Rock is rewarded with vistas over Paterson Inlet and Ulva Island. This is a short, easy uphill walk through bush to a rock, which, late in the afternoon, will reward you with the spectacular sunset that gives Rakiura its name.

From the wharf turn left into Elgin Terrace and then right into Excelsior Road. Excelsior Road is an uphill climb; watch for the Observation Rock track on your right, which will take you to the summit of the hill through a short bush track.

 Grade: Easy
Time: Allow 2 hours
How to get there: Water taxi from Golden Bay

Aparima/Riverton

The Maori name for the Riverton is Aparima, named after a high-born Waitaha woman, and today the river still retains this name. Some original estimates put the Maori population around 300, centred around an area later known as the Kaike.

Although pre-European Maori did not actively hunt whales, when European whalers moved into the area in the early nineteenth century, the relationship between Maori and whalers was mutually cordial. Maori provided vegetables, fresh water and wood, while young Maori men were attracted to the adventure of whaling; and American ships frequently recruited Maori. There is strong evidence that Queequeg in Herman Melville's famous whaling novel *Moby-Dick* is based on a Maori whaler.

Intermarriage was common between local Maori women and men from whaling ships. Around 1836 Captain John Howell established a whaling station at the mouth of the Aparima and Pourakino rivers, after working at Kapiti Island and Waikouaiti. While at first reluctant, he married Kohikohi, the daughter of Horomona Patu, a Ngati Mamoe chief from

Rarotoka/Centre Island, as his refusal to take a Maori wife was seen as an insult to the local people. With his wife he received a dowry of a large block of land between the Waimatuku and Aparima rivers. The house he built at the local kainga for his wife and family, known as Howell's Cottage or Te Whare Kohikohi, is the oldest European building in the South Island.

Kohikohi died around 1841, and in 1845 Howell married another Maori woman, Koronaki from Whenuahou/Codfish Island, with whom he had 17 children.

Hilltop is a small rocky outcrop that was once used to spot whales passing through the strait when Riverton was a whaling station. The islands of the strait are all clearly visible, including Stewart, Codfish, Centre and Pig Islands. To the west the view follows the coast to Colac Bay, the Longwood Range and, in the distance, the mountains of Fiordland. To the north lie the Takitimu Mountains, Eyre Mountains and the Hokonui Hills, and to the west Riverton, the Jacobs River Estuary, the white sweep of Oreti Beach and beyond that Bluff Hill.

While the views are similar from Mores Lookout, the appeal of this walk lies in the lush regenerating bush with the song of the bellbird following you all the way. These two walks leave from the same carpark.

Hilltop Lookout
Grade: Easy
Time: 15 minutes return

Mores Lookout
Grade: Easy
Time: 45 minutes return

How to get there: Head west from Riverton and turn left towards Riverton Rocks immediately after crossing the bridge over Jacobs River. After 800 m turn right into Richard Street and take the gravel road uphill to the carpark at the end.

5 Te Puka o Takitimu/Monkey Island

This island is called Te Puka-o-Takitimu, after the anchor stone of the waka *Takitimu* that journeyed from Hawaiki and was wrecked at the mouth of the Waiau River. Captained by Tamatea, the waka was struck by three waves so large that they have individual names: Otewao, Oroko and Okaka. They drove the waka far inland, where a cross-wave finally overturned it. The upturned waka then became the Takitimu Mountains.

The view across the wide expanse of Te Waewae Bay to Hump Ridge and the Princess Mountains is well worth the short detour. The tiny island is accessible at low tide and a short flight of steps leads up to the lookout viewing platform.

 Grade: Easy
Time: 10 minutes return
How to get there: 1 km southeast of Tuatapere off SH99

6 Lake Hauroko

Situated in the southern part of Fiordland National Park, this lake attracts few visitors, partly because of the location away from the main tourist trail and the fact that it's a 32-kilometre drive in to the lake, of which 20 km is pretty rough gravel. Beautiful, wild and undeveloped, Hauroko stretches deep into the mountains, is subject to very high winds and can quickly turn extremely rough.

In April 1967, local George Evans pulled his boat onto Mary Island in Lake Hauroko and decided to poke around the clefts in a rock face. To his great surprise, he found a skeleton held upright in a sitting position by manuka stakes and covered in a cloak. What George had found was the body of a woman of high rank dating back to the seventeenth century, who was later identified as Te Maiairea Te Riri Wairua Puru of Ngati Mamoe.

What makes the burial particularly curious is that the lake and the island were very remote from major Maori settlements, and that those who buried this woman were taking exceptional care to protect the location of the burial site.

Now known as the 'Maori Princess', the burial site is protected by a metal grille and is considered highly tapu. Stories soon circulated of a Maori curse that caused sudden squalls on the lake and is associated with the mysterious disappearance of three hunters in the 1960s – stories that local Maori dismiss as nonsense.

Mary Island is readily identifiable, as it is the only island in the lake. The best view of Hauroko and the island is from the Lake Hauroko Lookout. This track for the most part follows the lakeshore until the steep climb to the lookout, where you will be rewarded with spectacular views as far as Foveaux Strait. However, the track is a bit rough and steep towards the end of the walk.

For something less demanding, there is a flat easy loop walk through forest and swamp from the carpark.

Lake Hauroko Lookout
Grade: Medium/hard
Time: 3 hours return

Lake Hauroko Track
Grade: Easy
Time: 30 minutes

How to get there: From Tuatapere, drive 13 km north to Clifden on SH99 and then turn into the Lake Hauroko Road. Lake Hauroko is 32 km down this road, of which more than half is gravel.

7 Jacks Blowhole Walk

Both Jacks Bay and Jacks Blowhole are named after Tuhawaiki, better known to Pakeha as Bloody Jack. The name has nothing to do with bloodthirstiness, but rather Tuhawaiki's fondness for using 'bloody' as a swearword. The blowhole is also known to Maori as Opito or 'the navel'.

Tuhawaiki was a great Ngai Tahu warrior who played a key role in the defeat of Te Rauparaha near Cape Campbell in 1831. Again in 1835, with Taiaroa, he pushed back Ngati Toa forces in the South Island, and finally defeated Te Puoho near Mataura in 1836, after Ngati Toa had launched a surprise attack on Central Otago by sweeping unsuspected down the West Coast and through the Haast Pass.

In April 1840 he signed the Treaty of Waitangi on board HMS *Herald* at Ruapuke Island in Foveaux Strait, and he later travelled to Wellington in his own ship *Perseverance* to meet the governor. Known for his shrewdness, natural intelligence and vast knowledge, Tuhawaiki was also fond of being grand and had a special liking for dressing in splendid military uniforms. When he signed the deed of sale for the Otago Block, he called himself the 'King of Bluff'.

In 1844 Tuhawaiki drowned when his ship hit rocks south of Timaru at a location now known as Tuhawaiki Point. Nearby Tuhawaiki Island is also named after Jack and relates to the story that when Te Rauparaha trapped Tuhawaiki and his men on False Island to the north of Owaka River mouth, Tuhawaiki escaped by swimming to the island that now bears his name.

From the southern end of the beach at Jacks Bay an easy track across private farmland leads to the dramatic Jacks Blowhole, which you will hear before you see it. Over 200 metres from the sea, the hole is 55 metres deep, and the boom of the blowhole at high tide is especially impressive. A track goes around the blowhole with two lookouts enabling a good view of the crashing waves below.

From the track there are excellent views of Jacks Beach. The track is closed for lambing in September and October.

 Grade: Easy
Time: 1 hour return
How to get there: Turn off SH92 at Owaka and drive towards Pounawea. After 2 km turn right into Jacks Bay Road and drive the 8 km to the end of the road. The track begins at the southern end of the beach.

Bibliography

The Discovery of Aotearoa, Jeff Evans, Reed, 1998

Horouta, Rongowhakaata Halbert et al, Reed, 1999

Landmarks of Tainui, Finlay Phillips, Tohu Publishers, 2009

Nga Waka o Nehera, Jeff Evans, Oratia Media, 2009

The Puriri Trees are Laughing, Sissons et al, University of Auckland, 1985

Rangitane, JM McEwen, Reed, 1986

Reed Book of Maori Mythology, AW Reed, revised by Ross Calman,
  Reed, 2004

The Reed Dictionary of New Zealand Place Names, AW Reed, Reed, 2002

Te Arawa: A History of the Arawa People, Don Stafford, Reed, 1967

Te Takoto o te Whenua o Hauraki, Taimoana Turoa, Reed, 2000

Tuwharetoa, John Grace, Reed, 1959

Notes

Other books by Peter Janssen and New Holland Publishers

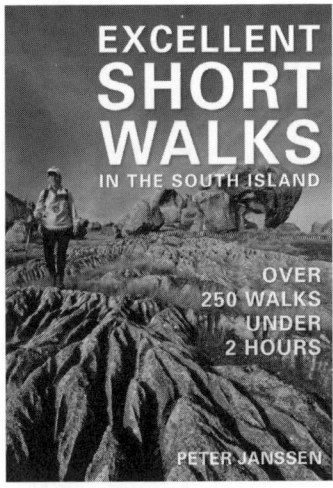

ISBN 978-1-86966-190-8

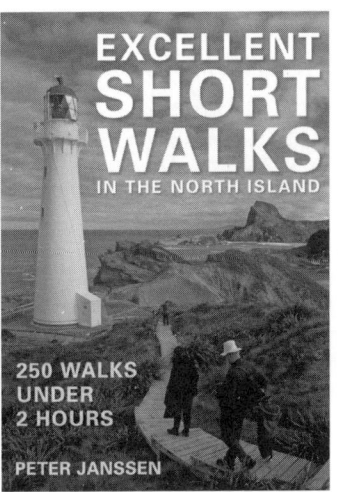

ISBN 978-1-86966-172-4

ISBN 978-1-86966-234-9

ISBN 978-1-86966-288-2

Other New Zealand outdoor guides by New Holland Publishers

ISBN 978-1-86966-227-1

ISBN 978-1-86966-206-6

ISBN 978-1-86966-200-4

ISBN 978-1-86966-318-6

ISBN 978-1-86966-218-9

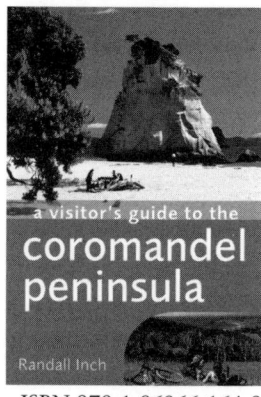

ISBN 978-1-86966-164-9

ISBN 978-1-86966-153-3

ISBN 978-1-86966-114-4

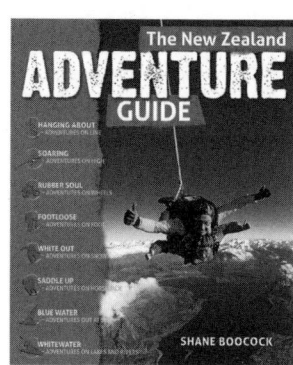

ISBN 978-1-86966-277-6